Pursuit of Excellence **THE OLYMPIC STORY 1980**

Pursuit of Excellence THE OLYMPIC STORY 1980

by

The Associated Press
and
Grolier

GROLIER ENTERPRISES INC.
Danbury, Connecticut

Grolier Incorporated

PRESIDENT AND CHIEF EXECUTIVE OFFICER: Robert B. Clarke
SENIOR VICE PRESIDENT, PUBLISHING: Howard B. Graham
VICE PRESIDENT, EDITORIAL DIRECTOR: Wallace S. Murray

EDITORS: Edward Humphrey, James E. Churchill, Jr.,
  Jeff Hacker
ASSISTANT EDITORS: Virginia M. Quinn,
  Daniel J. Domoff, Saundra France
EDITORIAL ASSISTANT: Catherine A. Vaughan
INDEXER: Jill Schuler

DESIGN: Murray Fleminger
LAYOUT: Eric Akerman, Franklin N. Sayles,
  Abbie Carroll Wilson
COVER DESIGN: Abbie Carroll Wilson

DIRECTOR OF MANUFACTURING: Harriet Ripinsky
MANAGER, MAIL ORDER MANUFACUTURING: David Bonjour
MANAGER, PRE-PRESS SERVICES: A. N. Qureshi
ASSISTANT, PRE-PRESS SERVICES: Joseph Corlett

Grolier Enterprises Inc.

PRESIDENT AND PUBLISHER: Robert W. Schramke
SENIOR VICE PRESIDENT, ASSOCIATE PUBLISHER:
  Henry J. Lefcort

The Associated Press

PROJECT DIRECTOR: Dan Perkes
EDITOR-IN-CHIEF: Ben Olan
PHOTO EDITOR: Thomas V. diLustro
EDITORIAL ASSISTANT: Carl Reuter
CONTRIBUTING WRITER: Hal Bock

ISBN 0–7172–8158–2
The Library of Congress Catalog Card Number 80-67767
COPYRIGHT © 1980 by GROLIER ENTERPRISES INC.

All rights reserved
No part of this book may be reproduced without
special permission in writing from the publishers.

Printed in the United States of America

FOREWORD

In a White House ceremony honoring the members of the 1980 U.S. Winter Olympic team President Jimmy Carter declared, "For all of you, the measure of your achievement is the effort and the dedication you gave to making a great team and to giving it all you had. . . . That pride in personal achievement and in honoring the ideals of the Olympics . . . is even more important than any medal.

"Some people live their whole lives without ever devoting themselves to one major attempt for achievement. It's hard for them to appreciate what it means to get up before dawn, year after year, when others are enjoying themselves, to endure pain and exhaustion and disappointment, to give not just your time and energy but your entire self to achieving a great goal.

"We often hear it said that there are no more heroes. We're all supposed to be too sophisticated for the recognition of heroes. But our Olympic athletes are heroes. They endure long and brutal training schedules. They make hard sacrifices. . . . They do it to reach their greatest potential. . . ."

At the same time, the president reiterated his belief that the "Soviet invasion of Afghanistan has violated peace and the principles of the Olympics" and that as a result the U.S. athletes should not participate in the 1980 Summer Games in Moscow.

This volume chronicles the development of the boycott movement and especially the play of the Lake Placid Games, not just the heroes and the organizational problems, but also the feats of the athletes who did honor to themselves by just participating and by fostering the Olympic ideal—"swifter, higher, stronger."

XIII Olympic Winter Games

Lake Placid, NY

CONTENTS

Athletes reflect

Just being part of the Olympic Games has affected my whole life. It opened new horizons for me. It made me expect more of myself. There is a tremendous satisfaction in doing whatever you do the best that you can do it. That goes for wrapping a package, designing a bouquet, or performing a surgical operation. I think that, above everything else, is what I have retained from my Olympic experience.

Participating in the Games added a new dimension to my life. To have people from all over the world, people we know little or nothing about, coming together, sharing the same commitment to the competition and to athletic excellence—well, that was a tremendous growing experience for me.

I think competing in the Olympics, calling on every ounce of ability that you have within you, putting it together in the harmony of performance, helped prepare me for my life's work in medicine and surgery. I am grateful that I have been able to continue participating in the Olympic movement as an officer of the United States Olympic Committee.

Tenley Albright, figure skater
gold medalist, 1956

Winning an Olympic gold medal was like joining a special secret club and getting a membership that lasts forever. It took utter, total dedication, a determination to be the best in the world at that particular moment.

I was only 15½ when I won my medals, but I worked as hard as anybody, no matter what age. It was what I wanted. Rome was going to be my Olympics. I remember sitting on a sidewalk curb in Detroit, crying tears of joy after the trials, realizing I had made the team, knowing that I had finally accomplished what I had been working at for so long.

For a year before the Games, I didn't walk on sand because there was a theory then that doing that could hurt a swimmer's performance. Whatever I was told to do, I did. I wanted those medals so badly.

I think other athletes are more impressed with an Olympic medal than ordinary people. That's because they understand the dedication and work involved. But I'd do it all over again in a minute. There was a tremendous sense of camaraderie on our swimming team in 1960.

Lynn Burke, swimmer
gold medalist, 1960

on the Olympics

Winning America's only gold medal in the 1964 Olympics in Innsbruck changed my life. It made me look for further goals, for higher standards for myself.

When I returned home, there were the usual parades and welcome home ceremonies. But when they were over, instead of going back to being a barber in a small Michigan town, I decided to reach for something more. That gold medal gave me the impulse to succeed, the desire to make something more of myself. Participating meant a lot, of course. I guess the press saw me as a long shot, but I thought I had a good chance at a medal. And when I won the competition, well, that was a great moment. That is the instant you work for and when you achieve that goal, you remember the moment forever.

Speed skating offered a great deal to me. When I was competing, I traveled all over the world because of my sport. Now I try to give something back by serving as vice president of the U.S. Speed Skating Association. I was privileged to take the oath for the officials at the 1980 Games.

Terry McDermott, speed skater
gold medalist 1964, silver medalist 1968

No one remembers I was the World Cup winner. They just remember the gold and silver Olympic medals. Skiing is a sport for oneself. The Olympics are different; it is a feeling inside you. There is the press and so much public attention, and the Games come only once every four years.

The athletes, not the hoopla, created a special aura for me.

Every country is at the Olympics. There are so many people. Athletes are there from all over the world. One can talk with all sorts of sports people. It is a good atmosphere for friendship to form.

You can't approach the Olympic Games as a special race. You have to approach them as a normal race. In the World Cup, a skier always has to be good. At the Olympics, one race, and that's it.

It seems it is not possible to separate politics from the Olympics, but all of us concerned with them must continue to try. The Games must be for the athletes of the world and not the politicians.

Rosi Mittermaier, Alpine skier
gold and silver medalist, 1976

An "Olympics in Perspective"

From the beginning, the XIII Winter Games were billed as the "Olympics in Perspective." With the rising cost of each festival of Games threatening the very life of the institution, organizers and promoters of the Lake Placid Olympics promised a no-frills operation that would "return the Games to the athletes." Emphasis would be placed on constructing the best possible sports facilities and seeing to it that the events were run smoothly and efficiently. The masses of spectators and the media, who would bring important revenues to the entire area, would have to be properly managed, but they would take second place to the competitions themselves.

The events that took place between Tuesday, February 12, and Sunday, February 24, did put the emphasis on athletes rather than on extravagant showmanship, and in an odd way the Olympic ideal was served. The "glory of sport and honor of our teams," commemorated in the Olympic Oath, prevailed. For the home crowd there was euphoria over the victory of the U.S. hockey team and pride in the five gold medals won by Eric Heiden. For everyone there were surprises, disappointments, and thrills that helped them forget the ordeals of being in Lake Placid.

But if the Lake Placid Olympic Organizing Committee (LPOOC) carried off the athletic competitions smoothly, there were hitches in almost every other area. Athletics notwithstanding, nearly everything that could go wrong did go wrong. Organization, logistics, and even Olympic protocol all fell to pieces at times during the two-week festival.

The Games were only a few days old before people began calling them the "Olympics in Chaos." A mismanaged bus system left thousands of spectators stranded in the bitter cold and ultimately caused New York Gov. Hugh Carey to declare a partial emergency. Massive traffic jams in and around Lake Placid further prevented transportation to and from the various sites. The ticket-selling and telephone systems were overloaded. And the International Olympic Committee (IOC) indulged in a public reprimand to the LPOOC for its bungling of the first medal ceremony on frozen Mirror Lake.

For some visitors, humor was the only way to cope with an entirely unhumorous situation. The most memorable comments came from the hard-bitten international press corps. A British journalist wondered whether John Brown, the famed abolitionist whose grave lies just south of Lake Placid, died waiting for a bus. Another was heard to say, "They always told us we could not be in two places at the same time. Here, we cannot be in one place at the same time."

Humor, however caustic, was beyond many. "It's disastrous. We never even got to our seats. And here I am waiting again for a bus," said Marie Dawe of Sagamore Beach, MA,

Lake Placid, NY, was heavily rebuilt for the 1980 Winter Olympics. Pins were cherished souvenirs.

one of hundreds of people who spent $300 for a ticket to see the opening ceremonies but missed them because of the transportation snafu.

Confronted by a band of disgruntled journalists, LPOOC press chief Ed Lewi was less than soothing when he reiterated the philosophy of an "Olympics in Perspective": "We never did say we were putting on the Olympic Games for spectators or for the press. We said the athletes would be No. 1 and everyone else would be No. 2."

During the week before the Games opened, workers in Lake Placid festooned the town with signs reading "Welcome World—We're Ready." But even as the athletes, support crews, media personnel, and spectators began arriving, the LPOOC faced Olympic-size problems. As if weather conditions, ticket sales, transportation, security, the gas supply, and the successful execution of all their plans and preparations were not enough for the Lake Placid organizers to be concerned about, there were two lawsuits and an international political dispute that could gum up the smooth running of the Games, as well as a threat to burn down the hotel in which the Olympic dignitaries would be staying.

The Games opened under a political cloud. On February 12, the first day of competition, the IOC held a meeting in Lake Placid at which it rejected the proposal of U.S. President Jimmy Carter that the Summer Games be moved from Moscow to protest the Soviet invasion of Afghanistan. After three days of discussions, IOC President Lord Killanin announced that all 72 members attending the meeting had agreed that the Summer Games should go on as scheduled. Carter in turn called on the U.S. Olympic Committee to reach a "prompt decision against sending a team" to Moscow and announced that he would be working with a number of other governments to set up alternative international games. The possible boycott brought into question the whole future of the Olympic movement.

A second political issue that caused headaches for the Olympic Committee was a familiar one: whether to allow Taiwan to take part under the name of the Republic of China. In 1976, Taiwan's 43-member Olympic delegation was barred from competing in the Montreal Summer Games under the banner of the Republic of China, its official IOC designation. The action was taken because the Canadian government had recognized The People's Republic of China. The Taiwanese were invited to participate under the name of Taiwan and to march in the opening ceremony with their national flag, but they refused to abandon the designation of Republic of China and withdrew before the start of the Games.

In 1979 the IOC ruled that China could participate in the Lake Placid Games and that Taiwan could take part only if it changed its name, flag, and national anthem. The Taiwanese again refused but still sent a 27-member delegation to Lake Placid. Seeking a revocation of the IOC rules, they filed suit in the New York State Supreme Court in Plattsburgh and in a court in Switzerland, home of the IOC. On Thursday, February 7, Justice Norman Harvey struck down the IOC regulation and declared the Taiwanese eligible to participate under their own name. But the LPOOC filed an appeal; on February 11 a state

Security was a prime concern. Above, a New York State trooper stands guard at the speed skating rink. Some 800 troopers, 75 FBI agents, and various Secret Servicemen and State Department officials were specially trained for duty at the quadrennial event.

appellate court reversed the decision and on February 12 the state's highest court also held against Taiwan. With not enough time to appeal to the U.S. Supreme Court, the delegation packed up and went home. Said spokesman Thomas Hsueh, "The mere suggestion that we have to accept any flag but our national flag is a downright insult."

Political tensions, the memory of a terrorist attack at the 1972 Summer Games in Munich, and the last-minute threat of arson made security a primary concern in Lake Placid. At the III Winter Games in 1932, it took 53 state troopers and four horses to keep the peace. In 1980, an army of almost 1,000 security personnel was mobilized. Among them were some 800 New York State troopers, 75 FBI agents, and law enforcement officers of the U.S. Secret Service and State Department.

Security was tightest at the 36-acre Olympic Village, situated in the hamlet of Ray Brook, about seven miles west of Lake Placid. The facility would be converted into a medium security prison after the Games, and although some complaints were heard about the size of the rooms and other aspects of the accommodations, few of the 1,600 athletes housed there could complain about safety. The village was surrounded by two high fences edged with razon ribbon and equipped with electronic sensors. At least one trooper was stationed inside each building, while jeeps patroled the perimeter and armed teams roamed through the surrounding woods. A contingent of state policemen stood on guard at every athletic event, while hundreds of troopers managed traffic and provided protection for the 50,000 tourists jamming into the village every day. The FBI covered the 1,800 foreign athletes and official guests; the State Department concentrated on Olympic and other dignitaries; the Secret Service protected visiting heads of state and U.S. leaders; customs officials stepped up security at the Canadian border; and aviation authorities were on the lookout for unauthorized fliers.

(Continued page 18)

X-rays and television monitors were utilized to check all luggage entering the Olympic Village. Below: Dr. Reed Kaplan and a "patient" demonstrate first aid procedure to security personnel.

ABC BRINGS THE WORLD TO LAKE PLACID

With the advent of the 1980 Olympics, according to the prevailing hyperbole, the world had come to America—or at least to Lake Placid, NY. But those who stayed home didn't miss much of what went on there, except maybe the traffic jams. For Lake Placid also came to the world, courtesy of the American Broadcasting Company.

ABC, a veteran of seven previous Olympics, obtained the rights to televise the Lake Placid Games with a payment of $15.5 million. The coverage was more extensive—and more costly—than ever before. ABC descended upon the Olympic Village with $70 million worth of equipment and an 800-member "team" that dwarfed the U.S. athletic contingent. It was the first time an American network had covered every Olympic event, and more than 100 ABC cameras were stationed throughout the site. Alpine skiing alone occupied 25 cameras, scattered from the top of Whiteface Mountain to the finish line; nearly 50 miles of cable were laid to connect them to the control center. Ten cameras in the Olympic arena focused on the hockey and figure skating events. Others were positioned along the bobsled run and the cross-country ski trails, or scanned the scene from helicopters hovering overhead.

It all added up to more than 50 hours of programming on U.S. television, much of it during prime time. In addition, ABC used its equipment to supply or "feed" continual live broadcasts to foreign networks, thus reaching an audience in the hundreds of millions.

To cover the events, ABC enlisted the services of crack commentators, notably Jim McKay as anchorman and veteran sportscaster Curt Gowdy, handling the luge and bobsled competitions. Frank Gifford and former U.S. ski team coach Bob Beattie covered alpine skiing and Chris Schenkel reported the ski jumping. Al Michaels, along with former Montreal Canadiens goaltender Ken Dryden, offered enlightening commentary on hockey, but never let verbiage dampen the excitement of the games. Former speedskater Sheila Young Ochowicz teamed with veteran sportscaster Keith Jackson to bring out some of the finer points of the speedskating competitions. Dick Button's expert coverage of figure skating was perhaps the most vivid and insightful

of all. He did not hesitate to give his informed opinion about skaters and performances.

All the goings-on were coordinated from the Broadcast Center, an immense, low building that housed administrative offices, editing rooms, studios, and eating facilities for ABC and foreign television personnel. The center—looking remarkably like a futuristic spacecraft with its flashing lights, control panels, and monitors—was commanded by Roone Arledge, president of ABC News and Sports. "Unquestionably, he's the genius of the industry," said Dennis Lewin, one of ABC Sports' top producers, who works closely with Arledge. "No one can put on an Olympics night after night and be right as often as he is."

Indeed, many of Arledge's decisions proved right. An example was the ABC policy concerning delayed telecasts. The network had decided not to announce the outcome of a taped event before showing it, but to present the competition as if it were live. "If there is one person in the country who doesn't know how it turned out, I don't want to be the one to tell him," said host Jim McKay. The policy was put to good test for the U.S.-Soviet hockey game, which ABC presented during prime time, three hours after it had been played. Thanks to the restraint of McKay and company, the thrill of the U.S. team's amazing win was not the least bit diminished by the delay.

The network's Olympic preview, "The Adirondack Gold Rush," kicked off the nearly two weeks of broadcasting. The preview spotlighted many of the athletes to watch during the Games and included breathtaking aerial views of Mount Van Hoevenberg and Whiteface Mountain. The show gave ABC the chance to be artistic and they didn't waste the opportunity. A replay of Franz Klammer's magnificent 1976 downhill run was followed by a tribute to downhill skiers, with the rock song "Power of Gold" as the accompaniment. Slalom specialist Ingemar Stenmark was shown skiing in a slow motion film set to the tune "Nobody Does It Better." Slow motion technique was also used effectively to examine the figure skating teams of Tai Babilonia-Randy Gardner and Irina Rodnina-Aleksandr Zaitsev. A tribute to 1932 bobsledder Billy Fiske was dramatically presented in a film vignette.

The technical expertise of ABC was in evidence throughout the telecasts. Those 100-odd cameras paid off in stunning visual effects. They took the viewer hurtling down the bobsled run in a film that presented the perils of the course as the competitor meets them. They followed the slalom skiers as they careened their way down the mountain, giving the TV audience a better view than was possible for any on-the-scene observers. The cameras caught small, moving touches: hands reaching to warm the women skiers' frozen faces after they completed their runs; goalie Jim Craig, after the ultimate hockey victory, anxiously scanning the crowd for his father; tears running down the cheeks of Soviet skater Irina Rodnina as she listened to her national anthem from the winners' podium.

Inevitably, not everyone was enchanted throughout. There were those who felt that the deluge of Olympic programming included far too many interruptions of the events for the sake of repetitious advertisements. Others noted that the otherwise all-seeing eyes of ABC managed to miss many of the massive problems encountered by visitors to Lake Placid. Don Meredith's down-home looks at the local scene did not appeal to the pure sports fan, and the more casual viewer found tedious the "up-close-and-personal" profiles of too many performers.

The closing ceremonies—including parades, speeches, an ice skating show, and other exhibitions—lasted 3½ hours, and ABC's determination to stick with them until the flame was extinguished seemed to drain even the durable McKay.

But most television viewers, it appeared, were willing to endure occasional overkill for the opportunity to experience vicariously the heart-stopping thrills, the agony of defeat, and the hot flush of victory.

From specially constructed stands, 25 cameras televised the Alpine skiing events.

The Adirondack countryside offered a beautiful setting for all of the events, especially the ski jumping. Right, skiers Phil Mahre and Cindy Nelson model the official American uniform.

The Coca-Cola robot intrigued all, especially the non-Americans. Housing (below) for 2,000 athletes, coaches, and managers was located in the hamlet of Ray Brook, 7 miles from Lake Placid. The facility was to be turned into a minimum-security federal prison following the Games.

Whether it was because of the extensive security measures, the remoteness of the town, cold temperatures, or any other condition, there were no major violent crimes during the 13-day period of the Games. Counterfeit $20 bills did turn up in several stores, and some $10,000 worth of television monitors were stolen from various competition sites. By the time the Games were over, there had been at least 7 felony arrests and 320 arrests and citations for traffic violations—including 20 for drunk driving, 48 misdemeanor arrests, and 113 accident investigations. The most celebrated crime of the 1980 Winter Games was the attempted theft of an Olympic flag by U.S. speedskater Peter Mueller. At 1:30 A.M. on February 20, Mueller was caught trying to take down a flag near the ice rink across from Town Hall. He was arrested on a charge of attempted petty larceny but released by a Lake Placid Village Court judge the next day at the request of Essex County District Attorney John McDonald.

The job of providing security was also simplified by President Carter's decision not to attend the Games. Whether to remain in Washington to work on economic matters and the Iranian crisis, or whether to avoid the inevitable discomfort and strained conversation of a meeting with Lord Killanin, Carter sent Vice-President Walter F. Mondale to declare open the Games.

But if Jimmy Carter was the most conspicuously absent personage, the more disturbing vacancies were those of Marie Dawe and the hundreds of other ticket holders still waiting for buses to the Olympic stadium. Petr Spurney, the general manager of the LPOOC, had said he visualized these Games as a showcase for mass transportation. On Monday, February 11, a day before the ice hockey tournament would begin and two days before the opening ceremonies, only 80 of 300 buses had arrived in town. The problem stemmed from a labor dispute over the use of Canadian drivers.

The first big wave of spectators was shuttled into town by bus drivers who barely knew their way around. Massive traffic jams on the three major roads into Lake Placid left thousands of visitors waiting behind in wintry parking lots. Because the town simply could not accommodate the influx of spectators, many were forced to lodge as far away as Montreal. Those seeking to drive to the Games were forced to leave their cars 16 miles (26 km) outside town. Major pickup points—such as Keene,

American athletes, including the Mahre brothers, join Soviet gold medalists Irina Rodnina and Aleksandr Zaitsev (right) at a party on the eve of Jimmy Carter's deadline for the withdrawal of Soviet troops from Afghanistan. If USSR troops were not withdrawn, the president said that the United States would boycott the Summer Games in Moscow. The Soviet forces remained in the Asian nation.

NY—were teeming with cold, angry ticket holders. Some waited 2½ hours for buses that were supposed to be running every 15 minutes.

The situation grew worse over the next several days. Although the thick blankets of snow that began falling could only enhance the beauty of the region and add to the manmade snow already covering the ski courses, plummeting temperatures caused misery for the frozen thousands waiting in line for buses. The volunteer emergency medical force reported several cases of frostbite. Mrs. Sally Ebersbach of Syracuse, NY, waiting at the Keene parking lot under several blankets and behind a wool ski mask, said she had read reports of the bus problems but had too much money invested in tickets to stay home. "I thought the news reports were exaggerated," she went on. "I thought it just couldn't be this bad."

Auto Rive-Sud, the Montreal firm originally hired to run the bus system, continued to be plagued by labor problems and equipment shortages, and the Rev. J. Bernard Fell, president of the LPOOC, called a committee meeting Thursday night, February 14, to discuss the problem. The organizers got a commitment from Greyhound Bus Lines for 50 buses and drivers, 33 of which roared into town the next morning. Later that Friday, the Executive Board of the IOC called an emergency meeting with U.S., New York State, and LPOOC officials to seek further solutions. On Saturday, Gov. Hugh Carey declared a limited transportation emergency, which allowed the LPOOC to waive bidding procedures and other bureaucratic delays. The state did not take over the beleaguered shuttle system, but it did contribute 15 school buses Saturday morning and sought to obtain another 38. The decree also lifted normal restrictions on the hours bus drivers can work in a single day.

Meanwhile, "The North Country Boys"—as Fell and his committee associates called themselves—had other matters to remedy. Perhaps the most embarrassing foulup occurred on Thursday night at the first medal ceremony of the Games. Thousands of spectators moved onto the ice at Mirror Lake only to hear cracks as loud as the sound of rifle shots. The ice held, but that was about the only thing that didn't go wrong. The ceremony began a half hour late; the gold and silver medalists in the 30-km men's cross-country race, Nikolai Zimyatov and Vasili

A labor dispute over the use of Canadian bus drivers precipitated a major transportation crisis at Lake Placid. Many persons were stranded in the cold and snow for hours and missed the events for which they held expensive tickets. The crisis began to subside after Gov. Hugh Carey declared a limited transportation emergency.

Rochev of the Soviet Union, did not attend because they had never been notified; no flags were hoisted during the various national anthems because the poles that had been rushed over from the opening day stadium couldn't be fitted into the concrete bases and lay on the ice beside the award stand; and there were no fences to keep spectators and the press away from the stage. To top off the evening, an obviously unnerved Lord Killanin dropped a medal off the ceremonial pillow and spent several awkward moments looking for it in the snow. LPOOC officials were called on the carpet at the emergency meeting of the IOC on Friday and were issued an official reprimand for the lapse in protocol.

Ticket sales presented another crisis. Not only would money have to be refunded to those who never reached the competitions but overloaded phone lines left new ticket-seekers listening to busy signals. Said one ticket agent: "It's like placing a call to Harry Houdini." The New York Telephone Company reported that the rate of calls per line was 50% greater than in the busiest sections of New York City. After realizing how much it had underestimated service needs, the phone company scrambled to add more lines and lay on several operators. Most of the 2,500 ticket-related calls each hour still went unanswered, and some events were held before thousands of empty seats.

At the height of all the frustrations, the Rev. Fell angrily suggested that all spectators be banned from Lake Placid. (He later retracted the statement.)

As far as the shopkeepers on Main Street were concerned, Lake Placid was a ghost town anyway. What was supposed to be a bonanza for the tiny Adirondack community had turned into a boondoggle. Merchants who laid in huge inventories and boosted prices to double or triple their normal level were not drawing customers. With all private vehicular travel forbidden, only an occasional state trooper's car was seen cruising the main business thoroughfare. There was only a smattering of pedestrians, except during breaks in activities at the nearby Fieldhouse and skating rink.

The owner of a corner restaurant near the main Olympic center, advertising "Buffet Breakfast $5.95, Lunch $7.95, Dinner $12.95," said he felt midtown business was suffering from a psychological effect.

Although the transportation snarls caused a decline in attendance and reduction in some prices, the cost of everything, especially food, remained high.

THE MEDALS

The victorious athlete bending to receive a gleaming medal of bronze, silver, or gold is a familiar and moving sight at the Olympic Games. In the years since the first modern Olympics in 1896, when the practice of awarding medals was begun, the Olympic medal has become the best-known symbol of amateur athletic achivement.

Although the average person may not have noticed, the medals awarded at Lake Placid were unique to the 1980 Winter Games. Under the supervision of the host committee, a new medal is designed and struck for each Olympic Games. IOC rules stipulate only the size of the medals (60 mm in diameter and 3 mm thick) and the amount of bronze, silver, or gold they must contain. The rest is up to the designer.

Tiffany & Company of New York, commissioned by the Lake Placid Olympic Organizing Committee to design the 1980 medals, combined traditional motifs with natural images from the Lake Placid region. The obverse of the medal is dominated by a hand holding aloft the Olympic torch, with the Adirondack Mountains forming a backdrop. The design also incorporates the traditional five interlocking rings and the legend, "XIII Olympic Winter Games." A bough of Adirondack white pine graces the reverse side of the medal, along with the words, "Lake Placid 1980" and the name of the event for which the medal was awarded.

The initial design was altered several times before it met with the approval of the LPOOC. The muscular hand that originally grasped the torch was deemed "Nazi-like" and was modified to produce a less ominous effect. The committee also objected to the pine cones and needles depicted by Tiffany. They didn't look like *Adirondack* pine, of which local citizens are justifiably proud. The pine is native to only two places in the world: the Adirondacks and a region of the Ural Mountains in Russia. The committee promptly mailed a fragrant sample of the genuine article to the Tiffany designers. These matters settled, the committee had one last problem. It seemed that the Olympic torch on the medal was blocking a certain Adirondack peak where one of the committee members owned a farm. Could the mountains be moved slightly to the left? The designers complied.

Tiffany, meanwhile, was encountering problems of a more practical nature. From the time of Tiffany's price estimate to the time the medals were struck, gold and silver had more than doubled in price. But Tiffany held to its original estimate, absorbing much of the cost of the medals.

The medals, struck by the Medallic Art Company of Danbury, CT, continued to increase in value as the Games approached. By January the first place medal, struck in silver and plated with six grams of 22-karat gold, had an intrinsic value of $552. The seven ounces of sterling silver in the second place medal gave it a value of $315.

But for the athletes standing proudly on the awards podium, the vagaries of the metals market had nothing to do with the true value of the medals. They would always represent the highest standards of athletic endeavor.

The women's 1,500-m speed skating medal.

"People look down Main Street, see no cars moving and think all the shops or stores are closed," he said.

One man who bought a pottery shop and converted it into a fast food stand said he was loaded down with food but had no buyers.

"We haven't had a handful of people in four days," he complained. "The trouble is all the out-of-town visitors are out in the boondocks somewhere, they are bused to the site of competition and bused home when the buses work. They never get to town."

Part of the trouble also must have been the high prices demanded at every turn. Although a few stores began posting half-price signs, the gouge continued. A cup of coffee was going for up to $1.50. One restaurant advertised a steak sandwich for $18.50. An Italian place offered a plate of spaghetti for $10.00. Hotel room prices were exorbitant. A centrally located motel jumped its rooms from $28.50 a day to $91.00 a day during the Games. Souvenirs also were bringing outrageous prices. One man bought three T-shirts for his kids. Price: $28.00. To the complaints about transportation, tickets, and the overall disorganization were added cries of "rip-off!"

During the 13 days of competition, the temperature varied greatly. At one point, the warmest clothing possible, including face protectors, was called for. At another time, shirtless sunbathing was enjoyed by the hardy.

With Eric Heiden taking five gold medals, the speed skating races drew large crowds. A steady snow fell during the 5,000-meter event. Figure skaters Kristiina Wegelius of Finland (below, left) and Mike Seibert of the United States inspect the ice castle, which was near the Olympic Village.

Exemplifying the general confusion surrounding the 1980 Winter Games, hundreds of copies of a spurious start list for Friday (February 15) night's pairs figure skating were placed in the mail boxes and bins at the press center. Reporters looked at the sheets and blinked. There wasn't a familiar name on the list, and scheduled to skate in the sixth position were Lois Lane and Clark Kent of Yugoslavia.

Then all of a sudden things began to look up. Even though, at about 10:00 A.M. on Tuesday (February 19), a power failure briefly knocked out electricity at several competition sites, the power loss did not delay any of the scheduled events. The medal award ceremonies were going without a hitch, and ticket sales were brisk. Most importantly, the bus system showed signs of improvement early in the week, and by Wednesday it was running almost as smoothly as the LPOOC had planned. Newly arriving spectators were pleasantly surprised at the efficiency with which they were moved. Temperatures and spirits rose markedly. On Main Street business was booming even at those prices.

"We're finally getting things together here and the Olympics are almost over," said Craig Adams, a clam shucker at an impromptu Oyster Bar. "If we had another couple of weeks it would flow smoothly."

A major reason for the turnaround was the emergence of the U.S. hockey team as perhaps the most exciting group of athletes ever to perform in the Winter Games. Enthusiasm grew with each victory, and the celebrations brought throngs of revelers to

The surprise success of the American hockey team led to wide jubilation by the partisan crowd.

the streets of Lake Placid. The 4–3 upset of the Soviet Union on Friday night (February 22) was followed by wild rejoicing that lasted through the night and into the next day. The final victory over Finland on Sunday set off the happiest and most raucous celebration Lake Placid—or perhaps any other town—had ever seen. There were singing, cheering, and snake dancing on Main Street. "Great! Super! Unbelievable!" raved Carlton Barnett of St. Louis, MO. "After all the problems in getting around this town, this makes these whole miserable two weeks worthwhile." The Rev. Fell, only ten days after suggesting that all spectators be banned, agreed that the victory had "made everything worthwhile." Perhaps for the first time in the Games, television audiences were envious of those who had made it to Lake Placid.

If the "Olympics in Perspective" had made the 1,300 athletes from 37 countries the primary concern and had relegated the spectators and press to a very distant second, it was the No. 1's who provided the lasting memories for the No. 2's. For the United States there was a great deal to cheer about, as well as several disappointments. The hockey team had caught the fancy of Americans who had never known the difference between a face-off and a field goal. Eric Heiden's record five gold medals in speedskating were an awesome feat. Phil Mahre's silver medal in the men's slalom, coming less than a year after a serious injury, was testimony to his courage. For those who had expected victories for singles figure skaters Linda Fratianne and

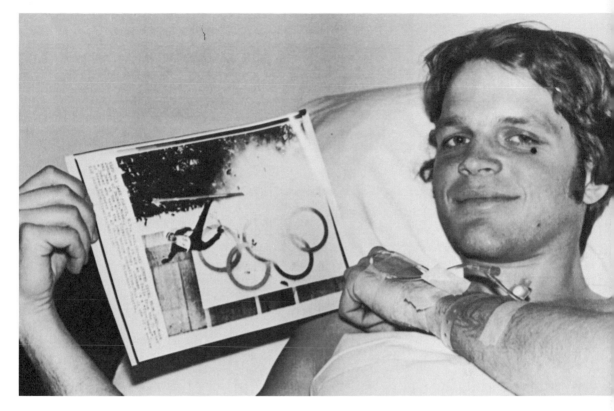

From a Lake Placid hospital bed, Mark Johnson displays a photo of himself taking a spill in the 70-meter jump. The Duluth, MN, skier suffered several fractures of his spinal vertebrae. The number of serious injuries incurred during the Games was minimal.

Charlie Tickner, silver and bronze medals, respectively, were disappointments. Those who could appreciate their hard work and gritty perseverance were proud. The most shocking disappointment for the United States, however, was the sudden withdrawal from the pairs figure skating competition of Tai Babilonia and Randy Gardner due to his groin and abdomen injury.

Sweden's Ingemar Stenmark became king of men's Alpine skiing with two gold medals. Hanni Wenzel won the first-ever gold medals for the tiny principality of Leichtenstein; all told, Wenzel won two golds and a silver. Brother Andreas also took a silver, making them the first brother and sister to win Alpine medals in the same Games. Leonhard Stock of Austria, who went to Lake Placid as an alternate, was the surprise winner in the men's downhill. Another long shot who won an unexpected gold was speedskater Annie Borckink of The Netherlands, a 28-year-old nurse who turned in the fastest 1,500-m race of her life. In Nordic skiing, the stars were Nikolai Zimyatov of the Soviet Union, who won three gold medals, and Ulrich Wehling of East Germany, who became the first male athlete to win a gold medal in three different Winter Games.

In the race among nations for medals, East Germany won a total of 23 (9 gold, 7 silver, and 7 bronze), but the Soviet Union took the most gold (10), as well as 6 silver and 6 bronze, for 22 overall. The United States was a distant third, with 6 gold, 4 silver, and 2 bronze.

Not all of the outstanding performers received official Olympic medals. There were many athletes whose best efforts were not recognized only because they didn't happen to win. To help rectify that injustice, The Associated Press awarded medals of "extraordinary merit" to some of the lesser lights who exemplified the Olympic spirit as much as the Eric Heidens, Ingemar Stenmarks, Hanni Wenzels, and Nikolai Zimyatovs. The gold medal for extraordinary merit went to Arturo Kinch of Costa Rica, who was his team's only competitor, doubling also as flagbearer, trainer, counselor, and national delegate. The 23-year-old skier, 145 pounds of grit, took a nasty spill in the men's downhill, injuring a leg. He tried again in the giant slalom, tipped a gate, and tumbled into the snow. On crutches, Kinch had to be restrained from tackling the hill again in the slalom.

The silver and bronze medals for extraordinary merit went to Faride Rahme of Lebanon and Guizhen Wong of China, who finished 34th and 35th (next-to-last and last) in the women's giant slalom. Their claim to immortality: they didn't beat the mountain, but the mountain didn't beat them.

With all the controversies, all the problems, and all the pressures to perform well, the athletes themselves enjoyed a pleasant and meaningful two weeks. Despite earlier complaints about the Olympic Village, most of the athletes—the Soviets notwithstanding—were quite happy once they moved in. Everyone thought the food was good—Soviets, French, and Swiss included. The main attraction at the Olympic Village—the hit of Lake Placid, as far as most were concerned—was the game room. Full of blinking electronic video games, Foosbol tables, and row upon row of pinball machines, the game room provided relaxed and pleasurable competition after the day's skiing, skating, and sledding were over. There was many an empty dance floor in the discothèques of Lake Placid.

For entertainment, athletes and visitors alike could enjoy the latest disco steps. However, the game room was the prime meeting point and gathering place.

A special "Arcade Tricathlon," sponsored by the leading tabletop game manufacturers, drew 35 entries into a five-day competition. Each contestant played a pinball machine, a video game, and Foosbol table soccer. The winner of the first-place lucite trophy was 15-year-old Canadian ski jumper Steve Collins; Alex Michaelides of Cyprus was second; Paul Gibbons of Britain was third.

The award for behind-the-scenes reporting at the pinball room went to David Silk, a forward on the U.S. hockey team. As far as Silk could tell, male athletes from the different countries fit perfectly their stereotypical national traits. The Italians, he claimed, whistled wolfishly at women athletes. The Chinese spent most of their time playing electronic Ping-Pong. Most disturbing to Silk was the pastime of the Soviets and East Germans. "They spend their time playing a game called Submarine, picking off American battleships," said Silk. "Geez, you ought to hear them carry on when they get one."

In terms of finances, the "Olympics in Perspective" did not keep the perspective the LPOOC had in mind. The final cost estimate was a cool $200 million—$50 million more than the "final" budget—and the taxpayers of New York State would likely be the ones to make up the difference. In terms of benefits to Lake Placid and the Adirondack tourist area, the Games were perhaps not the best publicity. But in terms of camaraderie and pure excitement of competition—and those, after all, are what the Olympics are really about—the 1980 Winter Games in Lake Placid, NY, were both enormously successful and not soon to be forgotten.

Petr Spurney, the general manager of the LPOOC, summed up well: "When you go to a once-in-a-lifetime experience," he said, "the wait in line is part of the experience."

In the game room, the Foosbol tables were always jammed.

FINAL MEDAL STANDINGS

Nation	G	S	B
Soviet Union	10	6	6
East Germany	9	7	7
United States	6	4	2
Austria	3	2	2
Sweden	3	0	1
Liechtenstein	2	2	0
Finland	1	5	3
Norway	1	3	6
The Netherlands	1	2	1
Switzerland	1	1	3
Great Britain	1	0	0
West Germany	0	2	3
Italy	0	2	0
Canada	0	1	1
Hungary	0	1	0
Japan	0	1	0
Bulgaria	0	0	1
Czechoslovakia	0	0	1
France	0	0	1

An "Olympics in Perspective" 27

Lake Placid Revisited

A new chairlift was built at Whiteface Mountain for the 1980 Games.

Against the backdrop of New York's Adirondack Mountains, between Storytown U.S.A., where fictional characters come to life, and Santa's Village, North Pole, where tourists find Santa in his workshop even in August, sits Lake Placid, a little mountain town with a fairy tale all its own. Founded in 1850 and incorporated in 1900, Lake Placid made the most of its surrounding natural resources to become a winter and summer resort. During the late 1800's and early 1900's exclusive clubs and large hotels were constructed to provide vacation activities for the leisured. Golf, tennis, horseback riding, croquet, and beautiful cotillions were enjoyed in the summer; skating, sleigh-riding, skiing, skijoring (being towed by a horse across the snow), and simply sitting by a fire were prime winter pleasures.

Melvil Dewey, the inventor of the Dewey Decimal library cataloging system, founded the famous Lake Placid Club in 1895. The club was one of the most famous in the United States; besides its own sports facilities it had its own post office, stores, water supply, and law enforcement department. Refurbished for the 1980 Games and called now the Lake Placid Resort Hotel, the club housed officials of the IOC.

Over the years the tiny town of Lake Placid has not changed much, not even in population. It has remained a tourist hamlet that depends for survival on luring visitors year round. It is buried in the forests of firs, pines, birches, and sugar maples in the 95,000 square miles of the nation's largest park, the Adirondack State Park. It is 150 miles from a major metropolitan area and is soothed by the serenity of lakes—sparkling Mirror, Clear, and Placid.

Per capita income is about $5,000 and off-season unemployment runs as high as 15%. The houses tend to be big and old, with huge open porches for summer. Capacious chimneys bespeak woodburning fireplaces for winter; steep-pitched roofs are clearly favored for their help in sliding the snow away. The quick, winding streams are a haven for trout, and the forests are alive with deer and other wildlife. At spring thaw the runoff from the mountains is clear enough to drink as it rolls over the rocks to the edge of two-lane roadways.

Dr. Godfrey Dewey, author, educator, and son of Melvil, was instrumental in bringing the 1932 Winter Games to Lake Placid. In fact, Dewey designed the original ski jump at Intervale, an area 1.5 miles from the village. The nation's only bobsled run began operation in Lake Placid on Christmas Day 1930 and an Olympic Arena opened just in time for the 1932 Games. Facilities for Alpine skiing, which was not part of the competition in 1932, did not come into being in the area until 1938. It would be another 20 years before the Whiteface Mountain Ski Center, operated by the state's department of environmental conservation, opened its doors.

The town of Lake Placid, located in the heart of the Adirondack Mountains, was founded as a year-round resort. By the late 1920's, the center had become the "St. Moritz of America" and a movement had begun to bring the Winter Olympics to the town. The photo above is a general view of Main Street, looking south, in December 1926; right, the A. G. Spaulding & Brothers sporting goods store, also taken in the same year.

Prior to the development of the airplane and other means of rapid transit, only a small, privileged group of North Americans—the wealthy and those who lived in certain sections of the nation—was in a position to enjoy winter sports. On the other hand, snow was common and easily accessible in most of Europe; in fact, most Scandinavian children grew up on skis. Consequently it was natural that the first two Winter Games were held in established winter sports areas—Chamonix, France, and St. Moritz, Switzerland. It also followed that the European (Scandinavian) athletes would—and did—dominate the first two Winter Olympics. However, things changed in 1932. Not only were the Winter Games held on American soil for the first time but also, for the first time, the United States won more medals than any other nation.

Four of America's six gold medals came in speed skating. Jack Shea, the 21-year-old son of a local butcher, captured the 500-meter and 1,500-meter events, while Irving Jaffee, who learned to skate while delivering newspapers in New York, won the 5,000 and 10,000 events. (In 1980 Shea was supervisor of the township of North Ebba, which includes Lake Placid.)

However, the darling of the Games was Norway's Sonja Henie, who swept first place votes from all seven judges in winning the second of her three figure skating gold medals.

The 1932 Games were a giant morale booster, coming at a time when the United States really needed one. It was an irony that Lake Placid, a rich man's playground, should become the means of lifting some of the gloom of the nation sunk in economic depression.

The Olympic Stadium, containing ice hockey and speed skating rinks and seating for 3,360 spectators, was built on Main Street for the 1932 Games. The cost was $200,000. During the summer, the facility was used for horse shows, flower shows, boxing matches, and special exhibits.

The III Winter Olympic Games opened at Lake Placid on Feb. 4, 1932. Jack Shea, a native of the town who recited the Olympic oath in behalf of the athletes, took gold medals in the 500- and 1,500-meter speed skating events. The American ski team, coached by Julius Blegen (extreme left), was unsuccessful in its efforts to win America's first medal in skiing. The Swedish ski team (below) dominated the 15-kilometer cross country as Sven Utterström and Axel T. Wilkström captured the gold and silver, respectively.

In the years following, Lake Placid made eight bids to bring the Winter Olympics back. From the pulpit of St. Agnes Church a pastor led his congregation in prayers to land the prestigious worldwide sporting event and boost the village's tourist economy.

According to Jack Wilkins, 58, a native and an original director of the 1980 Lake Placid Olympic Organizing Committee (LPOOC), the village was turned down for the 1952 Games because it lacked a reputation for dependable snow conditions. ''We had had a dry Olympics in '32,'' noted Wilkins.

''We didn't get it in 1960. The bid went to Squaw Valley. But we never gave up hope, or prayers,'' said the Rev. Philip Allen, pastor of St. Agnes Church. Over the years, local officials continued to lobby the sporting federations. Finally, on Oct. 23, 1974, the IOC announced that Lake Placid had been selected as host for the 1980 Winter Olympics. Advances in snow-making and refrigeration had negated the argument regarding undependable snow conditions.

''We just stuck with it,'' said Wilkins. ''There was a group of people who knew we could do it—not just thought we could do it. That's why we kept at it.''

Between 1932 and 1980, Lake Placid was the scene of numerous world championship winter events. Over the years, the little resort put more local residents on Olympic teams than any other community, regardless of size. According to Wilkins, Lake Placid is ''a very proud and committed community.''

(Continued page 38)

Three hundred and seven athletes from 17 nations, including skiers from Czechoslovakia (top, left) participated in the 1932 Games. Controversy developed during the speed skating competition. The Europeans were accustomed to skating only against time; the American style was to jockey for the best position. Following the events, most enthusiasts agreed that the American way was more exciting. Hubert and Curtis Stevens, two brothers whose family owned Lake Placid's famous Stevens House, won the two-man bob in world record time. After defeating West Germany, 4–1, Canada took its fourth consecutive gold in ice hockey. The sport was part of the summer program in 1920.

Following the IOC announcement of Oct. 23, 1974, that the Winter Games would return to Lake Placid in 1980, the town underwent a major construction and rebuilding program. New hotels, restaurants, and housing for the athletes were built. Sports facilities were either constructed or remodeled.

A 400-meter refrigerated speed skating oval (below) was built in the center of Lake Placid on the campus of the high school (right). A large sign near the oval announced that the town was ready for the Olympic Games.

Some experts considered the ski jumping towers at Intervale Hill, one mile from Lake Placid, as the architectural achievement of the Games. The 70-meter jump has seven starting positions (see photo above). The 90-meter jump is 257 feet high and contains an elevator.

Viewing the Games as an "Olympics in Perspective," Lake Placid residents—including the Rev. Bernard Fell, a former policeman who would become president of the LPOOC—began to prepare for the Games immediately following the IOC announcement of 1974. New hotels, guest houses, and restaurants were built and the requisite sports facilities were either constructed or remodeled in preparation for the Games. Some $200 million in local, state, and federal funds were spent.

Although the transportation system in and out of Lake Placid during the first week of the Games, the size of the rooms at the Olympic Village, the high prices for almost everything, and confusion at the town's only traffic light led to many complaints and some irate criticism, the ski jumps, luge and bobsled runs, fieldhouse, and other venues received unusually high marks from contestants and spectators alike. The LPOOC also was praised for seeing to it that the events went off on schedule and were run efficiently.

The smallness of the town added a distinct charm to the Games, and a friendly atmosphere was prevalent to an unusual degree throughout the 13 days. The trading of souvenirs and other items, especially multicolored Olympic pins, became widespread. On Sunday, February 24, the day the Games ended, the shops of Lake Placid had a good day—the sale of flags, T-shirts, and posters was excellent.

After the flame had been extinguished, the LPOOC found itself with an estimated total deficit of more than $6 million and unpaid bills to several major suppliers and contractors. The committee pleaded unsuccessfully with Washington for an additional $3.5 million in federal loans, and some town residents suggested that the torch itself be sold to help defray costs. With the bonanza over, many local businesses found it difficult to make ends meet. Two of the most prestigious hotels in town filed for bankruptcy. All in all, the economic future of Lake Placid was left unresolved. It was unclear whether all the publicity and new construction would revive the tourist economy or whether the expense of maintaining all the facilities would be too burdensome for the small mountain town.

A large ice sculpture was designed in front of the Olympic Arena, which was built for the 1932 Games and reconstructed and refurbished for 1980. The building connects with the Fieldhouse, which contains seating for 8,000 persons, Olympic-size and U.S.-size ice sheets, offices, lounges, and rooms for the figure skaters.

The Opening Ceremony

Massed Olympic flags precede the march-in as the ceremonies opening the XIII Winter Olympics begin.

One million flowers, 2,000 birds, 5 planes, 40 hot air balloons, 25,000 helium balloons, and a skydiving team were part of the colorful ceremonies that officially rang in the XIII Winter Olympics on Wednesday, February 13, 1980. Under an overcast sky in a cold wind, with temperatures at 25°F (−4°C), the traditional parade of athletes spread a sea of color across the Olympic stadium. Teams from 37 nations—wearing colorful winter gear, ranging from bright red parkas to tan ranch outfits—marched in behind their flags and name placards and took up their positions in the center of the field before a crowd of 23,000 persons. With the exception of the United States delegation, the Canadian team received the most applause. Only days before, Canada was credited with rescuing a group of Americans from possible captivity by extremists in Tehran, Iran.

During a preceremony program, three parachutists, each carrying a flag—the Greek, the Olympic, and the American—had dropped with great precision on their target inside the stadium.

U.S. Vice-President Walter Mondale, standing in for President Carter, presided from the presidential box. Sitting with the vice-president were Lord Killanin, the president of the IOC, Hugh Carey, governor of New York, and Jacob Javits and Daniel P. Moynihan, the state's two senators.

In his welcoming speech, Governor Carey expressed the hope that the Games might be "contests without conflict." Bernard Fell of the LPOOC spoke of the pride Lake Placid would feel if "we can say that what we did here contributed to the preservation of the Olympic Games."

During a pre-ceremony program, parachutists bringing the Greek, Olympic (above), or U.S. flags landed precisely in the Olympic stadium. Right: the West German team marches in behind its flag and placard.

Following the march-in, 37 teams assembled in the center of the field. As the host, the U.S. team was last, behind the USSR and Yugoslavia. The Americans wore ranch-type outfits designed by Levi Strauss. From the presidential box, Vice-President Walter Mondale, New York Gov. Hugh Carey, and the state's two senators, Daniel P. Moynihan and Jacob Javits, viewed the festivities with Lord Killanin of the IOC and representatives of the organizing committee.

The torch was lit in Olympia, Greece, (above, left) and then traveled to Lake Placid so that Dr. Charles Kerr could ignite the flame (page 43).

THE OLYMPIC TORCH

A short time after Vice-President Mondale officially opened the Games, Dr. Charles Kerr, a 44-year-old psychiatrist from Tucson, AZ, who enjoys jogging, carried the torch into the Olympic stadium. After climbing 13 stairs which signified that the 1980 Lake Placid Games were the 13th Winter Olympics, Dr. Kerr dipped the torch into a big saucer that immediately burst into flame. An automatic lift then raised the saucer to the top of a 49-foot tripod so that the flame would be visible from the various competition sites.

Amid girls waving pom-poms and the sounds of school bands, the torch had arrived in Lake Placid on Friday, February 8. Most of the populace of the town turned out in biting cold to receive the torch, which had been lit in a simple ceremony in Olympia, Greece, on January 30 and flown to Langley Air Force Base, VA. Fifty-two Americans, who had been selected from a pool of applicants and who represented all the states and the District of Columbia, took turns carrying the two-foot high, two-pound torch the 1,000 miles from Virginia to Lake Placid. Each torch-bearer covered a distance of 18 to 30 miles. Special stopover ceremonies were held along the route. The custom of bringing the torch from Greece to the Olympic site by relay began at the 1936 Summer Games and at the 1952 Winter Games. Although the relay for the Summer Games has always originated at Olympia, various starting points were used for the Winter Games until 1964. At that time, Olympia became the starting point for the winter torch relay as well. In accordance with Olympic rules, the organizing committee is responsible for transporting the torch.

The flame at Lake Placid consumed 10,000 gallons of liquid propane gas. Two 1,000-gallon tanks were installed to make sure that the flame burned without interruption throughout the Games. A subsidiary of Texas Eastern contributed the fuel.

Some 25,000 balloons were released as the opening ceremony ended. Earlier, the Twin City Skating Club had performed "A Musical Expression of Friendship."

Lord Killanin thanked the community of Lake Placid for its vast preparations in anticipation of the Games and introduced the vice-president. Mr. Mondale declared: "On behalf of the president of the United States and the American people, I am pleased to declare officially the opening of the XIII Winter Olympics, held this year at Lake Placid."

With a fanfare of trumpets, and to the strains of the Olympic hymn, the Olympic flag was raised on its tall pole. Then the mayor of Innsbruck, Austria, where the last Winter Games were played, handed the embroidered satin official Olympic flag to Lord Killanin, who handed it to Robert Peacock, mayor of Lake Placid, for deposit in the town hall for the next four years.

A three-gun salute was fired, and then the last of the carriers of the sacred flame from Olympia ran to the lowered cauldron whose fire would illumine the Games. Tipping his leather-handled bronze torch to the cauldron he lighted it.

The end of the flag ceremony was the signal to release hundreds of doves, which soared into the chill sky.

American speed skater Eric Heiden took the Olympic oath on behalf of the athletes, and Terry McDermott, a 1964 speed skating gold medalist, did the same for the officials and the judges.

The Star Spangled Banner was played and sung and as its notes faded away a cascade of colored balloons drifted over the site. The Games could begin.

Alpine Skiing

U.S. downhiller Karl Anderson throws caution—and himself—to the wind in attacking the course on Whiteface Mountain. Said Austrian skiing great Karl Schranz of the event: "No coward will ever win."

The most lasting picture of the 1976 Olympic Winter Games was the crouched figure of Franz Klammer in a heart-stopping plummet down the Austrian Alps. Amid the cheers of his countrymen, Klammer charged to a gold medal in the downhill skiing competition. It was a magnificent show of going for broke and one that was still vivid four years later.

One thing that Alpine skiers can't worry about is going too fast. There is no room for fear. "You have to be aggressive," says U.S. men's coach Harald Schoenhaar. "You have to fight. You're attacking the hill, you're attacking those gates, and you're attacking the clock. You can't be afraid of anything." It was the aggressiveness and lack of fear displayed by Klammer in 1976 that the men and women racing down 4,867-ft Whiteface Mountain in 1980 sought to match.

According to the International Ski Federation (FIS), the governing body for Olympic skiing competition, the Alpine courses laid out on Whiteface are among the fastest and most challenging in the world. If their assessment was not universally shared—and it wasn't—there could be little criticism of the effort made to prepare Whiteface. Nine miles of courses were laid out especially for the 1980 Games, some with a vertical drop of 800 meters and an incline of up to 34°. To ensure proper conditions, snowmaking facilities were expanded and improved. The new air-water system has the capacity to cover 9.6 miles of the mountain's 16 miles of ski trails. It can cover the entire Olympic downhill course with 16 inches of snow in 16 hours. For the first time in the history of the Winter Olympics, skiers would compete on man-made snow from the top to the bottom of every course. Because European teams were not accustomed to artificial snow and would have to adjust to its somewhat different consistency and texture, several arrived in the United States weeks before the Games to train at other ski areas—such as Hunter Mountain, NY, and Stowe, VT—where machine-made snow is used.

Men's Downhill

On the morning of the men's downhill the sky was partly overcast, and it was snowing. Six inches had fallen overnight. The fast, solid base put down in the dry weeks before the Games was blanketed by a fluffy layer that would only slow the skiers at points along the course. And so in the early morning hours 200 volunteers were brought in to sweep off the newly-fallen snow. The 3,009-meter run was restored to perfect condition for the race—hard and fast.

The opinion of some competitors was that the course was not so difficult as the FIS had claimed. "To compare it with the downhills in Europe is a joke," said Phil Mahre, the top U.S. contender for a medal. "The last third of the course, you just get in your tuck and stay there." The top of the course was steep and technically demanding, with several sharp turns. The only viable strategy was to ski cleanly and aggressively through the upper parts of the course—Hurricane Alley, Lake Placid Turn, Sno Field, and Dynamite Corner—maintain top speed in the fast middle sections—Niagara, Victoria, and so on—and

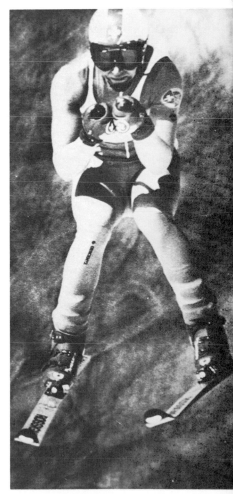

Intrepid Leonhard Stock, left, speeds past another gate on his way to a gold medal in the downhill. Stock went to Lake Placid as the alternate on a powerful Austrian team. Silhouetted against the trees, Switzerland's Peter Mueller, below, maintains the "tuck" position even as his skis leave the snow.

stay in the streamlined "tuck" position for a smooth glide through the slower, flatter bottom of the run. Although some of the skiers may not have been thrilled by the course, there was a tall, sharp-featured, 21-year-old clerk from a small village in the Austrian Tyrol who obviously found it to his liking.

When Austrian team officials hoisted a triumphant Leonhard Stock to their shoulders after the race, their jubilant countrymen broke into song. The choruses of *Immer Wieder Austria* (Again and Again Austria) must have warmed the coaches and managers as much as they did the smiling champion. That a new name had been added to the list of great Austrian downhillers—Toni Sailer, Egon Zimmerman, Karl Schranz, Klammer, and now Leonhard Stock—certainly was cause for celebration. But the relief of team officials had as much to do with the events of the preceding days as with the race itself.

The controversy surrounding the Austrian downhill team actually began in January, when the nation's ski federation decided to cut the great Klammer from the Olympic team. The hue and cry of seven million Austrians was so loud that team manager Karl "Downhill Charlie" Kahr was forced to go on national television to explain. Klammer had been a great racer, but his recent results were not of Olympic caliber and there were too many other good skiers vying for spots on the team. Kahr was right on both counts, and the public bought it. That, the federation thought, was that.

New problems, however, were just around the corner. The final ski-off for the Olympic squad, to be held in Chamonix, France, was canceled for lack of snow. The ski federation then named to the team what it considered its best prospects: Peter Wirnsberger, Sepp Walcher, Werner Grissman, and Harti Weirather. Leonhard Stock, who only a month before had been skiing in a sling and cast because of a broken collarbone, was selected as the alternate. It was commonly understood that only

sickness or injury would keep any of the top four out of the competition. But Leonhard Stock had different ideas and was out to make a place for himself. He was simply spectacular in the official trial runs in the days preceding the race, recording the fastest times in two out of three trials. Keeping him off the team threatened another scandal. Two nights before the competition, Downhill Charlie told the team that all five would have to race the next day for the final four spots. In the morning, however, Kahr announced that Stock and Weirather were definitely on the team and that the other three would have to race for the two remaining spots. The result was an angry shouting match and near fisticuffs between skiers and managers. But the race-off was held and Walcher, the 1978 FIS champion and one of the prerace favorites, was out. "We have already finished our first Olympics," said Grissman after the race-off.

By the time their second Olympics—the real one—came around, the Austrian downhillers were at a competitive edge. Stock was the ninth skier to make his run, and he attacked the course with confidence. Because his specialty is really the giant slalom, the difficult turns at the top of the run were much to his liking. His split times at intervals along the course were blistering, and he finished at 1 minute 45.50 seconds, the best time so far by 1.5 seconds.

But still to come were many of the world's greatest downhillers. Stock was still breathing hard when Peter Mueller of Switzerland, one of the heaviest prerace favorites, came down the course. Mueller's run was uncharacteristically flawed, however, and his time was well slower than that of the leader. Stock watched tensely as more skiers came across the finish line. The Canadian team, led by Ken Read, posed a major threat. Known

Steve Podborski (above), one of the Kamikaze Kanadians, flies to a surprise bronze medal in the downhill. Harti Weirather (right) needed two strong practice runs just to make the final Austrian team.

as the "Kamikaze Kanadians," their reckless, breakneck style was patterned after the legendary run of Klammer in 1976. Read hurtled out of the starting gate shortly after Mueller. "All week long," he said later, "we kept telling ourselves, 'it's only one race; anything can happen.' Well, it happened." Not even 15 seconds into the race, Read suffered a heartbreaking mishap. One of his bindings released and he tumbled off the course, out of the race.

After all the skiers had finished and the snow had settled, Stock's time was still the best by a comfortable margin. Peter Wirnsberger of Austria, who also made the team only the day before, took the silver with a time of 1:46.12. Third was Steve Podborski, a Kamikaze Kanadian, in 1:46.62. Pete Patterson of the United States finished a surprising fifth, just behind Mueller.

Stock's victory was his first ever in a world-caliber downhill competition. "I was hoping I could have a good run here," he said. "I was looking forward to it, but I never thought I could win the gold medal." Perhaps reminded by the strains of *Immer Wieder Austria*, Stock spoke of his predecessor and brought to mind some of the earlier controversy. "I was glad to be able to succeed Klammer," said the new champion. "I'm a little sad, though, that Klammer was not here. There will never be another Franz Klammer."

The downhill medalists stand victorious at the award ceremony. Below, Stock is embraced by fellow Austrian Karl Schranz.

Alpine Skiing 49

A superb glider, Austria's Annemarie Moser-Proell found the women's downhill course much to her liking. "I dislike easy runs where one has time to think," she once said. "Thinking is bad." Ignoring the bitter cold and a hard-driving wind, Moser-Proell burned up the course and won her first Olympic gold medal.

Women's Downhill

As Annemarie Moser-Proell awaited the start of the women's downhill, Alois Bumberger, the Austrian women's Alpine coach, rubbed the skier's knees to keep them from going numb and warmed the inside of her boots with a hair dryer. At 11:30 A.M. it was still only 7°F (-14°C) and the wind was blowing at 25 miles per hour. The first five skiers battled the wind and cold racing down the hard-packed course at speeds of nearly 80 miles per hour. Frostbite was a real danger. As each skier crossed the finish line, she was met immediately by a medic who removed her goggles and warmed her face with his hands.

Annemarie Moser-Proell has cold, pale blue eyes—like icicles. To those who don't know her, the stare is chilling. She has been called intimidating, arrogant, termperamental, and insufferable. She has also been called the greatest woman downhill skier of all time. Her fierceness is but the temporary disposition of an athlete concerned only with winning. "She wants to win," said Bumberger. "Only victory counts." Indeed the 26-year-old restaurant (Café Proell) owner from Kleinarl in Salzburg Province, Austria, had won everything in sight during her 12-year career in world-class competition—with one exception. She had won a total of 61 World Cup races and six overall World Cup trophies. What she had never won was an Olympic gold medal.

At age 18, Proell was touted to win two or even three gold medals at the Winter Games in Sapporo, Japan. She was a major disappointment, settling for silver medals in the downhill and giant slalom. Taking the gold in those two events was a young Swiss named Marie-Theres Nadig, a rival for years to come. Said Proell, "I was not concentrating on the races. I was thinking about other things." Thereafter she did not think of much else. On the dashboard of her car appeared a metal plaque which read: NEVER FORGET SAPPORO. Before the Innsbruck Games in 1976, however, Proell married and went into retirement. She thought she had hung up her skis for good. She managed to sit around for 1½ years before the lure of gold drew her back.

Early in 1979 there was fear that Moser-Proell might meet the same fate as the legendary Karl Schranz of Austria, who was barred from the Sapporo Games on charges of professionalism. Moser-Proell had appeared in a television commercial with her husband, advertising a detergent. Later she sent her fee to the Austrian Ski Federation and returned to the World Cup circuit. A subsequent probe by Olympic officials cleared the veteran skier of all charges. In the early part of the 1980 World Cup season, the 5'-7" Moser-Proell trimmed down to 148 pounds and established herself as a major Olympic contender.

The women's downhill course on Whiteface Mountain is similar to the men's—difficult and steep at the top and flat at the bottom. The 2,698-meter run begins at Cloudspin with a very steep grade; alternates between flat and steep sections through Crossover, Chicane, and Waterfall; and begins to flatten out at Grand Central, about 1,115 meters from the start. The course then maintains about a 15° slope through Fifth Avenue—a long, straight schuss—until reaching the Boreen Bump at the 2,000-meter mark. The course ends at Ziel Schuss. As on the men's course, the key is to be very aggressive at the top and carry as much speed as possible to the lower sections.

Charging out of the starting gate, Moser-Proell quickly tucked her poles under her arms and assumed the low crouch of a straight-away schuss. With strength and control she retained her tuck position through the tight, sharp turns and at the same time followed a line that brought her several feet closer to each gate than any other skier. Despite the raw conditions, Moser-Proell turned in what some considered one of the best downhill runs ever by a woman. Her time was a sizzling 1:37.52.

But while others congratulated her, Moser-Proell stayed calm until Nadig, her longtime rival, finished her run. Anne-marie was taking nothing for granted. Coming down three racers later, Nadig was in the middle of a fine run when she was jarred by a violent rush of wind. It cost her valuable seconds, but she was at least strong enough to stay on the course. ''I almost went into a fence,'' she said. ''It was not a fair competition because of the wind. Some had gusts and some didn't. They shouldn't have started under these conditions.''

Her rivalry with Moser-Proell as intense as the cold, Swiss star Marie-Theres Nadig had trouble in the wind but still managed to finish third.

Two American women won praise, if not Olympic medals. Cindy Nelson (right), who competed in all three Alpine disciplines, was awarded the International Ski Federation silver medal for the "world combined championship." Heidi Preuss (below) was a surprise fourth-place finisher in the women's downhill event. Prior to the Games, she had completed only one full year of World Cup competition.

Nadig's time—1:38.36—went up on the scoreboard, and Moser-Proell thrust her arms in the air. "When I saw Marie-Theres come across the finish line, I knew I had a 99% chance of winning because she was my toughest competitor," the Austrian said. "I was obliged to win the downhill gold medal here because it's the only thing I haven't won."

In the cold, icy air the years of frustration—and the chilling stare—melted away in one marvelous moment of triumph.

Without the wind Nadig might have won the silver medal, but she had to settle for a bronze, as Hanni Wenzel of Liechtenstein, skiing 12th, narrowly beat her for second place with a time of 1:38.22. Wind or no wind, it did not seem likely that anybody could have beaten Moser-Proell. An Olympic gold medal meant too much to her. Said Nadig: "Annemarie just blew me off the course today."

Braving the cold to watch the world's best women downhillers blown off their stride by the icy wind and Annemarie Moser-Proell were 20,000 spectators, most of whom paid $28.30 for the privilege. The "hometown" crowd was given something to cheer about when 18-year-old Heidi Preuss of Lakeport, NH, crossed the finish line in 1:39.51—good for fourth place. It was a stunning performance for one so new to world class competition, but Preuss was hardly satisfied. "I was very disappointed when I saw my time and when I saw that '4' on the scoreboard. That's the fourth time I've placed fourth at World Cup level. It really burns me."

Also unhappy with her run was Cindy Nelson of Lutsen, MN, a bronze medalist in the 1976 Olympic downhill and considered the best chance for the U.S. women's team at Lake Placid. Nelson finished in a tie for seventh place with Torill Fjeldstad of Norway at 1:39.69, and she too was disappointed. "I feel like I'm one of the best in the world, and I didn't ski like it. I just wasn't concentrating. My mind was a little behind what was happening. I wasn't anticipating."

A favorite of the spectators and media on chilly Whiteface was Faride Rahme of Lebanon, a country with little snow and few places for an Alpine skier to train. It was Faride's first downhill in world competition, and even she conceded there was no hope of taking a medal. "I know I won't win, but I just want to ski well," said Rahme. "There's a chance I might get 10th place," she added unrealistically. An injured ankle and training times more than a *minute* slower than the *also-rans* in the field made her the bettor's choice for last place. Her enthusiasm undiminished, Rahme made it down the run. She finished 27th in a field of 28 (one skier fell and did not finish the race). Her time of 2:42.88 was 56 seconds behind the 26th-place finisher and 1 minute, 5 seconds behind Moser-Proell.

With commendable determination and sportsmanship, Faride Rahme (above) attempted her first Olympic downhill race at the 1980 Games. The Lebanese skier, accustomed to more temperate climes, wore a mask to protect her face from frostbite. Austrian skiers Anton Innauer and Annemarie Moser-Proell (left) display countenances as glowing as their gold medals, awarded for 70-meter jump and women's downhill, respectively.

Pure strength is one of the attributes that has put Ingemar Stenmark a notch above other world-class skiers. Above, the Swedish star miraculously avoids a fall with one hand.

Men's Giant Slalom

Andreas Wenzel of Liechtenstein, who had taken a narrow lead into the second and final run of the men's giant slalom (GS), ended up satisfied with a silver medal. "I'm not disappointed," he said. "I had an idea this would happen."

Others also had the idea. Indeed there were few expressions of surprise when Sweden's Ingemar Stenmark won the gold medal. He had long since established himself as probably the best giant slalom skier in history, having won every race he entered in nearly two years. Still, Stenmark was not invincible and nobody knew it better than he. It would take two strong runs to win the gold, and he was angry with himself after a third place finish in the first run. The taciturn Swede refused to speak with reporters but the next day admitted that the obstacle had been of his own making. "I put myself in a situation I shouldn't have."

The first run was held on Whiteface Mountain's new Parkway course. The 1,354-meter, 56-gate run begins on a very steep schuss to the first lift crossing, then decreases in slope gradually over the next 400 meters. The rest of the course alternates between steep and flat, before reaching the finish at Ziel Schuss, a 150-meter-long schuss with a 38-meter drop. "I'm real pleased with the GS," said Phil Mahre. "It's not too steep and not too flat. There's a lot of rolling terrain."

But if Mahre and the other skiers were pleased with the course, they could not have been pleased with the weather conditions. At start time—11:00 A.M.—the mercury hovered near zero, and a blustery wind caused the wind-chill factor to dip to −25°F (−32°C).

Austria's Hans Enn (left), Valeri Tsyganov of the USSR (above), and Liechtenstein's Andreas Wenzel display the speed and control required in the giant slalom.

The day after sister Hanni had won a silver medal in the women's downhill, Andreas Wenzel sped to the fastest time in the first heat of the men's giant slalom. Hanni and Andreas were in excellent position to become the first brother-sister Alpine medal-winning act in the history of the Games. Skiing in the 11th position, Wenzel clocked 1:20.17 for the run, .14 of a second faster than Austria's Hans Enn and .32 of a second better than the feared Stenmark. The latter was not his usual flawless self. He skied without his characteristic rhythm and nearly fell at the fourth gate from the bottom. Making the turn, his skis began sliding out from under him, and Stenmark was all but on his side before putting out a hand and pushing himself upright. Few other skiers could have avoided a fall. In fourth place after the run was Italy's Bruno Nockler, followed by Joel Gaspoz, an 18-year-old Swiss rookie. The fastest American was Phil Mahre, in 14th place. Of the 78 skiers, 14 did not finish and one was disqualified for missing a gate. One who did not finish was Peter Luescher of Switzerland, the overall World Cup champion, who fell not far from the end of the run.

"I think I can be a little faster tomorrow," said Andreas Wenzel. "I think I can ski a little better but it will be hard to win. Stenmark is in a very good position to attack on his second run." Given Stenmark's penchant for skiing the first run cautiously and then attacking the course on the second, most competitors agreed that he was the man to beat. Even Stenmark cannot, or will not, explain his uncanny ability to propel himself past the frontrunners, no matter how far back he gets. He has won races coming from as far back as 23rd place after one heat. "Psychologically, it's very tough on us," Wenzel admitted.

The second run was held in temperatures approaching 20°F (−7°C), a break for the racers after the sub-zero weather the day before. Competition took place on the shorter (1,303-meter, 55-gate) Thruway course. Thruway is a little less rolling than Parkway, starting on a 200-meter section that drops nearly 50 meters. It then levels off slightly until the halfway point, called Calamity Lane, a 233-meter-long schuss that drops 61 meters. The course gradually flattens out again, before ending at Ziel Schuss.

In fourth place after the first run of the giant slalom, Bruno Nockler of Italy finished sixth. The Italian Alpine ski team had a disappointing showing overall, not winning a single medal in men's or women's competition.

After a patent come-from-behind victory in the giant slalom, Sweden's Ingemar Stenmark (far left) shares a laugh with third place finisher Hans Enn of Austria. Andreas Wenzel, from little Liechtenstein, is pleased with a silver medal-winning performance.

Sixty-three skiers started the second run, and the first five down the course went in reverse order of their standing after heat 1. Gaspoz and Nockler registered unimpressive times and wound up in 7th and 6th place, respectively. Next was Stenmark. He was extremely nervous in the starting gate but had managed to avoid some of the pressure in the previous 23½ hours. "I didn't think about the race until half an hour before," he said. "Then I thought only about how I should ski."

Stenmark's nervousness was apparent at the top of the course, as he fought to establish a rhythm. "I started out badly, and I had a choice," he recounted after the race. "I could attack and risk running out of the course, or I could take it easy and ski around the gates. I had this decision to make at every gate." As he approached each gate it became obvious that his every decision was to attack. Not satisfied to ski around the flags, he hit each one with his shoulder as he passed. Regaining his impeccable rhythm, Stenmark was again perfection personified. His time of 1:20.25 gave him a total of 2:40.74 for the two runs and posed a formidable challenge to Enn and Wenzel.

Joel Gaspoz, above, could manage no better than seventh, but the Swiss team was encouraged. Gaspoz was still a teenager and a rookie on the world class circuit.

Neither of them was quite up to the challenge. Enn, skiing next, posted 1:22.20, nearly two full seconds slower than Stenmark. His combined time of 2:42.51 was good for a bronze medal. Wenzel skied aggressively, as he knew he must. His time of 1:21.32 was fast, but still more than one second slower than that of Stenmark. His total time of 2:41.49 won him a silver medal. One of the fastest times of the day was recorded by a young Yugoslav named Bojan Krizaj, whose strongest event—the slalom—was still to come. A clocking of 1:21.25 moved him from 7th place after the first run to a 4th place finish. The top U.S. performance was put in by Phil Mahre, whose total of 2:44.33 left him in 10th place.

After the race Phil Mahre and twin brother Steve, who finished 15th, were asked why Stenmark could not be beat. "That's hard to say," said Phil. "It's almost unexplainable. He's an excellent technician. He's just an amazing skier."

Steve was more analytical. Stenmark, he said, "knows how to delay his turn and then put the pressure on at the right time. He makes good, clean turns all the time—that's the key."

Whatever the reasons, the simple truth was stated by a gracious Andreas Wenzel. "Stenmark is the most worthy gold medalist. I had an idea this would happen."

Ingemar Stenmark

Speed, speed, just speed, that's all I think about.

—INGEMAR STENMARK

Before every Olympic Games, athletes say they have never trained so hard in their lives. But Ingemar Stenmark, the 23-year-old Swedish slalom specialist who many say has revolutionized Alpine skiing, has never worked out so little before a season.

"It's more important for me to feel the joy of skiing when it comes to the big, important championships. I don't want to get bored with skiing. That's the reason why I cut my training schedule," Stenmark said.

In spite of the late start, Stenmark continued his domination of World Cup competition during the early part of the 1980 season. He finished first in two of five slalom events and did not lose at all in his specialty, the giant slalom. Three consecutive giant slalom victories in the 1980 season extended his unbeaten streak to 14, his last defeat coming in March 1978. Stenmark won the overall World Cup championship in 1976, 1977, and 1978, and would have won again in 1979 had it not been for a change in the scoring system that penalized a skier not participating in all three Alpine events. (Stenmark does not ski in downhill competition.)

But with all his successes, the single most important skiing title—an Olympic gold medal—had eluded him. Going into the 1976 Games at Innsbruck, young Stenmark was considered a favorite but managed only a bronze medal.

Stenmark's triumphs after the 1976 Games elevated him almost to the level of a god in his home country. "Winter's Bjorn Borg," Swedes called him. When Stenmark races, the schools in Stockholm close down for one or two hours, the factories close, and the streets are all but empty. Everyone is at home watching the race on television. But Stenmark's enormous popularity also created intense pressure to bring home gold from Lake Placid. "The pressure I'm under doesn't stop growing," he said. "For my fans, victory is all that counts. A second place means nothing to them."

The shy, taciturn Swede limited his remarks to the press but dedicated himself to at least one victory at Lake Placid. "The Olympic gold medal is the most important thing for me now," was about all he would say.

The pressure grew even more heavy on his 6', 170-pound frame after placing third in the first run of the giant slalom. But he did not disappoint. The next day he charged down the course in his characteristically rhythmic, fluid turns and won the event by a comfortable margin. After the race King Carl XVI Gustaf and Queen Silvia of Sweden, who traveled to Lake Placid for the Games, spoke privately with Stenmark. "He congratulated me and the rest is between him and me," Stenmark reported. With

Stenmark had a lot to smile about at Placid.

In the heat of competition even a superb skier like Stenmark never relaxes.

some of the pressure off, Stenmark went out three days later and won the gold medal in the special slalom, again with an impeccable second run.

The son of a bulldozer driver, Ingemar Stenmark was born and reared in the village of Tärnaby (pop. 500) in Swedish Lapland. It is located about 100 miles south of the Arctic Circle, and in the long winters there are only two hours of daylight. Reindeer roam the hills. Stenmark began skiing at the age of five on a small hill in back of his house. Stenmark's father explained that he must either use his natural talent as a skier or become a bulldozer driver. Ingemar decided to be a skier. "It was a thing I could do alone," he says now.

At age 13 he was discovered by coach Hermann Nogler, who immediately recognized his ability: "I watched him for a week, and I said to myself, 'That boy will be a world champion.' You could see the natural talent, the single-mindedness, the way he was hard on himself." At age 17 he participated in World Cup competition, and it wasn't long before he won his first giant slalom. His fluid style and enormous leg strength—he can high jump almost five feet from a standing position—made him the king of Alpine skiing in a few short years. Elan, the Yu-

goslavian-based company that makes his skis, is said to pay more than $250,000 a season to the Swedish ski association for the use of Stenmark's name. Olympic rules allow much of it to be returned to him.

Very much a loner—rarely participating in the ski circuit social life and seldom seen taking a drink—Stenmark spends a great deal of time in the reaches of Lapland, running through the forest, alone or with his dog Zorro. His other training methods (when he does work out before the season) include gymnastic exercises, walking a tightrope, and riding a unicycle. In addition to Swedish, he speaks English, French, German, Italian, and Serbo-Croatian. His comments are usually brief.

Before the Lake Placid Games, however, Stenmark could talk at length about the pressures of being the best. "It's more and more difficult each year. To win the Olympics—two golds—is going to be hard, more difficult mentally. Sometimes the whole business is too much for me. I only feel relaxed when I am skiing—by myself."

Not surprisingly, after he had won the two golds, his attitude toward skiing changed, "I have nothing more to achieve," he said. "I ski just for fun now," he added.

The cheering of American fans was "a big boost," said Christin Cooper, the best U.S. finisher in the women's giant slalom.

Women's Giant Slalom

Liechtenstein has its own postage stamps but no postal system. The mail is handled by Switzerland. The tiny principality has no air force or navy, none of its own television or radio stations, and not even its own currency (this, too, is Swiss). Most of the 25,000 inhabitants speak German, and the national anthem is called *Above on the German Rhine*. The music is the same as *God Save the Queen*.

At 5'4", 125 pounds, Hanni Wenzel is one of the tiniest skiers on the women's international circuit. Already a silver medalist in the downhill, she set off four days later to capture a gold medal in the giant slalom. Liechtenstein had never won a gold medal in either the Winter or Summer Games. Olympic audiences had heard *God Save the Queen* often enough, but it had always been a Briton atop the victory stand.

The first run of the women's giant slalom was held on the Thruway course, a day after the men had concluded their competition on the same run. Although the course was shortened to 364 meters and 51 gates for the women, it was no less challenging. A turn near the top of the run was so sharp that several skiers lost control and crashed. Four of the 15 top-seeded skiers,

including favored Marie-Theres Nadig, fell in the course and were unable to finish. Nadig fell at the fourth gate, allowing her left ski to slide out from under her. Daniela Zini of Italy and Regina Sackl of Austria also fell at about the same spot. Ursula Konzett of Liechtenstein had several close calls at the top, then fell after the midway point.

The weather had a lot to do with it. The temperature had risen to a springlike 41°F (5°C), and the snow was soft. After only three or four skiers had left the gate, ruts were already cut into the course. Skiers in the lower seeds had little chance of turning in fast times. For everyone, the greatest danger was sliding skis. In some instances this caused disaster, and in many others it cost valuable seconds. "Since it is all man-made snow and none of it is natural, it is very dense. The skis slide away from you. You lean in a little and you're gone," said Christin Cooper of Sun Valley, ID, who held 9th place after the first run.

Skiing in the sixth position, Wenzel had to contend with an already rutted course. The conditions were difficult, and adjustments had to be made. "I would have preferred harder snow," she said in her native German after the run. "I planned to come down smooth and not take too much risk on this snow. I had very good concentration." Wenzel did ski the course smoothly,

France's Perrine Pelen exhibits the technique that helped catapult her to third place and a bronze medal on the second day of the giant slalom event.

Irene Epple of West Germany said she was nervous, but her pursed lips and narrow stare show the determination and concentration that brought her a silver medal.

losing time only when she skied too wide around some of the gates on the upper portion. Her time of 1:14.33 was the best of the day.

Close behind Wenzel was Irene Epple of West Germany at 1:14.75. Epple nearly lost a ski pole at the top of the course, letting it dangle briefly by its strap, but she recovered quickly. "Without that mistake I could have been closer, I don't know how much it cost me, but I know that I really wanted to attack after that," she said. Christa Kinshofer, another West German, held third place with a clocking of 1:15.19. Still in the chase were Erika Hess of Switzerland, who was fourth with 1:15.27, and Fabienne Serrat of France, who was fifth in 1:15.43. Another French skier, Perrine Pelen, was just two one-hundredths of a second behind Serrat.

The 1980 Games represented the first time in Winter Olympic history that the women's giant slalom was run in two heats. Because of a rules change by the International Ski Federation in 1978, the women skied two runs on separate days. The new format had an effect on the skiers. After the entire competition was over, Hanni Wenzel explained: "I was very nervous before my run today. I'm sometimes nervous in World Cup races, but this was different. It was more intense. I think having the two runs on separate days causes that. In between, you have too much time to think about losing." Irene Epple also felt the effects of the added pressure. "I guess I was too nervous," she said after the race. "I didn't ski relaxed enough."

The second run was held on the Parkway course, 1,315 meters and 59 gates long for women. The sloppy conditions of the previous day were made even worse when the mercury dropped some 40°F (22°C) overnight. The course was very hard and icy, especially at the bottom, and the consensus was that it was more difficult. Common reactions were: "The course was a lot icier today than yesterday, and it was too risky." "I didn't have a feel for the snow." "It was very icy."

One skier seemed to have few problems on the course, negotiating its subtle dangers in a manner that left her competition envious. "I'm impressed by Hanni's technique," said Irene Epple. "She has the ability to put her edges in the snow, and she changes weight from one ski to the other so quickly." Although Wenzel's time of 1:27.33 was only the third fastest of the day, it was easily fast enough for the gold medal. Her combined time of 2:41.66 was nearly a half second faster than that of Epple. Nervous and wary of the ice, Epple made mistakes on the upper part of the course and could not make up the time. She was clocked at 1:27.37, giving her a silver-medal-winning total of 2:42.12.

The day's fastest run was posted by France's Perrine Pelen, whose 1:26.96 vaulted her from sixth place to third with an aggregate time of 2:42.41, just one-hundredth of a second ahead of teammate Fabienne Serrat. Pelen, a pert 19-year-old from Grenoble, wasn't surprised by her leap into third place. "I thought I could win the bronze," she said. "I was only three-tenths of a second out of third place, and I skied much better today."

Christa Kinshofer of West Germany, in third place at the halfway point, slipped to fifth with a time of 2:42.63. Finishing sixth, at 2:43.19, was Annemarie Moser-Proell, the gold medalist in the downhill. Erika Hess, in fourth place after one run, was among four skiers who didn't finish the race. She caught her right ski on a gate and fell midway through the course. Christin Cooper was the top American, with a 7th place finish. Cindy Nelson and Heidi Preuss finished 13th and 17th, respectively.

When Hanni Wenzel, wearing a white ski suit with gold leggings, crossed the finish line with her arms raised, there were no more than a dozen countrymen to cheer her. It was a far cry from the raucous welcome for Stock, Stenmark, or Moser-Proell in previous days. But in little Liechtenstein, the celebration was as noisy and as joyous as in Pittsburgh on Super Bowl Sunday. Liechtenstein still had no postal system, but it did have an Olympic gold medal. Little Hanni Wenzel called it "the culmination of my whole career." Not yet, Hanni.

Only three fourths of a second separated the top three finishers in the women's giant slalom. Wenzel of Liechtenstein, center, Epple of West Germany, left, and Perrine Pelen of France acknowledge the cheers of the crowd before receiving their medals. The event was held during two days for the first time in the Olympics.

Men's Slalom

The United States had never won an Olympic gold medal in men's Alpine skiing. After the first run of the 1980 special slalom, however, Phil Mahre of Yakima, WA, was in a strong position to become the first. Mahre, who said he was "really charged up for today," took advantage of his No. 1 starting position and skied smoothly and consistently through the 549-meter, 66-gate course. He knew his time—53.31 seconds—was good, but no one knew just how good until several other skiers had come down the course. As others crossed the finish line and their slower times went up on the scoreboard, the partisan U.S. crowd grew enthusiastic. Flags were waved and cheers were heard, but it was a quiet—almost disbelieving—excitement.

The two slalom courses were side by side on the eastern slope of Whiteface Mountain. At the 10:00 A.M. start time, the temperature was a cool 16°F (−9°C), and the snow was hard packed. Those who survived the first run in the morning would ski the adjacent second course in the afternoon.

The steep first run was made especially difficult for the lower seeds by the chatter marks etched in the snow by earlier racers. The course took its toll, as 28 of the 79 competitors did not finish and 4 more were disqualified for missing gates. Among those who did not make it to the afternoon heat were World Cup champion Peter Luescher of Switzerland, who fell in a tangle of slalom poles near the top of the course; Liechten-

Ingemar Stenmark (center) exults in his second gold medal of the Olympics with silver medalist Phil Mahre (left) and third place finisher Jacques Luethy.

stein's Paul Frommelt, who skied over a gate and fell; and Steve Mahre, who was tripped up only two gates out of the start.

Christian Orlainsky fell near the bottom of the run, but crossed the finish line anyway; a protest was lodged against him for missing a gate, and the Austrian finally was disqualified. Also disqualified was the Yugoslavian challenger, Bojan Krizaj. The young slalom specialist pulled to a stop in the middle of the run, apparently having lost his way through the gates. Claiming that a pole had been misplaced, Krizaj was given another chance and recorded a fourth-place time of 53.79. Upon reviewing films of his first descent, however, the FIS ruled that there was no basis for a rerun and Krizaj was out.

Another favorite, Christian Neureuther of West Germany, managed to complete the course but had to settle for a fifth-place 54.37 after sitting back on his skis near the top and almost falling. Andreas Wenzel turned in a slow time of 54.63 after knocking over a gate near the bottom of the course and then skiing over it.

But not all the competitors fell, stumbled, or were disqualified, and Mahre watched hopefully as the other skiers came down. The television audience caught a glimpse of him kissing his skis as he watched. Jacques Luethy of Switzerland and Hans Enn of Austria, skiing fifth and sixth respectively, turned in identical times of 53.70, to tie them for second place.

Ingemar Stenmark, the sensational Swede who was favored to win his second gold medal of the Games, was to ski in the 13th position. But it wasn't the unlucky number on his bib that bothered him so much as the late starting position and the condition of the run. "I'm not superstitious," he said. "Thirteenth was a bad position to ski from, so I took it easy on the first run." Despite taking it easy, Stenmark put in a respectable time of 53.89, .58 of a second behind Mahre and good for fourth place. Stenmark was in much the same position as he had been in the giant slalom—not far behind the leader and with his aggressive second run still to come. But Mahre was the leader at the end of the first run.

The second run, scheduled to begin immediately after all competitors completed the first, was delayed briefly by new-falling snow. By the time the heat began, 12:54 P.M., the temperature had climbed to 25°F (−4°C). The second course was slightly shorter than the first—541 meters, 60 gates—and not nearly so treacherous because of the new snow. Of the 47 skiers who made it to Round 2, nine did not finish and one was disqualified, none of them top contenders for a medal.

For the second run, the skiers again started in reverse order of the top five places. Neureuther of West Germany was therefore the first to try the course, and he raced through the still-falling snow in a very good time of 50.77. Stenmark was up second, a decidedly better position than in the morning heat. With his patented second-run aggressiveness, Stenmark bolted through the gates in sharp, rhythmic turns. He raced down the mountain without incident to a lightning-fast time of 50.37 seconds. His combined time for the two runs was 1:44.26. "I knew I had a good second run, but I knew Phil had a chance too," Stenmark said. "I didn't make any mistakes, but I think I could have skied faster."

Jacques Luethy had an impressive first run in the slalom, tying Hans Enn of Austria for second place. His bronze medal was the top finish by a Swiss skier in men's competition.

It didn't matter. Luethy and Enn, both of whom needed runs of 50.55 to move ahead of Stenmark, clocked 51.36 and 51.42, respectively. Luethy's total of 1:45.06 did prove fast enough for the bronze medal. Mahre, skiing fifth, needed only a 50.94 to bring home the first-ever U.S. gold in men's Alpine. He missed by half a second. Describing his run as "pretty frantic," Mahre had trouble almost from the very beginning. "It was the third or fourth gate," he said. "I knocked down a pole, and it rolled under me three or four more gates. I got really sideways later, and I almost came to a full stop. I didn't know if I was going to make it down. I never really got my rhythm."

Fallen gate or not, rhythm or not, Mahre's second-run time of 51.45 and total of 1:44.76 made him the first American man to win an Olympic Alpine skiing medal in 16 years. The only other American men to win Alpine medals were Billy Kidd and Jimmy Heuga, who took a silver and bronze, respectively, in the Innsbruck Games of 1964. Mahre's performance also gave the United States its first Alpine medal—by a male *or* female—of the 1980 Games. The U.S. squad had been optimistic going into the Games, but the results were disappointing. Men's team leader Bill Marlot called Mahre's success "a great morale builder for the rest of our team. Too bad it didn't come earlier in the Games."

It was with good reason, therefore, that Mahre felt "pretty jubilant" after claiming his medal. "I'm really happy to win the silver," he said. "Winning a medal for the United States was the main thing. I have to hand it to Ingemar. He outskied me today. He deserved to win."

As for Stenmark, he too made history. His victory in the slalom made him only the third man ever to win more than one gold medal in Alpine skiing at a single Olympics. Austria's Toni Sailer in 1956 and France's Jean-Claude Killy in 1968 each won all three Alpine events. The self-effacing Swede, however, was not overly impressed with his place in the record books. "I had already won one gold medal, and that should be quite

The U.S. Ski Team maintained training headquarters in Killington, VT, and was flown into Lake Placid by helicopter. Living outside the Olympic Village made for fewer social distractions and more serious practice sessions.

Phil Mahre

In Alpine skiing, it's you against the mountain and the clock. You can't ever hold back. It's all or nothing. No time outs. No coasting.

—PHIL MAHRE

When Dr. Richard Steadman, a surgeon and the medical chairman of the United States ski team, opened the injured left ankle of Phil Mahre (pronounced Mayer) after a painful spill in World Cup competition on Whiteface Mountain in March 1979, he took one dismayed look and exclaimed, "God *damn!*" It was more than a broken ankle. Steadman called it "the ultimate broken ankle, a break of both the ankle and the lower leg with a complication of the weight-bearing surface of the joint." The roof of the joint was shattered, and to reassemble the fragments Steadman had to insert three screws and a metal plate, secured by four more screws. To Phil Mahre, the physical pain was surpassed only by the disappointment of losing a strong bid for the overall World Cup championship.

Less than a year later, the 5'-9", 165-pound Mahre returned to the slopes of Whiteface to capture an Olympic silver in the slalom. Three screws had been removed, but the plate and four holding screws remained. The metal in his ankle was mute testimony to the sometimes savage nature of his sport. The metal around his neck was testimony to his grit. The arduous rehabilitation program began almost immediately after the surgery, and within six months he was ski racing again. By the time the Olympics rolled around and he was nearly ready, Mahre found questions about his injury almost as tedious as the long hours of rehabilitation. "That's all anyone wants to talk to me about," he said. "Look,

the ankle is fine. It doesn't bother me. When it's very cold, the metal plate gets cold but it's no problem." But there were problems, and U.S. coaches said the ankle was only 85-95% sound.

Mahre's effort, on the other hand, was 100%. Being a slalom specialist, he was not disappointed with a 14th place finish in the downhill; his 10th place showing in the giant slalom was his best of the season in that event; and his silver medal in the slalom made him feel "pretty jubilant." His overall performance won him the International Ski Federation (FIS) gold medal for the lowest combined penalty-point total for the three Alpine events.

Phil's twin brother Steve, who also skied in the Lake Placid Games, was troubled by his own ankle injury. A tie for 15th place in the giant slalom and a fall in the slalom were disappointing. Although Phil was acknowledged as one of the best ski racers in the world, Steve was considered almost as good. Steve is the younger brother by about four minutes, and he said of Phil, "I've been trying to catch him ever since." Although they are both intensely competitive, the 22-year-old twins deny any sibling rivalry.

Team director Hank Tauber notes other similarities in attitude. "They're tough. Fiercely independent. Unspoiled." Tauber attributes it to their "pioneer life." Born in the middle of seven brothers and sisters, Phil and Steve grew up in a town called White Pass, a gas station-general store, diner, and ski area in the Cascade Mountains of Washington state—population: about two dozen, many of them Mahres. Their father, David, is the mountain manager, and their mother, Mary Ellen, answers the telephones. The boys grew up clearing trees, digging ditches—and skiing. As youngsters, the Mahres had only to walk out the front door and buckle on their ski boots. They taught themselves how to ski and were each other's best coaches. According to their mother, the boys' competitiveness "started when they were crawling."

From the beginning, the brothers were known as renegades. They had a cavalier disregard for summer training, choosing instead to race motorcycles. They would go into the first days of the World Cup season with only two or three days of skiing. Says father David, "Their attitude is, 'When the time comes to ski, we're ready.' "

Steve is married and lives in Yakima, WA, about 50 miles from their birthplace. After his divorce in the summer of 1979, Phil moved in with his brother.

enough," he remarked. "History is not important. The most important thing is that I am satisfied with myself."

On another matter, Stenmark could offer no firm answers. Asked how he would celebrate, he replied: "I don't know. I never won so many medals in the Olympics before."

Women's Slalom

Of the 49 skiers entered in the women's special slalom, the last Alpine event of the Games, only 19 completed the two runs. The first heat, 461 meters long with 52 gates, eliminated 21 racers, including every Austrian in the first seed. They called it the "Austrian Waterloo." Annemarie Moser-Proell, the downhill gold medalist and a favorite in the slalom, sat back on her skis going through the sixth gate and was unable to recover; teammates Regina Sackl and Lea Soelkner also fell. Other victims included Marie-Theres Nadig, Tamara McKinney of the United States, and Regina Mosenlechner of West Germany. The second heat was not much better. Seven more competitors did not make it to the finish line on skis.

Harald Schoenhaar, the U.S. men's coach, attributed the tumbling exhibition to the snow. "Man-made snow is made in cold temperature," he said. "It's like styrofoam snow. Every skier knows you can't afford to get your weight in, but you saw a lot of good skiers do that today. On man-made snow, if you follow instincts and let your weight come in, you're going to slide out."

The sky was partly cloudy for the morning heat, the thermometer read 23°F (-5°C), and there were moderate winds. Despite the strange, sticky snow, Hanni Wenzel told coach Jean-Pierre Fournier, "I feel great and I like the course." Liechtenstein had already celebrated, and Wenzel had already marked the "culmination" of her career. It was easy to be relaxed. "I was in a good position to attack," said Hanni after it was all over. "I had nothing to lose since I had already won a silver and a gold medal."

Skiing ninth out of the gate, Wenzel could feel even more relaxed because she had already seen Moser-Proell fall out of the competition. Wenzel swept down the run in good form—and on her skis—to a crisp 27.71 intermediate time and a final clocking of 42.50. It was the fastest time for the first run. Nearly as impressive, however, was the 42.74 performance of 19-year-old West German giant slalom specialist Christa Kinshofer. The biggest surprise of the morning was 21-year-old Soviet veteran Nadezhda Patrakeeva, who turned in a time of 43.42 for third place. Her best finish in 1980 World Cup slalom competition had been a fifth place; in the 1978 World Championships at Garmisch, West Germany, she finished 27th. Perrine Pelen of France, a bronze medalist in the giant slalom, was fourth with 43.46, followed by Erika Hess of Switzerland in 43.50, Mariarosa Quario of Italy in 43.63, Christin Cooper of the United States in 44.23, and Fabienne Serrat of France in eighth place with 44.40.

In the afternoon, it was the French who met their Waterloo on the 465-meter, 53-gate second run. Both French women entering the heat in the top 10 were undone by the steep, twisting course and the gluey snow. Pelen got a pole tangled with her legs before the midway point and fell, and Serrat took a similar spill. Irene Epple, a silver medalist in the giant slalom, Abbi Fisher of South Conway, NH, and three other skiers also did not finish.

Despite the long casualty list, it was not through attrition alone that the winners earned their medals. Erika Hess of Switzerland, at only 17 years of age, skied the difficult course with the expertise of a veteran and took the bronze with a run of 44.39 and a combined time of 1:27.89. Hess said she had received a great deal of help from her aunt, also a ski racer, and from Hanni Wenzel, who trains with the Swiss team.

The silver medal was a mild surprise for young Kinshofer of Germany. Regarded as a better giant slalom skier, Christa recorded the best slalom finish of her career in a major race. Her time of 43.76 for the second run gave her an impressive aggregate of 1:26.50. "It was a very good day for me," Kinshofer said. "I wanted to fight for first. I thought I had a chance to win, but I'm glad to get second."

As it turned out, there really was no fight for first. Hanni Wenzel was simply too good. "When I walked the course before the race, I didn't think the course was good for me," she said. "But when I started the race, I was able to attack and had no problems." No problems at all. As she had done in the morning, Wenzel clocked the best time—42.59—in the second run. Her total of 1:25.09 was an unheard of 1.41 seconds faster than runner-up Kinshofer. Wenzel's victory gave her two golds and one silver for the Games, making her only the second woman Alpine skier to take home so much metal from one Winter Olympics. In 1976, Rosi Mittermaier of West Germany won the downhill and slalom and placed second in the giant slalom.

Mariarosa Quario of Italy was fourth in the competition, only three one-hundredths behind Hess, with a total of 1:27.92.

Tamara McKinney of Olympic Valley, CA, falls on the first run of the women's special slalom. The U.S. women's team had a tough go of it, but the youth and ability of 16-year-old McKinney and others held promise for the future.

Hanni Wenzel

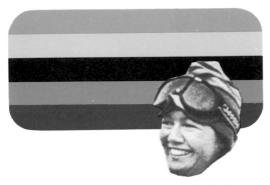

You can't just count on the Lake Placid Olympics. In just one race, anything can happen. You can't build up your season for just one event.

—HANNI WENZEL

In her comment prior to the Lake Placid Games, Hanni Wenzel did not mean to imply that she was not planning to do well. She was, but she was not going to consider the world off its axis if her hopes were jolted in one event. As it turned out, Hanni was right: anything *can* happen. Counting on it or not, Wenzel won big—and not just in one event. Her two gold and one silver medals matched the record performance of Rosi Mittermaier in the 1976 Winter Games. Wenzel replaced the old pro, Annemarie Moser-Proell, as the queen of Alpine skiing and established herself as the one to beat in the new decade.

The 23-year-old "Liechtenstein dumpling," as the diminutive (5'4") Wenzel has been called, comes from a family of skiers. All seven of Liechtenstein's athletes at the 1980 Winter Games were Alpine skiers, and of them three were Wenzels. For the first time in the history of the Winter Olympics a brother and sister won Alpine medals in the same Games. Andreas Wenzel, 21, took the silver medal in the men's giant slalom. The total of four medals won by Hanni and Andreas equaled about one for every 6,000 residents of Liechtenstein. The third member of the Wenzel trio, 19-year-old Petra, finished 19th in the women's giant slalom.

As Hanni stood on the victory rostrum to collect her first gold medal—for the giant slalom—25,000 pairs of eyes were glued to the television in a tiny mountainous corner of central Europe. The normally staid principality of Liechtenstein was ga-ga. Hundreds of blue and red flags draped windows and lined the streets in the capital city of Vaduz, which resounded with the noisy tributes to the blond haired, brown eyed "Golden Hanni." Every restaurant and bar was jammed, and the celebration went on into the early hours of the morning. Prince Franz Joseph II sent a telegram of congratulations. A group of Vaduz businessmen set off for Lake Placid just to shake her hand. Lore Wenzel, Hanni's mother, who had been too nervous to watch the second run, was invited to a special dinner in one of Vaduz's most exclusive restaurants. Her husband, Hubert, was in Lake Placid as the manager of the Liechtenstein team.

Hanni was born in West Germany but has lived in Liechtenstein since she was a year old. As all great skiers, she took to the slopes almost as soon as she could stand on her own two feet. Andreas and Petra were not far behind. "She helped me until I was 15 or 16," says Andreas. "Then I got too strong. Do I help her now? No. She is the best in the world."

Indeed, Hanni was already becoming a world class skier when Andreas was 16. At the age of 19 she won the slalom title at St. Moritz. At the 1976 Innsbruck Olympics she took a bronze medal in the slalom. And in 1978 she won her first world championship. At Lake Placid she

Hanni and Andreas Wenzel became the first brother and sister to win Alpine medals in the same Games.

A proud Hanni Wenzel hoists the flag of Liechtenstein after winning the women's slalom. It was her second gold medal of the Games and the second ever for Liechtenstein. Supporting her are silver medalist Christa Kinshofer (left) and bronze medalist Erika Hess.

was the fastest, most elegant, and technically best competition on the slopes. "She has such great technique," said West Germany's Irene Epple, runner-up in the giant slalom. "She really gets her edges into the snow, and she has the ability to change weight from one ski to the other so quickly." Hanni Wenzel loves high speeds—not only on the slopes. She has a passion for motorbikes. Brother Andreas, on his part, is fanatical about fast cars. Speeding down the steep, winding roads of their native countryside is not a surprising pastime for two of the world's most exciting ski racers.

Hanni has spent many years of her training with the Swiss teams and said that "it has been a very big advantage." The national character of her own people, she says, also is a factor in her success. "We're individualists, very strong-willed." Of all things, Liechtenstein's size may be one of its strengths and a primary reason why the tiny principality emerged with four medals. After Hanni's second medal, Peter Ritter, president of the Liechtenstein Olympic Committee, tried to explain how a country with only 25,000 residents could become such a power in amateur skiing. "Our sports federation is very small," noted Ritter. "That is one of our secrets. We have very close contact with our athletes. We handle their problems directly, with no intermediaries involved. It's a matter of human relations." Ritter also said he believes Liechtenstein has a "healthy climate" for promoting athletics. "We're a small country with everything to gain and nothing to lose. Our athletes are not subjected to as much pressure from the public as are athletes from Austria and other places. In addition, we have good coaching and good training facilities."

Wenzel's final victory, in the slalom, gave her a wide margin in winning the FIS gold medal for overall performance. The FIS medal is not Olympic—it is awarded as a world championship.

Still only 23 and at the top of the ski world, Wenzel nevertheless foresees the day when she will hang up her boots. "I've been racing a long time, but maybe I will continue. It's still fun. Two more years, maybe." She is seeking a license that would enable her to set up official professional contracts and gain her living through skiing after she retires. Andreas and Petra, meanwhile, are expected to stay on the World Cup circuit for several more years.

Another Italian, Claudia Giordani, was fifth in 1:29.12. Christin Cooper was the highest-placing American, in eighth with 1:29.28. Patrakeeva, the surprising Soviet of Round 1, slipped from third place to sixth after nearly falling close to the finish. At the bottom of the pack, in 19th place, was the Lebanese, Faride Rahme. Not only did she finish the race, as most others had not, but her combined time of 2:28.48 was only about 30 seconds slower than the 18th place finisher, a definite improvement over her downhill performance. In 18th place at 1:59.01 was Guizhen Wang, the only Chinese in the competition.

So ended the Alpine skiing competition in the 1980 Olympic Winter Games. Franz Klammer was not there, but Leonhard Stock and Annemarie Moser-Proell carried on the tradition of Austrian downhill excellence. Sweden had two kings at the Games, Carl XVI Gustaf and Ingemar Stenmark. The music of *God Save the Queen* was in fact Liechtenstein's national anthem being played for Hanni Wenzel—twice. The Kamikaze Kanadians crashed, Austrians and others met their Waterloo, a Yugoslav lost his way down the mountain, four screws and a metal plate saved the home team from complete embarrassment, and the artificial snow made every bump, jump, and turn a Whitefaced thrill.

ALPINE SKIING CHRONOLOGY

Whiteface Mountain

Thursday February 14 — Leonhard Stock of Austria wins the gold medal in men's downhill, with a time of 1 minute 45.50 seconds. Countrymen Peter Wirnsberger finishes second, and Steve Podborski of Canada takes third.

Sunday February 17 — Veteran Austrian star Annemarie Moser-Proell wins her first Olympic gold medal, capturing the women's downhill in a time of 1:37.52. Hanni Wenzel of Liechtenstein takes the silver and Marie-Theres Nadig of Switzerland the bronze.

Monday February 18 — In the first run of the men's giant slalom Andreas Wenzel of Liechtenstein takes a slim lead over Hans Enn of Austria and favored Ingemar Stenmark of Sweden.

Tuesday February 19 — With an all-out attack on the second run, Ingemar Stenmark races to a gold medal in the men's giant slalom. His combined time of 2:40.74 easily beats Wenzel and Enn.

Wednesday February 20 — On a messy course, Hanni Wenzel of Liechtenstein takes the lead in the first run of the women's giant slalom. Next are two West Germans, Irene Epple and Christa Kinshofer.

Thursday February 21 — Hanni Wenzel skis to a gold medal in the women's giant slalom with a combined time of 2:41.66. Epple finishes second, followed by France's Perrine Pelen.

Friday February 22 — With a lightning-fast second run, Ingemar Stenmark (1:44.26) beats the United States' Phil Mahre to win the gold medal—his second—in the men's slalom. Jacques Luethy of Switzerland finishes third.

Saturday February 23 — Hanni Wenzel wins her second gold medal by taking the women's slalom in a total time of 1:25.09. Christa Kinshofer of West Germany is second, followed by Erika Hess of Switzerland.

MEDAL WINNERS

	Gold	Silver	Bronze
MEN'S DOWNHILL	Leonhard Stock (AUT)	Peter Wirnsberger (AUT)	Stephen Podborski (CAN)
WOMEN'S DOWNHILL	Annemarie Moser-Pröell (AUT)	Hanni Wenzel (LIE)	Marie-Theres Nadig (SUI)
MEN'S GIANT SLALOM	Ingemar Stenmark (SWE)	Andreas Wenzel (LIE)	Hans Enn (AUT)
WOMEN'S GIANT SLALOM	Hanni Wenzel (LIE)	Irene Epple (GER)	Perrine Pelen (FRA)
MEN'S SLALOM	Ingemar Stenmark (SWE)	Phil Mahre (USA)	Jacques Luethy (SUI)
WOMEN'S SLALOM	Hanni Wenzel (LIE)	Christa Kinshofer (GER)	Erika Hess (SUI)

Biathlon

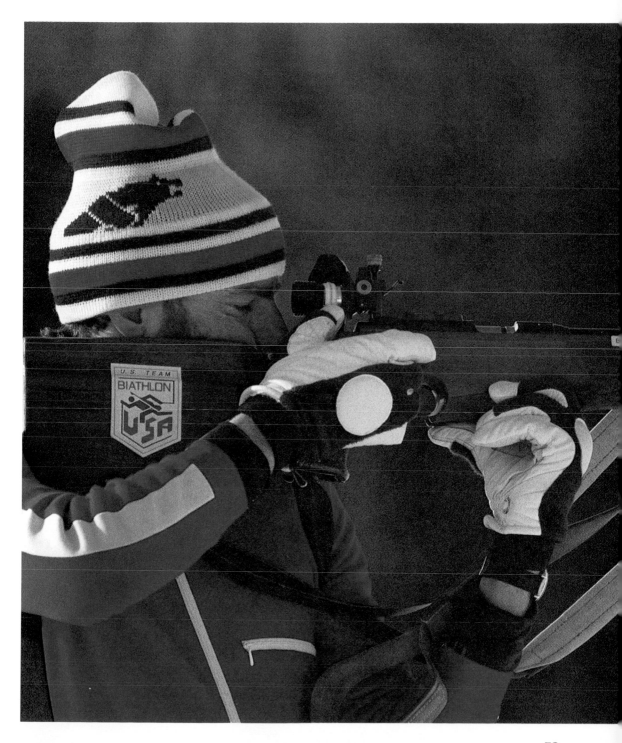

The biathlon, among the more recent of the Winter Games—it was added in 1960—is much better known in Europe than in other parts of the world. That may help to explain the steadiness of the Scandinavian and Soviet biathletes' successes in the Games. The name biathlon, from the Greek words meaning "dual contests," hardly conveys the difficulty of the sport. Its two component disciplines have been described as making the oddest possible marriage of efforts. One is cross-country skiing, an extremely physical activity that demands great exertion from the biathlete. The other is rifle marksmanship, the success of which requires a nearly motionless body. And to make the test as tough as possible, the two activities must be done alternately.

Lyle Nelson, a former U.S. Army officer who is a dedicated biathlete, describes the sport as more exciting than baseball any day.

"There's a challenge that's unique to biathlon," says Nelson. "You've got to transfer from the totally physical endeavor of skiing to the psychological challenge of shooting a rifle. It's really mentally demanding."

Don Nielson, a member of the U.S. biathlon team, described the sport as one in which "you run like a rabbit and then turn into stone." Cross-country skiers have the highest oxygen intake of any athletes in the winter sports, which means that their chests are heaving and their pulses pounding when they come to the firing ranges. There, of course, as everyone who has ever fired at a target knows, they want to be as calm as possible. So they must contrive to pant without wavering the sights off the targets. It's a very tall order.

Although dissimilar, the two skills of the biathlon are not unrelated. Early Scandinavian hunters skied in search of game nearly 4,000 years ago. Later, skiing and shooting were combined for military purposes, and were used with great success by Finnish ski troops, during the 1939–40 Finno-Russian War, to overcome the militarily superior Soviet invaders.

The first World Championships were held in Austria in 1958. The sole event was a 20-kilometer race by individuals. The single restriction then was that the rifle had to be a bolt-action piece with iron sights. There were four sets of targets, three at a range of 250 meters and the fourth at 100 meters. For the longer range the biathlete was prone. The 100-meter target was shot at while standing on the skis.

Whether firing in the standing position, above, or the prone, the biathlete saves time by keeping his skis on. Undue haste here is costly. Ammunition dropped has to be found in the snow, dried off, and used, or a miss is recorded.

A relay for four biathletes skiing 7.5-kilometer segments became part of the World Championships in 1965 and of the Olympic Winter Games in 1968.

A 10-kilometer sprint was added in 1974 to the World Championships. It became part of the official program in the 1980 Lake Placid Games.

For reasons of cost and practicality the range was reduced to 50 meters and the targets were scaled down in proportion. For the first time, at Lake Placid .22 caliber rifles were required. They still had to be bolt action and equipped with iron sights. The rifles are shoulder-slung for skiing, then unslung at the ranges and loaded.

Only men take part in the three biathlon races. Whereas in the early competitions it was good shooting that determined good finishes, the prizes today go to the biathletes who combine skill in cross-country skiing with shooting accuracy.

20-Kilometer Individual

The first event, the 20-kilometer race for individual biathletes, took place on February 16. Throughout, the 49 competitors were pelted by heavy snow driven by a strong east wind. Visibility was low and in general the course was slow. The biathletes were started at one-minute intervals on this routine: ski 5 kilometers to the first range and, in a prone position, shoot 5 rounds; get up, sling rifle, ski 3 kilometers in a loop, coming back to the range to fire 5 rounds in a standing position; ski 3 kilometers and shoot 5 rounds from a prone position; ski 4 kilometers and, prone, fire 5 more rounds; then ski with all speed the 5 remaining kilometers to the finish line.

To the biathlete's elapsed time between start and finish, time was added for any targets missed. For the total of 20 targets, each had 20 rounds of ammunition. Every bull's eye left the biathlete free of penalty. If, from his distance of 164′ he missed the 1⁹⁄₁₆″ bull's eye but hit the 3⅛″ target, he had to accept a 1-minute penalty. If he missed altogether, he got a penalty of 2 minutes.

Despite the Adidas-labeled cap, everyone knew bib number 42 was worn by Anatoli Aljabiev. His running stride, below, ate up the course.

Biathletes representing 18 nations entered the event, and only two Argentinians failed to complete the course. Only one of the contestants—Anatoli Aljabiev of the Soviet Union—came in minus shooting penalties; his flawless eye on the range won him the gold medal. The 29-year-old army lieutenant was not the fastest skier, as his coaches along the route told him, but his marksmanship carried him through. Aljabiev's total time was 1 hour, 8 minutes, 16.31 seconds. Only 11.48 seconds slower was Frank Ullrich of East Germany. He protested being penalized for missing the bull's eye three times, saying it was only twice, but in the two hours after the race in which protests may be lodged, no East German posted any protest. Ullrich, the 1979 World Champion, took the silver medal.

The bronze went to his teammate, Eberhard Rosch, who acquired only two penalty minutes, but was not so swift on his skis. His combined time was 1 hour, 11 minutes, and 11.73 seconds.

The best showing by a U.S. biathlete was Martin Hagen's. He had eight penalty minutes and an elapsed time of one hour, 21 minutes, 2.95 seconds, which put him in 36th place.

Ullrich had expected to dislodge the Soviets from their domination of biathlon, but his confidence was not general. One of the Finnish coaches picked Aljabiev as the man to watch, for the simple reason that he was the winner in the Olympic trials and "he shoots as if he was being helped by radar."

10-Kilometer Sprint

The 10-kilometer sprint was new in the 1980 Games, and, at least to the old biathlon hands, so was the demonstration of spectator interest. It wasn't so long ago that biathletes had to explain what they did, even when they were seen on skis and with rifles. They had to resign themselves to giving their utmost effort in a sport that, because of its nature, was expected to remain a participant rather than a spectator sport.

Not so at Lake Placid on February 19. Some 1,500 spectators made their way to Mount Van Hoevenberg for the contest in which 50 biathletes were entered. One Chinese was disqualified, but the other 49 all completed the course.

The sprint starts the contestants at 1-minute intervals. They race 2.5 kilometers to a target area, assume the prone position and as rapidly as possible load and fire five shots at five breakable targets. As in the 20-kilometer, the prone targets are 1⁹⁄₁₆″ in diameter and the marksmen have one shell per target. For a miss, a penalty is exacted: a 150-meter loop has to be skied. That is the equivalent of 30–40 seconds of elapsed time.

From the first targets, the biathletes run, pole, and schuss on their narrow (1⅞″) skis over a 5-kilometer course to the second targets. They are fired at from standing position, which means an even shorter interval between the exertion of skiing and the requirement to stand as nearly stock still as possible. These targets are 3¹⁵⁄₁₆″ in diameter and again the penalty for missing one is a 150-meter loop to be skied before haring off on the final 2.5 kilometers of the race.

Frank Ullrich, one of the fastest skiers in the biathlon ranks, made two-pole starts of great power. His marksmanship, while very good, was just enough flawed to lose him precious points in the 20-kilometer event.

Anatoli Aljabiev

It's impossible to lose, with such sportsmen as the Russians.

—ANATOLI ALJABIEV

Anatoli Aljabiev was not entirely a stranger in Lake Placid when the XIII Winter Games convened. He had won the 20-kilometer biathlon race in pre-Olympic competitions held there in 1979. So biathlon fans had good reason to expect him to be a serious contender. He was— and then some. Not only did he take the gold medal in his specialty, but he also won the bronze in the 10-kilometer event and anchored the gold-winning Soviet team in the 30-kilometer relay.

The 29-year-old Red Army lieutenant, the son of a raftman, was born in the town of Velsk, a district center on the Vaga River, some 335 miles from the White Sea port of Arkhangelsk. Because the area is snow-covered six months of the year, the children take up skiing at an early age. Little Tolya's older sisters, Galya and Zina, were avid skiers and they eagerly taught him. Later, as a school boy, he became an enthusiastic boxer, and was good enough to appear in competitions. By the time he was called to Leningrad for military service, his puny look was deceptive. The 5'4", 141-pound athlete was both strong and tough.

In ski races conducted by his service club he caught the attention of the sports club coach, who began to direct him to the biathlon. His cross-country skiing stamina steadily improved, but the heavy army rifle then used by biathletes was his master as much as he was its. Until 1978 his best showing was a silver medal in the Soviet championships of 1976.

The change to small caliber rifles for the international biathlon gave Aljabiev what he needed. Under the guidance of veteran biathlete Valentin Pshenitsyn he began to shine. By the time he was entered in the Lake Placid competitions in 1979 he was a triple threat, ready to compete in both individual races and relay.

In the XIII Winter Games, his investment in all-out skiing and rather deliberate shooting paid high returns. He shot perfect scores in both the 20 kilometers and the relay, and missed only one target in the 10 kilometers.

Back in Leningrad after the Games he greeted a brand new second son, born to his wife Aleftina. The older boy, Nikolai, is already on skis, under the watchful eye of his champion father whose hope, as he finishes the final year at the physical culture institute, is to keep training successfully enough to qualify for the 1984 Games in Sarajevo.

Jubilant teammates toss a happy Aljabiev after his victorious anchoring of the four-man relay.

Big Frank Ullrich (GDR), flanked on his right by Vladimir Alikin (URS), and with an arm around bronze medalist Anatoli Aljabiev, beamed acknowledgement of the applause when the medals were given after the 10-kilometer event.

This time Frank Ullrich's faster time on skis paid off. Even though he missed two targets and had to ski 300 extra meters, he reached the finish line in 32 minutes, 10.69 seconds. That was 42.41 seconds faster than Vladimir Alikin (URS) clocked, and he had no penalties added. The third man in, with a time of 33 minutes, 9.16 seconds, was Anatoli Aljabiev (URS), whose flawless shooting in the 20-kilometer race was not repeated. His one penalty side loop made the difference between getting the silver and the bronze. No doubt the wind was a malefactor. Several of the pre-race favorites missed their targets because a strong wind sweeping across the range made shooting very tricky.

A power outage affected the electric scoreboard, the public address system, and all the television cameras zeroed in on the race. There was a delay in reporting the intermediate and final finish times of nearly all the competitors until some time after most of them had completed the race. When the scoreboard did light up once again it carried only the six best results, and at that point all results were declared unofficial.

Where even the best got into difficulties it was not surprising that the less adept did, also. The twelfth man to start, Yves Blondeau of France, in his one appearance in the Games, had the worst shooting of all the competitors—8 misses. At a minimum they added more than 4½ minutes to his clocked time, and left him in 39th place.

30-Kilometer Relay

History repeated itself. In 1968, when the relay was made part of the Games, a Soviet team won the gold medal. A member of the team was Alexander Tikhonov. In 1972, 1976, and again in 1980, the gold went to the Soviet team, and each time Tikhonov was part of the victorious quartet. After his team was safely through the ordeal Tikhonov said it was his last Olympic competition. He had run the second leg of his team in the second fastest time of the four, and used 13 of his 16 shells to break all his targets. That, too; was the second best showing. So he was retiring from strength.

The relay, the final biathlon event in these Games, begins with the first-leg members of all the teams scrambling from the starting line for the position at the head of the pack. Fifteen teams were entered. Each member of a team skis 7.5 kilometers, fires at five targets from a prone position, five from a standing position, and then "hands over" to his next teammate by actually touching him. The targets are 1%16″ in diameter and 50 meters distant for the prone firing, and each contestant has eight shells allowed him for the five targets. The discs are 3¹⁵⁄₁₆″ across for the standing position, and again there are eight shells allotted.

Every miss is penalized, as in the 10-kilometer sprint, by an added loop of 150 meters to be skied.

A biathlete's clothing, above, like the speed skater's "skin," is light in weight and tight-fitting. Knitted caps are favored. Gloves must be warm, but they must also be flexible enough to handle ammunition. Some racers, like those in the clumped start of the relay, left, favor leggings or knee-length socks.

There is no prescribed rifle for the biathlon. Each national group works to develop the best one for the athletes' needs: light weight, easy to handle, accurate. None can incorporate telescopic sights or be automatic.

Besides the requirements that they be bolt-action, small bore, and equipped with only iron sights, the rifles can be very various. William Spencer, shooting coach of the United States team, gave considerable credit to the Vostock rifle the Soviet team used. It was a .22 caliber model made in the Soviet Union and available only to the Soviets. It weighs about 10 pounds and is a beautifully efficient piece. (At the price of $700 it should be.) One of its advantageous features is a bolt that is pulled straight back for loading. (The U.S. rifles require lifting up the bolt before it can be pulled back.)

On the East German team, first leg Mathias Jung and third leg Frank Ullrich skied like demons—their legs were both faster by 35 seconds than the best of the Soviet skiers—and both of them shot down their targets without incurring penalties. The East Germans and Soviets were neck and neck until shooting errors cost the East Germans a total of 450 additional meters of skiing. The East Germans clocked 53.72 seconds more than the Soviets, precious seconds that decided gold and silver awards.

The Soviet victory was clinched when Anatoli Aljabiev hit all his five targets in the standing position on the last leg in a thrilling marksmanship duel with East Germany's Eberhard Rosch.

By a margin of only 41.50 seconds West Germany nudged out Norway, to capture the bronze medal, their first one ever in Olympic biathlon races. The two teams were about evenly matched in skiing, but Norway had three shooting penalties to Germany's two.

In the weeks before the Games, the United States team members had been given generally good marks for their skiing, but their shooting was considered weak. In the event, their shooting was flawless. Only the victorious Soviets' was better. For 40 targets without errors the Soviets used 52 shots, the Americans 53, and the French 55. But slower skiing made the difference, leaving the French in 5th and the Americans in 8th place.

Eberhard Rosch (GDR) and Aljabiev at the target range in the course of the relay convey a strong sense of the origins of their sport: winter-bound hunters resorting to skis to traverse the snow-covered land.

There are said to be a million biathletes in the Soviet Union, and there are untold thousands in East Germany. In the years between 1975 and 1980 the 40 or so American biathletes had increased to about 300. Perhaps that seven-fold increase was the reason that more than 2,000 people went to Mount Van Hoevenberg for the relay, the largest crowd ever for a biathlon event in the United States.

Three biathletes accounted for 8 medals in the Lake Placid Games: Ullrich (1 gold, 2 silver); Aljabiev (2 gold, 1 bronze); Rosch (1 silver, 1 bronze).

BIATHLON CHRONOLOGY

Mount Van Hoevenberg

Saturday February 16
Anatoli Aljabiev combines perfect marksmanship with excellent cross-country skiing to win the 20-kilometer race and give the Soviet Union a third gold medal for the event since 1960. Lyle Nelson, the United States biathlete, is sidelined. His replacement, Glen Jobe, misses six targets, ends in 38th place.

Tuesday February 19
Frank Ullrich skis with such power that, despite two penalties, he takes the 10-kilometer biathlon sprint from the two Soviet contestants who were the strongest competition. Vladimir Alikin shoots perfectly, and Anatoli Aljabiev misses once, in achieving silver and bronze medals, respectively, for the Soviets. Lyle Nelson, Donald Nielsen, and Peter Hoag represent the United States. They place 19, 44, and 45, respectively.

Friday February 22
With Alikin as lead and Aljabiev as anchor the Soviet Union races to their fourth consecutive gold medal in the 4 × 7.5-kilometer relay. The East Germans, with Ullrich and Rosch, ski masterfully, but miss three targets. The Soviet shooting is flawless. So is the American, but slow skiing puts the team in 8th place.

MEDAL WINNERS

	Gold	Silver	Bronze
20-KILOMETER	Anatoli Aljabiev (URS)	Frank Ullrich (GDR)	Eberhard Rosch (GDR)
10-KILOMETER	Frank Ullrich (GDR)	Vladimir Alikin (URS)	Anatoli Aljabiev (URS)
30-KILOMETER RELAY	URS (V. Alikin, A. Tikhonov, V. Barnaschov, A. Aljabiev)	GDR (M. Jung, K. Siebert, F. Ullrich, E. Rosch)	GER (F. Bernreiter, H. Estner, P. Angerer, G. Winkler)

Bobsledding

"**S**cared?" blurted Willie Davenport, repeating a question. "Sometimes I can feel my heart flutter. You know what they say in those TV commercials? 'Don't squeeze the Charmin.' Man, I'm *always* squeezing the Charmin."

Actually, Willie's nerves probably would not tingle even if he looked down the throat of a lion, but he is realistic about his recently adopted favorite pastime, bobsledding—sliding down an icy chute on a half ton of lumber and steel at speeds of 80 miles per hour.

The former Olympic hurdler knows that one little mistake and the bobsled could careen off the course, sending fragments and bodies flying. People have been known to get killed that way.

"It's a natural feeling," he added. "Everybody who does something dangerous has to be afraid. If you're not scared, you get loose and make a mistake. Fear keeps you alert.

"If a parachute jumper tells you he's not scared, he's either a liar or a lunatic."

Gary Sheffield, the coach of the 1980 U.S. team, feels that while bobsledding "is a super sport, there's always that chance of a crash. That's what makes it the sport it is." Sheffield has also pointed out that "many bobsledders have a hard time explaining how they do it, or why. . . . I did it for 22 years. It cost me a lot of money. You have to like speed, I guess. It's self-rewarding."

It is also very demanding, requiring a surprising amount of training and practice. According to Eugenio Monti, former Olympic gold medalist and world champion, "each member of the team has to be strong. The riders have to give a good push, the brakeman must be strong with his body, shifting his weight when necessary, but never braking during a race. The driver must also be strong. He must feel the course."

Although "the champagne of thrills" enjoyed enormous popularity among the watchers at the first Lake Placid Olympics in 1932, Mrs. Eleanor Roosevelt, the wife of the governor of New York, was invited to take a bobsled ride to demonstrate the safety of the machine. The soon-to-become first lady accepted, causing many to worry. However, the run was completed without accident.

Although the sled has been a basic form of transportation for centuries, the sport of bobsledding did not originate until the early years of the 20th century. It emerged from tobogganing, which was conceived by a group of adventurous American and British vacationers in Switzerland about 1890. To increase the speed of the toboggan, runners were soon added to it. A heavier sled was then developed to lower the rate of serious accident. Since the crew learned to "bob" on the course's straightaways to increase speed, the new device was called a bobsled.

The bobsled run at Mount Van Hoevenberg, 6.5 miles from the center of Lake Placid, was originally built for the 1932 Olympics. For the 1980 Games, the walkway, spectator galleries, timing installations, refrigerated piping, and lighting were added.

Bobsledding, the "champagne of thrills" for the participants, was a great magnet for the Lake Placid spectators.

The first official bobsled competition took place at St. Moritz, Switzerland, in 1898, and with the formation of the International Bobsleigh and Tobogganing Federation (FIBT) in 1924, the sport gained international recognition. Artificial bobsled runs had begun springing up throughout Europe by 1904. The first national championship was held in Austria in 1908 and the first world championship occurred in 1927.

The four-man (driver, two riders, and brakeman) bobsled race was part of the competition at the first Winter Olympics in Chamonix, France, in 1924 and a two-man (driver and brakeman) race was introduced eight years later at Lake Placid. Teams from central and southern Europe, especially Switzerland, Germany, and Italy, have for the most part dominated at the Olympics.

America's first bobsled run was built for the 1932 Olympics and U.S. teams captured both events that year. Hometown boys, Hubert and Curtis Stevens, members of the family that owned the Stevens House—an elegant hotel located on Lake Placid's highest hill, won the two man in world record time. The Mount Van Hoevenberg run, near Lake Placid, remains the only one in the United States. When the Olympics were held in Squaw Valley, CA, in 1960, there was no bobsled competition. The Mount Van Hoevenberg run was rebuilt and upgraded for the 1980 Games. Refrigerating coils were added to aid ice formation and synthetic concrete lips were constructed to prevent sleds from flying off.

The run is regarded as extremely fast, perhaps the world's fastest and most dangerous. Many European courses are called "Kinderbahns, children's runs" in comparison. The exceptional speed of the run was expected to aid the experienced bobsledders in the 1980 Olympics. In many ways, it must have. A Swiss team, led by world champion Erich Schaerer, won the two-man event and an East German sled, driven by Meinhard Nehmer, a 1976 gold medalist, captured the four man.

The first two runs of the two-man competition were held on Friday, February 15, and the last two on the next day. The four-man event occurred on Saturday and Sunday, February 23 and 24. Each nation could enter two sleds in each race. Total time decided the order of finish.

The Two Man

Swiss bobsled driver Erich Schaerer—getting a powerful assist in each start from brakeman Josef Benz—overpowered the two-man bobsled field on Saturday, February 16, with consecutive times of 1:02.29 and 1:02.44 to win the gold medal.

The 34-year-old businessman from Zurich, who was the reigning world four-man champion driver, so dominated the two-day competition that he had the fastest time in three of the four heats. His runs included a "nearly perfect first run" for a course record of 1:01.87 on Friday, the 15th, and a second one of 1:02.76. The Swiss team's combined time of 4:09.36 beat by more than 1½ seconds East Germany's Bernhard Germeshausen, who was a member of both gold-medal-winning teams in 1976, and Hans Jurgen Gerhardt. Another East German sled,

THE BOBSLED

Today's bobsled is made of fiberglass and is designed principally for speed. Its prime parts are a steering wheel which is slightly smaller than the one on an automobile, two solid axles with two runners attached to each, a front cowl to lower wind resistance, bars welded to the sides for push-offs, and seats for the participants. Although there is a brake—a bar with a serrated edge between the runners that can be pressed against the ice—braking during the run is not permitted in international competition.

According to the International Bobsleigh and Tobogganing Federation, the four-man and two-man sleds may not exceed 507 and 363.2 pounds, respectively. The length of the sled and the width between the runners are restricted. The gauge of the runners is also governed, and only sleds constructed for the sitting position are legal.

Like all sleds, the bobsled is descended from the sled of ancient times, which was merely a strip of animal skin between two strips of wood. Technological advances have occurred throughout the years. Art Tyler, a member of the bronze-winning U.S. team at the 1956 Olympics, was the first to install a cowl on the front of the sled. Previously, bobsleds were entirely open. Tyler simply built an aluminum ball, cut it in half, and installed it on his sled.

Recently, Dale Smith, an electrical engineer from Troy, NY, who invented a device for detecting police radar, designed the "T-Package" for bobsleds. The "T-Package" records on magnetic tape the bobsled's velocity, acceleration, kinds of movements, and pressure on the metal runners. According to Smith, it is "designed to tell us the effects of any change we make in the sled or to tell us what changes we should make."

Although European bobsled designers and the American Bobsled Research Association, located in Schenectady, NY, are constantly searching for the perfect or fastest sled, U.S. bobsled coach Gary Sheffield believes that it is the driver, not the sled, that really counts. According to Sheffield, "if you have the best equipment in the world and give it to everybody, the best driver will win."

The search for the perfect or fastest sled is a continuing challenge to ingenuity.

HURDLER WILLIE DAVENPORT TAKES UP THE BOB

Record-setting and Olympic-medal-winning hurdler Willie Davenport was one of the most celebrated personalities at the XIII Winter Olympics. Not only was he one of the first blacks to participate in the Winter Games (two others also competed at Lake Placid) but the 36-year-old Louisianan tried to become the second athlete ever to win gold medals in both the Winter and Summer Games. American boxer Eddie Eagan took the gold in the light heavyweight division in 1920 and 12 years later was a member of the gold-winning four-man bobsled team. Willie Davenport won the 110-meter hurdles in 1968, was a bronze medalist in the same event in 1976, and was a member of the No. 1 four-man American bobsled team in 1980.

Although Davenport did not ride a bobsled until December 1979, he qualified for the four-man team two months later. He was selected because of his exceptional speed. American bobsledders felt that Davenport could provide a strong push during the first 50 meters of the bobsled run which would give the sled momentum.

While serving as a member of the U.S. Olympic Committee, one of the first athletes to so do, Davenport became acquainted with Alan Hachigian, a former bobsledder who had become head of a private investigative and security systems firm in Plattsburgh, NY. Hachigian pointed out to Willie that there is no reason why a hurdler could not become a bobsledder. According to Hachigian, the "same things—speed, balance, and coordination"—are needed in both sports. Davenport soon developed a similar viewpoint.

In terms of mental attitude, Davenport believes that the approach to both bobsledding and track is about the same. "Athletics is athletics. You have to have the same mental attitude no matter what you're doing," Davenport said. The Southern University graduate believes that both sports require the same amount of physical effort but that more weight training is required for bobsledding. In fact, Davenport and the other members of the bobsled team who were recruited by Hachigian—Jeff Gadley of Plattsburgh, Bob Hickey of Keene Valley, NY, and Jeff Jordan of Athol, NY—spent the months of September and November at the Olympic training center in Colorado Springs,

CO, working out with Olympic weight lifters and doing a lot of sprints.

Although some confusion and discontent resulted from a newspaper statement attributed to Davenport, charging that "bobsledding is a rich white man's sport," Bob Hickey, the team driver, refused to consider coach Gary Sheffield's suggestion that the roster be changed. Davenport meanwhile denied making the statement.

The Davenport team, which had established a course record during the U.S. team trials at Mount Van Hoevenberg, finished 12th in the Olympic competition with a combined time of 4:06.11, 4.6 seconds behind the winners.

Despite his participation in the 1980 Winter Olympics, Willie Davenport said that he had no intention of trying for a driver's license as a bobsledder. "My Louisiana driver's license is all I plan to get.

"I work for the city, coordinating federal programs for youth and I own a business that sells pumps and pump parts. I'd like to concentrate on that."

Former hurdler Willie Davenport won a place on the American bobsled squad because he is fast.

driven by Meinhard Nehmer, Germeshausen's driver in 1976, finished third with a combined time of 4:11.08. A Swiss sled, driven by the current European two-man champion, Hans Hiltebrand, was fourth.

Throughout his bobsledding career, Schaerer had his sights set on an Olympic medal. According to his mechanic, "All his training pointed to that. World championships, European championships, they mean nothing." Following the win, Schaerer said, "The only thing I wanted to do on the second (final) run was get down the hill safely. I wanted to avoid a crash at all cost."

The greatest excitement of the final day of the two-man competition was provided when Howard Siler, a 34-year-old insurance man from Brushton, NY, and Dick Nalley of Indianapolis completed their first run in 1:02.65, a time bettered in that run only by Schaerer's sled. The Siler team failed, however, to duplicate its excellent time in the final round, finished with a combined time of 4:11.73, and was awarded fifth place. It was the best American finish in the two-man event since 1956. The No. 1 U.S. sled, formerly known as the Dew Drop Inn and carrying Brent Rushlaw and Joe Tyler, both of Saranac Lake, NY, was sixth.

Siler, who was disappointed at not winning a medal, said, "We've worked hard on our start, but when you go up against the best in the world, you've got to be ready. I'm proud to have our best finish in 24 years, but after the four-man sleds, I'd like to retire from driving and try my hand at coaching."

Joe Tyler expresses similar sentiments, "We've made maybe 125 runs on this track this winter. The Europeans have 200 or 300 runs before they get here. You've got to consider them professionals. I'm a professional, but on another level."

Switzerland's No. 2 two-man team, Erich Schaerer and Josef Benz, captured the gold. They defeated the runner-up East German sled by 1.57 seconds. East Germany's other entry finished in third place.

The Four Man

Meinhard Nehmer's runs down Mount Van Hoevenberg gave the 1976 Olympic champion his third gold medal on Sunday, February 24, as East Germany and Switzerland scored a medal sweep in bobsledding. For the sixth straight Winter Games, the United States, once a bobsled power, failed to capture a prize. A crowd estimated at 17,000 watched the final runs as light snow fell and the temperature was slightly below freezing.

Other members of Nehmer's winning sled were Bosdan Musiol, Bernhard Germeshausen, and Hans Jurgen Gerhardt—all medalists in the two man. The East German team outdistanced the field of 16 sleds from nine countries with a combined time of 3:59.92. The time included a first run of 59.86 seconds and a third run of 59.73 seconds, the fastest run in Olympic history.

When queried about East Germany's two subminute runs, American coach Sheffield said, "They certainly were outstanding, but they didn't surprise me. I knew it was in this track, and I knew we had the best drivers in the world testing it." Howard Siler commented, "I knew someone would break a minute but I didn't think it would be broken that bad. They smashed it."

The finish by the Nehmer team was nearly one second ahead of the runner-up Swiss sled, driven by the two-man gold medalist Erich Schaerer. East German's No. 2 sled, with Horst Schoenau as driver, was just behind and received the bronze medal. Austria's two sleds completed the course in 4th and 5th places and the No. 2 Swiss team was 6th. Injury prevented the Canadian sled from participating in the final two runs.

The No. 1 U.S. sled, driven by Bob Hickey and carrying former Olympic hurdler Willie Davenport, finished 12th in 4:06.11, more than five seconds behind the winner. America's No. 2 sled, driven by Siler, was 13th in 4:06.2. The failure of the top American sled to win a medal deprived Davenport of the distinction of being the second athlete in history to win medals in both the Winter and Summer Games.

Above: a four-man American team does a practice run. Sixteen sleds participated in the four-man bobsled event. Despite much publicity and high hopes, the American sleds finished 12th and 13th. American driver Bob Hickey said that the American performance would have been better if the U.S. teams used the same type of sleds as the Europeans. Hickey noted that the European sleds "have better aerodynamics and suspension" (photo right).

With two subminute runs, the East German team (left) took the gold medal. Switzerland's No. 1 sled (below) was less than a second behind and won the silver.

Hickey said he was happy with 12th place, but said the Americans could do better if they had the same equipment as the Europeans. "There's no guesswork in their equipment. In our equipment you're always guessing, taking a chance. They have better aerodynamics and suspension on their sleds," Hickey said.

According to Siler, the bottom line is financial. "Americans have trouble financing their sport."

Nehmer expressed surprise at the Americans' finish. "We certainly expected them to do better in the four-man races than they did in their two-man sleds," he said. According to Horst Schoenau, the Americans "try to be too intense with their training on Mount Van Hoevenberg. They should get out and try other bob runs to build their spirit by testing themselves against other countries."

Following the XIII Winter Olympics, the bob run at Lake Placid was opened to the public. Any brave soul with an extra $5 and willingness to release the state from responsibility for possible injury could partake of "the champagne of thrills."

Meinhard Nehmer

Meinhard Nehmer is a natural driver . . . a man like him comes along once every 50 years.

AMERICAN BOBSLEDDER SANDY KELLIN

Meinhard Nehmer, an East German farm implement dealer, ended his bobsledding career by driving his blue, four-man craft to a gold medal on the final day of the 1980 Winter Olympics. The decisive victory gave Nehmer a third Olympic gold medal to go with the bronze he won earlier in the two-man race at Lake Placid. He was a member of the winning teams in both events in the 1976 Winter Olympics at Innsbruck.

In the four-man event at Lake Placid, Nehmer made the first and only subminute runs down the nearly mile-long course as his sleek bobsled neared 90 miles per hour. By his final run, Nehmer had such an insurmountable lead that he practically coasted to the finish. His combined time for four runs of 3:59.92 was nearly a full second faster than most of his challengers'. Of his victory, Nehmer said: "There is only one reason we won today. There is no secret. We were the fastest. As to why we were the fastest, all I can say is that we had a good sled, the right runners, and a good course."

His combined time in the two man was 4:11.08, .15 second behind the East German silver medal-winning team and 1.72 seconds behind the gold winning Swiss team.

Nehmer, who is also considered one of East Germany's best javelin throwers, was born Jan. 13, 1941, on the Baltic Sea island of Boblin. He took up bobsledding while recovering from a soccer injury in 1973. Three years later he became the third man in history to drive two gold medal-winning sleds in the same Winter Games. At Innsbruck, his four-run time was 57/100ths of a second faster than the runner-up and in the four-man race he was 46/100ths of a second ahead of the Swiss sled driven by Erich Schaerer.

Nehmer, who attributes his success in bobsledding to his love of fast automobiles, became familiar with the Lake Placid bobsled run during the 1978 world championships, which were also held at Mount Van Hoevenberg. He finished the two-man championship in second place and the fours in third. In 1979 he lost the 4-man world championship to a West German team by just 1/100th of a second but was first in the European fours.

Nehmer, his wife, Renate, a physiotherapist, and their son and daughter live in Suhl, 9 miles from the winter-sports center of Oberhof. He is a lieutenant in the National People's Army.

Following his success in the 1980 Winter Olympics, Nehmer said: "The people back home do not take me seriously when I say I am retiring, but I will not drive again. I will not miss bobsledding. . . . I am very pleased to have won the gold. It was very significant to end it this way. I am 39 years old and I have been doing this long enough. I am sure there are many more coming after me and I'd like to pass it along to others."

The bobsled medalist also hopes that giving up the sport will give him more time to study the latest developments in his field, farm machinery, and to spend on his favorite hobby, deep-sea diving. According to Nehmer, "training and racing down runs take up a lot of time."

The winning team was (l–r) B. Musiol, B. Germeshausen, M. Nehmer, and H.J. Gerhardt.

The East German and Swiss flags hang as the 12 medal-winning members of the four-man bobsled event gather for the presentation ceremony in the Olympic Arena.

BOBSLED CHRONOLOGY

Mount Van Hoevenberg

Friday February 15
Under partly cloudy skies, with the air temperature at 9°F (−13°C), the two-man bobsled competition begins at 9:30 A.M. The Swiss sled, driven by Erich Schaerer, scores the fastest time of the day (1:01.87) and is in the lead after two runs.

Saturday February 16
As expected, the Swiss sled maintains its lead and goes on to win the gold medal. The East German entries are the runners-up. The American team of Howard Siler and Dick Nalley has the second fastest run of the day and finishes in fifth place—the best results for U.S. bobsledders in 24 years.

Saturday February 23
The sky is cloudy, there is a light wind, and the temperature is 19°F (−7°C) for the first two runs of the four man. East Germany's No. 1 sled, driven by Meinhard Nehmer, a former javelin thrower, completes the first run in 59.86 seconds and ends the day in the first spot.

Sunday February 24
Nehmer's sled again races down the bob run in less than a minute, 59.73 seconds, and completes the fourth run in 1:00.30 for the gold. The Swiss No. 1 sled overtakes the other East German team to capture the silver.

MEDAL WINNERS

	Gold	Silver	Bronze
TWO MAN	SUI (E. Schaerer, J. Benz)	GDR (B. Germeshausen, H. J. Gerhardt)	GDR (M. Nehmer, B. Musiol)
FOUR MAN	GDR (M. Nehmer, B. Musiol B. Germeshausen, H. J. Gerhardt)	SUI (E. Schaerer, U. Baechli, R. Marti, J. Benz)	GDR (H. Schoenau, R. Wetzig, D. Richter, A. Kirchner)

Figure Skating

Pairs

Ever since it was made an event in the Olympic Games, pairs figure skating has been one of the premier spectacles. In London, in 1903, Anna Hübler and Heinrich Burger from Germany and two British couples, Phyllis and James Johnson and Madge and Edgar Syers, delighted the crowd with their agility in executing intricate figures together on the ice, and were awarded the gold, silver, and bronze medals respectively. In succeeding Games the medals went with regularity to pairs from Western European nations until 1948, when Canada's Suzanne Morrow and Wallace Diestelmeyer won a bronze. An American couple, Karol and Michael Kennedy, returned from Oslo with the silver medal in 1952, and eight years later, when the Canadian team of Barbara Wagner and Robert Paul captured the gold at Squaw Valley, Nancy and Ronald Ludington were awarded the bronze. Thereafter, the gold medal had been a Soviet monopoly. Twice, in 1964 and 1968, it had been Ludmilla (Beloussova) and Oleg Protopopov, dazzlingly elegant, who took the top honors. Then in 1972 it was Irina Rodnina and Aleksei Ulanov. Soon after, Ulanov ditched Rodnina for Ludmilla Smirnova, half of the silver-medal pair in 1972. But diminutive, strong-willed Rodnina paired with Aleksandr Zaitsev, and together they secured the 1976 gold medal for the Soviet Union for a fourth straight time.

Over and above her Olympics successes, Rodnina had achieved a formidable standing in the World Championships. She had worn the world crown for ten years when she skipped the contest in 1979 to have a baby. While Rodnina and her husband, Zaitsev, were otherwise occupied, a young American pair, Tai Babilonia and Randy Gardner, skated away with the World Championship. Despite Rodnina and Zaitsev's absence, the graceful American couple was practically flawless. In fact, a West German judge gave them a perfect 6.0 score.

Now, in Lake Placid, the long-reigning Soviet champions and the new World Champions were to come face to face in a contest that their very different styles of skating, their age differences, and the political tensions between their national governments had kept in the limelight for weeks.

As the American pair knew—none better—they were in for a battle. Following the World Championships, they had gone on a skating tour that took them to the Soviet Union. After an exhibition there, Rodnina went backstage to greet them. "She didn't have an ounce of fat on her," Gardner said. "And she'd been back on the ice for three days—which was six weeks since she'd had the baby."

In the past, the Russian duo, as subtle as a sledgehammer, had been winning titles with a variety of lifts, powerful skating,

A special excitement surrounded Tai Babilonia and Randy Gardner in Lake Placid. They were the 1979 World Champion figure skaters, the former rank of Irina Rodnina and Aleksandr Zaitsev of the Soviet Union. In Placid to defend their Olympic title, the Soviet couple was famed for speed and power, and a kind of cold precision. The younger Americans were known for their grace and beauty on the ice, for a kind of sixth sense whereby each knew the other's location without looking, and for their willingness to chance the most difficult moves. A classic confrontation was in store.

and perfect technique. Babilonia and Gardner, in contrast, had always been more lyrical and interpretive in their approach.

"Their strength is in their speed and power," Gardner said, by way of comparison. "Our strength is in our style, our power, and our choreography. So it balances out."

Yes, but would it? The nine judges would determine that, and there was no predicting the way their opinions would go. By definition, judging is subjective. In a speed race, instruments without emotional or personal bias can be employed to determine first, second, and so on. But what constitutes a great, as distinct from a competent, pairs figure skating performance? Some judges prefer athleticism, others perfect form, and others a combination. So the judging is likely to be controversial in figure skating. That knowledge made for cautious predictions.

"Tai and Randy are more elegant, they have more sparkle and, technically, they're better free skaters and spinners," said Gordon McKellen, a figure skater on the U.S. team in 1972 and now a coach in Rockford, IL. "But they lack the Russians' speed and movement and technical difficulty on their lifts."

The judges are supposed to be chosen from those countries that placed in the prior year's World Championships, but trade-offs may be made. For the pairs competition in Lake Placid the judges came from Australia, Canada, Czechoslovakia, France, Great Britain, Japan, the Soviet Union, and the United States.

The pairs program consists of two parts of unequal length. The first, the short program, is two minutes long and its elements are prescribed. In Lake Placid the six figures were a solo jump with double flips; an overhead one-arm axel; a backward inside death spiral; a solo spin, changing to a sitting position; a pairs spin, changing to a catch-waist camel spin; and a serpentine dance sequence. These elements were performed to music of the couple's choice, and their results counted one third of the total score. The short program took place on February 15.

Two days later came the free skating, which gave each couple five minutes to show off to the best advantage. Again, they chose their own music for their routines. So long as they conveyed an overall impression of unison and harmony they could do lifts, jumps, spins, and spirals; they could skate symmetrically (mirroring each other's moves) or in parallel (shadowing each other). They could separate and perform moves that were not identical. Whatever the judges rated them was two thirds of their total score.

The power of television can not be overstated. Its inquisitive eye had been on Tai and Randy so closely that their names had become as familiar as household words. And because they were being talked of as the Western contestants who had a good chance to beat the Eastern hopefuls—a chance that even the hockey players' mothers didn't believe *they* had—the Soviet skaters' names became equally familiar. The self-same couple had won the gold medal in Innsbruck in 1976, but until the battle for gold with Tai and Randy shaped up, you could have won money betting against anyone knowing their identity.

A near-capacity crowd in the Olympic Fieldhouse well before 9:00 P.M. on Tuesday, February 15, buzzed in anticipation of what the American couple's coach, John Nicks, had called a "classic confrontation" between strength and speed on the one

The short program for pairs was scheduled for 9:00 P.M. on Friday, February 15. During their morning practice (below) Tai and Randy worked out before the eyes and lenses of fans and camera buffs. If any of them had an inkling that something was amiss, it was only the knowing few who noted that some figures were not skated. Later, Randy would say that he could not do two of their planned moves.

side and grace and elegance on the other. Inevitably, there was another confrontation in everyone's mind. Both teams were favored to win a gold medal at the end of the competition, which was scheduled for Sunday, February 17, just three days before President Jimmy Carter's deadline for the Soviets to withdraw from Afghanistan or face staging the Summer Games without the presence of U.S. athletes. Against that threatening background the question was, how objective would the judges—three of them from East Europe—be in this most subjective of sports.

Nicks had not been averse to using psychological jockeying to aid the gold medal chances of the team he had coached. Saying that the longtime Russian champions were guilty of at least four technical violations during their five-minute free-skating performance at the European Championships in Gothenburg, Sweden, in January, he wrote letters of complaint to U.S. skating officials. Nicks smiled when asked if he were trying to rattle the Russians. "I'm doing what I think is right. The Russians have dominated things for so long, but I wouldn't want them to think they can continue to dominate by taking advantage of the rules," he said.

Nicks contended that Zaitsev held his wife by the leg when hoisting her off the ice during three of their eight lifts. The International Skating Union (ISU) rules clearly state that the man cannot place his hand below the woman's hip during a lift. Also, Nicks said that on one of the lifts, Zaitsev raised and spun Rodnina in the same movement—another ISU no-no.

Such violations would cost points if the judges saw them in the Olympic contests. Knowledgeable people, including several American coaches, didn't show much enthusiasm for the complaint, saying that the Soviets would not have any difficulty changing the lift at any time. "It would take Rodnina and Zaitsev five minutes to change them, they're so professional," said Ron Ludington, coach for the brother-sister team of Peter and Kitty Carruthers, the No. 2 U.S. pair.

The crowd was equipped with flags and flowers, and there were hand-lettered signs of encouragement: "Tai and Randy—USA Gold." The first pair to skate were the West Germans, pleasing but not exciting. They were followed by the East Germans, and then the British pair. The crowd liked the British, and booed when the judges gave them marks lower than expected. While the first teams were performing, their successors regularly appeared on the ice, to warm up near the entrance.

It was during that time that the crowd could have spotted the burgundy-costumed American couple. Those who did knew something was amiss. Unbelievably, Randy fell. Then again, and still a third time. Apprehension drifted like fog through the banks of seats.

But then, as the Britons' scores came up, Tai and Randy skated out to echoing cheers. Randy tried another double flip, the sort of move he can do in his sleep, and now everyone, fieldhouse and television audiences together, saw him fall. To the ice with him crashed his and Tai's gold medal hopes. Nicks waved his hand. The skaters in spangled burgundy left the ice without making a move of what was to have been the most important performance of their lives.

Randy Gardner, a superb athlete and dependable performer, sprawled on the ice was a sight to defy belief. It happened while the cameras were trained on performers at center ice, and only nearby spectators were aware of the trouble. But twice more he fell during the warm-up, unable to do sit-spins or routine jumps. In all but palpable sadness, Coach John Nicks withdrew Tai and Randy. With them went any real challenge to Rodnina and Zaitsev and 29 years of Soviet domination of pairs skating.

"There was no option," Nicks said. "Randy wanted to go on but I withdrew them. He had problems with the lifts and that would have been dangerous to Tai."

Within seconds the television audience knew what had happened. Through the expert commentary of former gold medalist Dick Button the millions not able to be in the fieldhouse learned that the Americans had withdrawn. Gardner had pulled a groin muscle in his left thigh practicing a double axel jump in Los Angeles two weeks before, according to U.S. team physician Anthony Daly. He again injured his groin, more seriously, the night before the short program, in a late-night practice session.

Daly, an orthopedic surgeon, said Randy had been receiving treatments for his injury since the pair arrived in Lake Placid on February 10. After the second injury, he was treated with ice, compresses, and anti-inflammatory medicine.

"I couldn't do two of the required elements because of extreme pain, so it was then I decided I had to numb it," Randy said, but with the numbing he lost feeling in his leg. "I couldn't feel my left leg, I couldn't feel the positions I was supposed to be in, but I didn't feel much pain either."

Daly said Randy's reaction to the shot, of Xylocaine, was "a reaction to the injury" and not the shot. "The dosage was not great enough to give a numbing effect, but he blocked out the pain completely." However, he admitted that the shot was a "last ditch" move that he was "not really in favor of. But Randy said he couldn't do it any other way. There was nothing else to do. Either withdraw, or try it, and he was such a courageous young man, we tried it."

It was a measure of their disappointment that people who should have known better criticized the decision to use a drug, saying that Randy could have endured without it. Two days after the shot was given, Dr. Daly said he was treating Gardner's injury with an ice whirlpool bath because the abdomen area was still swollen. The area was also black and blue, he said.

"Maybe the seriousness of this injury hasn't been stressed enough," he said. "The fact that he even tried at all is testimony to how courageous he is."

The young couple left the arena in tears. There was some solace in the flood of telegrams that began pouring in on them, and in knowing that the President had called to express sympathy and concern. The American skaters practicing for their events expressed sorrow at the injury that kept America's best team out of the pairs event.

"They were kind of like our leaders," said David Santee, America's No. 2 men's figure skater. "I know how hard they worked for this moment."

They had worked hard, and it had been possible because others worked hard for them. It is estimated that expenses for world class skaters can run from $15,000–$20,000 a year. There is the cost of lessons; a coach charges $35 an hour. There are rink costs—$70 for private practice sessions, and Tai and Randy often practiced five hours a day. And there are ballet lessons. Neither family is wealthy. Jack Gardner is a cost accountant and his wife, Jan, is a schoolteacher. Tai's father, Constancio, is a detective sergeant in the Los Angeles police department. He

Without Tai and Randy the United States had no gold-medal hopes in pairs skating, but it was not without talented entrants. The brother-sister pair of Peter and Caitlin Carruthers, newcomers on the international circuit, were fifth in both short and free-style competitions. They conveyed (below) a sense of athletic skating for the joy of it. The crowd loved them.

could have retired last year but decided to stay on the force for five more years while also moonlighting as a security guard to defray his daughter's enormous skating costs.

The hard work had begun 10 years before when Tai and Randy were told to hold hands and skate around the ice. They instantly disliked each other. "At the beginning I couldn't get them to skate together," said Mabel Fairbanks, a former skater who gave them instruction in their early years. "She said 'I won't skate with that boy' and he said 'I won't skate with a girl.' But I said 'you're perfectly matched for each other so let it work.'"

Slowly, a relationship developed, built on the realization that one couldn't achieve greatness without the other.

One by one the barriers and competition began to tumble. In 1974, they became the youngest pair ever to represent the United States in international competition. Tai was 12; Randy 14. Two years later, they won their first of five consecutive national pairs titles and in 1976 went to the Innsbruck Olympics, where they finished fifth.

For figure skaters especially, the Olympic gold medal can be an open sesame to instant riches. They can all thank Sonja Henie for that. "The gold medal in itself is not a guarantee," says Dick Button. "You've got to have some pizzazz, a sense of style, projection, and good management."

They have it, and to spare. As Button observed, "Tai is cute as apple pie and extremely talented. Her partner, Gardner, has great ability—a super athlete. They are a brilliant, innovative pair who perform beautifully as a team."

When the news of their withdrawal was known, and before anyone knew the seriousness of the reason, Dick Button's spontaneous reaction was, Don't quit! If you can't do everything planned, do what you are able. The anguish he articulated was shared by millions.

Manuela Mager and Uwe Bewersdorff, representing the German Democratic Republic, seemed to many to have merited higher marks in the short program than those that put them in fourth place. In the longer free-style program their beautiful performance significantly impressed judges to move the pair ahead of Pestova and Leonovich (URS) and win them the bronze medal.

And then, in a kind of desperate urgency that the dream not just fritter away in a walkover for the Soviets, the question began to be asked, why not put in an alternate pair? After all, hadn't Austria reconstituted its downhill ski team at the last moment, giving alternate Leonhard Stock a place on the team?

Yes. But the International Skating Union rules that govern Olympic figure skating and the rules of the International Ski Federation, which governs Olympic skiing, are greatly different. By the ISU rules, American entries for the Lake Placid Games had to be submitted by February 1; after that, there could be no substitutions, for injury or anything else.

When their turn came, Irina Rodnina and Aleksandr Zaitsev glided out before the dispirited house. For a second they looked tense, as people do who are doubtful about their reception. The fans were disappointed but they were sportsmanlike. There was welcoming applause for the Russians. No one could have imagined they had been out of competition for a year. They gave a nearly flawless performance that earned them several 5.9 marks and a warm ovation from the audience.

The free-skating program on Sunday evening, February 17, which was to have been the theater for the showdown, had a capacity crowd. The absence of Babilonia and Gardner robbed the event of any real drama. It was a foregone conclusion that

Marina Cherkosova and Sergei Shakrai, above, and Rodnina and Zaitsev, right, established the Soviet Union in second and first places, respectively, in the short program and then in the finals. How much of their silver-medal success Cherkosova and Shakrai owed to the withdrawal of Babilonia and Gardner made lively speculation.

Rodnina and Zaitsev would be first. They were. They performed as powerfully as ever, unmatched for sheer athletic ability and precise, synchronized skating, and they won ringing applause. Later, on the awards stand, the usually composed Irina, with her third gold medal on a broad ribbon around her neck, showed how much the battle to be best meant to her. Tears ran down her face as the crowd cheered the winners.

With them on the stand the Soviet couple had, on their right in the silver medal spot, a pair of their teammates, Marina Cherkosova and Sergei Shakrai. An attractive and talented team, they had placed second in the short program and had convincingly held on to that rank in the free skating. The bronze medals were hung on East Germany's Manuela Mager and Uwe Bewersdorff. They had moved through their free program with such assurance that they bumped the Soviet team of Marina Pestova and Stanislav Leonovich out of the third place they had won in the short program.

In fifth place, to the noisy joy of the packed house, was the sister-brother team of Caitlin and Peter Carruthers, enthusiastically making the most of their first international competition. At 18 and 20 the Americans showed up as clean skaters and good jumpers, who effortlessly established instant rapport with the audience.

When the medal-winning couples stood on the podium in the limelight, dwarfed by the vast ice arena, they could not help but realize how the crowd had wanted to see Tai and Randy there. The winners' pleasure was the greater, then, when the sportsmanlike spectators raised a thunder of applause for their success.

Irina Rodnina—Aleksandr Zaitsev

Skating is privileged.

—IRINA AND ALEKSANDR ZAITSEV

The 1979 achievement of Irina Rodnina and Aleksandr Zaitsev, the husband and wife pairs figure skaters, was a baby boy, Sasha. Before that interruption in their careers, they had never missed a beat. Together they had won six world pairs championships and the 1976 Olympic gold medal. Before teaming up with Zaitsev, Rodnina had won the 1972 gold medal and four world titles in partnership with Aleksei Ulanov.

As a youngster in Moscow Irina was both small and delicate, enough to worry her parents. She began skating at 9, because the fresh winter air was thought to be good for her. She showed talent from the start and through her army officer father was brought to the attention of the Central Army Club authorities. Attached to their club is a special children's sports school, and there Irina was entered and made a pupil of Stanislav Zhuk, a renowned coach.

Rodnina moved into the international limelight in 1969 by winning the 1969 European pairs championship with her first partner, Ulanov. Three years later, in Sapporo, they won the Olympic title. Soon afterwards, when Ulanov began training with Ludmilla Smirnova, who had won a silver medal in pairs skating in Sapporo, it appeared as if Rodnina were headed for retirement.

But the strong-willed skater wasn't settling for the discard. Through a nation-wide audition she found a new partner and, in 1976, a husband.

Aleksandr Zaitsev was born in 1953 in Leningrad, where he attended a sports school. He began figure skating when he was seven years old, showed promise, and eventually was sent to train with a famous coach. He became a member of the Soviet national Olympic team when he began skating with Rodnina. By 1973 they were dazzling crowds with their athletic performances. At 6' and 152 pounds, he is a foot taller than and almost half again as heavy as Irina, whom he lifts with a show of great power. Their precise, synchronized skating and strong acrobatic style are wonderful to watch.

By Western definition of what constitutes *amateur*, the Zaitsevs would have to be called professional amateurs. Both are technically graduate students of one of the Soviet Union's 23 physical culture institutes, whose purpose is to train athletic instructors and coaches. She is preparing a thesis on the history, organization, and management of figure skating. His concerns the physiology of figure skating. She is a third-year student, he a fourth. Usually, said Rodnina, a thesis must be defended within five years, "but they make special allowances for people with demanding training schedules."

Both are entitled to the equivalent of $450 a month. They pay no tuition fees, get their costumes free, have a spacious apartment in one of the fashionable sections of Moscow, and own a $22,800 Volga car, got through the army club.

After Sasha's birth, 30-year-old Rodnina had doubts about whether she could skate again. Her coach urged her to, with golden results. Tears streamed down her face as she stood with her husband on the awards platform, hearing the Soviet anthem over the cheers of the crowd. It had been a long way to go to get there, and attaining her third Olympic gold medal was the realization of a childhood dream. Her idol, Sonja Henie, was a three-time gold medalist and now so was she.

The Zaitsevs execute a flawless "death spiral."

Men's Singles

Figure skating competition, in which athletics and artistry merge, is demanding of both the body and the soul of the contender. In addition to flawless technique, the winning skater is one who displays a less tangible quality, a certain élan that goes beyond technical proficiency. In the 1980 Olympics, an elegant Briton proved to possess both the requisite elements.

Robin Cousins, 22 years old, had spent the previous two years in Denver, CO, training with fabled coach Carlo Fassi, the man who groomed gold medalists Peggy Fleming, Dorothy Hamill, and John Curry. Cousins was determined to fulfill a self-imposed three-year timetable by carrying off a gold medal from Lake Placid. Among those out to foil that design were reigning world champion Vladimir Kovalev of the Soviet Union and Jan Hoffmann of East Germany, the European champion and former world titlist. Hoffmann, a 24-year-old medical student, hoped to crown his amateur career with the one prize that had thus far escaped him—an Olympic medal. U.S. hopes for a medal centered on Charlie Tickner, the 1978 world champion who was banking on his strong artistic program to outshine the rather lackluster free skating of Hoffmann and Kovalev. After the first phase of the men's competition, the compulsory figures, Kovalev had dropped out of the race and Hoffmann was leading the pack.

Viewing the compulsories has been compared to watching grass grow and rust creep in. Hundreds of glazed spectators at the Lake Placid Olympic Fieldhouse found out why after paying $11.20 per ticket to watch 17 men trace six hours-worth of figure eights. Tedious they may be, but the compulsories are worth 30% of the overall competition. Skating first on one foot and then on the other, the skater attempts to carve perfect figures on the ice and retrace them several times. Crouching judges scrutinize the markings for clarity and accuracy of duplication. The

Robin Cousins, top, a spectacular free skater, Jan Hoffmann, left, star of the compulsory figures, and consistent Charlie Tickner made the men's singles dramatic.

Robin Cousins

I love a crowd and can respond to the people because without them there is no inspiration.

—ROBIN COUSINS

In 1977 British figure skater Robin Cousins mapped out a route to the 1980 Olympics. He aimed for a bronze medal at Ottawa in 1978, a silver in the 1979 world championships at Vienna, and ultimately, the gold at Lake Placid. He did not stray once from his itinerary.

Though he made it seem effortless, the path to that golden pinnacle was not an easy one. Cousins, who sprang from a middle-class family in Bristol, England, launched his bid for glory from a cheap room in London's seedy Camden Town. During those lean years the aspiring champion was very often completely broke. He needed every cent of the sponsorship money he received from the British Sports Council and various well-wishers.

The sponsors could consider their money well spent when, in January 1980, the lithe 22-year-old yanked the European men's title out from under the blades of arch-rivals Jan Hoffmann and Vladimir Kovalev. By then it was apparent that Robin Cousins had become Britain's best—and only—gold medal hope for the following month's Winter Games.

In a country where winter sports heroes are few and far between, Cousins came in for constant attention from the British news media, and public interest reached fever pitch after his Lake Placid triumph. Front-page headlines in *The London Evening News* trumpeted, "That's Our Golden Boy." The next day Cousins was offered $75,000 to take part in a "superskater" challenge match with Britian's 1976 Olympic champion John Curry.

But three years under the spotlight have not changed the quietly determined young man; his mother, Jo Cousins, affirms that "he's a very easy person to get along with, especially at home." Friends and associates agree that pressures off the rink have not altered Cousins' personality. The skater is an admitted "ham" who thrives on performing before big crowds: "I love the chance to show off and give something to somebody."

What he gives is, according to many, the finest free skating in the world. Intent on producing a flawless program, he chooses his own music and choreographs much of his routine, under the experienced eye of Coach Carlo Fassi. "I decide what I want to do, then Carlo decides how it best fits into the program," he has said. So involved is Cousins with the overall look of his routines that he designed his own costume for the Olympic long program.

His fluid, graceful style owes much to the movements of dance, and he delights in adapting the latest disco steps to his own icy medium. In fact, Cousins was dancing before he was skating. At age nine he took up figure skating as an alternative to ballet, to escape hated practice sessions at the bar. "It was a way to fly through the air without doing those silly little ballet exercises."

Needless to say, Cousins' soaring technique is constrained by the more pedestrian skating exercises; he placed fourth in the school figures at Lake Placid. His offhand demeanor drew criticism that Cousins was treating the event too casually. Jo Cousins set the record straight. "He is casual," she said, "but not about skating. His skating is his life. He is a perfectionist in all things."

Cousins dazzled with his free-skating program.

exacting routine is the bugbear of many a skater and more than one squared-off circle has been etched into Olympic ice.

Kovalev, normally an ace in the school figures, placed a disappointing fifth in the event. The Russian skater had missed four days of practice, a flu victim according to official Soviet reports (although there were those who said that Kovalev, a noted party-goer, had merely been enjoying himself too much). Whatever the reason, the Soviets later announced his withdrawal from the competition. Hoffmann held the top spot but the Americans Charlie Tickner and David Santee, both of whom expected to surpass the East German in free skating, were close behind in second and third place. Robin Cousins was down the line in fourth place, a turn of events that fueled American hopes. "I don't think anyone has won the Olympics who hasn't placed in the top three in the figures," declared Tickner's coach, Norma Sahlin. A correct statement, but one that did not reckon with the abilities of Robin Cousins.

For on the following day, Cousins skated an exhilarating short program that catapulted him into second place and knocked Tickner and Santee down a notch apiece. In an afternoon of skating that delighted the crowd, Jan Hoffmann maintained his overall lead after skating a competent short program. But Cousins took first in the event itself, skating so dazzlingly that his program was rated a perfect 6.0 by Canadian judge Alice Pinos.

The short program is a gauntlet of required moves that counts for 20% of the final score. The skater must incorporate seven specific jumps and spins, performed alone and in combination, into his two-minute routine. There is little margin for error.

The pressures of this demanding exercise affected the performance of Charlie Tickner, who placed fifth in the short program and slipped to third position overall. Attempting a triple salchow-double loop—an important mandatory maneuver—the 26-year-old skater landed incorrectly, damaging his chances for a gold medal and sparking a controversy over the fairness of the judges. Tickner's marks for the required elements ranged from 5.0 to 5.8; the latter mark was considered high, since a missed combination means an automatic four-tenths of a point deduction. Hostilities among coaches and officials brewed for several days, but Charlie Tickner was concerned only with his chances in the one remaining event, the five-minute free-skating program. "I've got to skate the best I can," he said. "I have to be very aggressive. I'd be happy with any medal—gold, silver, or bronze. I am the one I have to beat."

David Santee, a 20-year-old from Park Ridge, IL, ended a strong performance with arms raised in victory as he basked in the cheers of the crowd. Santee had been plagued by self-doubts until he bolstered his confidence with positive thinking tapes and inspiration from the movie *Rocky*. He skated one of his best performances ever, as did the third American team member, tiny Scott Hamilton, who thrilled the fans with a dynamic performance.

By the end of the short program, Robin Cousins had emerged as the man to beat. The free-skating, or long, program would count for 50% of the final score and, though Jan Hoffmann was in top place, it was Cousins who would pose the

Was he injured, as the Soviet coaches averred, or had he too well earned the sobriquet "Playboy of the Eastern World"? Whatever the truth, 1976 Olympic silver medalist and defending World Champion Vladimir Kovalev appeared for the compulsory figures, above. After doing three, he was withdrawn from competition.

The marvelous fluidity of Robin Cousins' skating carried the judges before it. His was the gold, and the magnitude of the triumph showed in his podium smile that was barely suppressed laughter. Jan Hoffmann, a medical student in his fourth Olympics, had the silver medal. Bronze went to Charlie Tickner, who showed the spirit the Olympics are supposed to instill. He would be proud, he said, to win a medal of any color.

greatest challenge in the most creative of the skating exercises.

Tensions, thick as the ice underfoot, mounted in the Olympic Fieldhouse as the skaters readied for their last, crucial routine. There were 16 competitors, but only five that counted: Hoffmann, Cousins, and the Americans Tickner, Santee, and Hamilton. The draw for skating order had put Cousins directly ahead of Hoffmann, adding to the pressure that already weighed upon the East German.

It was one of the closest competitions of all time. The graceful Cousins skated a program that, although delightful to watch, was admittedly not his best. He managed to overtake the highly disciplined Hoffmann by a narrow margin. Both skaters received 5.8's and 5.9's from the nine judges for technical merit, but Cousins' creative flair gave him the edge; he was awarded eight 5.9's for artistic impression. Hoffmann skated commendably, but his stalwart performance did not measure up to the British skater's fluid routine, which was punctuated by disco rhythms. The East German came away with the silver medal.

It was a disappointing evening for Charlie Tickner, who needed marks of 5.9 and 6.0 to be the first American since 1960 to win the gold in the men's singles. He was scheduled to skate last, an undesirable draw because the strain of waiting often takes its toll on a skater. When he finally took to the ice, Tickner had little of the spark that had previously distinguished his routines. But he captured the bronze, the U.S. figure skating team's first medal in 1980. Teammates Santee and Hamilton proved they were worth their salt by skating energetic performances that landed them in fourth and fifth place, respectively.

"I think with technical standards so high, you have to look for something extra," said Robin Cousins after succeeding countryman John Curry as the men's Olympic figure skating champion. "It's far too easy to go around and jump, jump, jump."

Women's Singles

The women's Olympic figure skating competition is always fraught with emotion, and the 1980 Winter Games were no exception. This year, perhaps, the tensions and pressures weighed even more heavily than usual upon the two main antagonists.

Midway through the women's program, it became clear that the three gold medal possibilities so eagerly touted for the U.S. figure skating team had dwindled to one. With the withdrawal of Randy and Tai from the pairs and only the bronze captured in the men's competition, all the American hopes and expectations came into focus and descended upon the slender shoulders of one woman.

In 1977 Linda Fratianne won the world championship in women's figure skating but lost it the following year to Anett Poetzsch of East Germany. Of that defeat she remarked, "It was easier winning it the first time because when you're the underdog you have nothing to lose." In 1980 Fratianne was decidedly not the underdog. At 19, she had regained her world title and won the last four U.S. championships; it was expected that she would form the next link in the golden chain of American figure skaters that included Tenley Albright, Carol Heiss, Peggy Fleming, and Dorothy Hamill. Fellow team member and sometime rival Lisa-Marie Allen put it another way: "Linda has been totally moulded and packaged to win the gold medal."

At Lake Placid, as in the past, Fratianne's major competition would come from Anett Poetzsch. In each of the past three world championships, Poetzsch held the lead after the compulsories and Fratianne worked her way up in the short and free-skating programs. In 1977 and 1979, Fratianne was able to climb all the way to the top, while in 1978 she was surpassed by the East German skater. The Olympic confrontation between the two old rivals, one from the East and one from the West, had the makings of high drama.

The pressure had already begun with the compulsory figures, always a difficult event for American skaters. European coaches drill their charges in the school figures which, like the music student's scales, are an abhorred but necessary part of training. Americans, on the other hand, devote much more time to the creative aspects of skating. So it was that Fratianne found herself placed third in the compulsories, behind Anett Poetzsch and the West German Dagmar Lurz. Though it came as no surprise, her standing left Fratianne with little room for error in the rest of the competition. "She'll have to do a super job now," said her coach, Frank Carroll. "She'll have to not miss anything in the short program and she'll have to skate the best in the long program. If she makes any mistakes, she's out."

"I just want to skate the best I can," said Fratianne.

That she did. While the compulsories belonged to Poetzsch, the short program was all Fratianne. Seven of the nine judges gave her the highest marks after a dynamic two minutes, in which she cleanly hit her triple salchow-double loop combination, the double flip, and the double axel. Wearing a flaming red outfit and skating to music from *Firebird*, the American convincingly won the short program and moved into a very threatening second-place position behind Poetzsch.

Anett Poetzsch in Lake Placid will be remembered for two things: the one-legged move, below, during which she held the other leg above her head, and the humorous program she skated to Louis Armstrong's rendering of "Hello, Dolly."

If decibels of audience applause decided medal winners, Linda Fratianne would have gone home with Lake Placid gold. She brought the packed Fieldhouse to its feet with her free-skating show. Her lower standing than Poetzsch's in the compulsories made the difference.

The East German, who has sometimes had problems in the short program, skated conservatively but maintained her overall lead. Lisa-Marie Allen, a lanky, blonde American who had finished eighth in the compulsories, skated an elegant program that shot her into sixth place overall. The biggest surprise of the event was the performance of the young Swiss skater Denise Biellmann, which earned second place in the short program and allowed the graceful 16-year-old to leap to seventh overall.

But all the questions that hovered over the ice after the short program were directed at one small American skater. Would Linda Fratianne, as she had in the past, propel herself into first position and a gold medal? "It's possible," was as close as she would come to a prediction. "I know Anett can skate a long program well. . . . It's going to be a battle."

Anett Poetzsch, meanwhile, was dealing with pressures of her own, for the results of the men's competition had placed as large a burden on her as on Fratianne. Jutta Mueller, the East German coach, wanted nothing more than to produce her country's first figure skating champion, and the abilities of Poetzsch and teammate Jan Hoffmann presented a golden opportunity. After Robin Cousins edged out Hoffmann in the men's competition, East German hopes for a gold medal centered on the 19-year-old woman.

The long program was the final phase of the women's event and the two top contenders were prepared for a battle. Poetzsch, on the advice of Coach Mueller, had trimmed off ten pounds during training and broadened her artistic scope in an effort to freshen her free-skating routine. Fratianne, too, had been working on her image, trying to overcome her natural shyness and project a more vibrant personality on the ice. Her fiery red costume and selection of Spanish music for the long program reflected her new persona.

The event, held on February 23 in the Olympic Fieldhouse, was attended by an enthusiastic crowd of 8,500. Fratianne, who skated first, performed a highly athletic program to the strains of music from *Carmen*. She had the house roaring and clapping when she hit two triple jumps in the first 30 seconds of her four-minute program, and she received a standing ovation at the finish. Her scores did not belie the crowd's enthusiasm. The five 5.8's for technical merit and five 5.9's for artistic impression seemed to guarantee her the gold. But despite her best efforts and the fervent hopes of the American crowd, Fratianne could not beat Poetzsch. The East German skated brilliantly to music from *Funny Girl*, collecting enough points to maintain her overall lead. Fratianne had to settle for the silver medal, even though she defeated Poetzsch in the free skate. "The competition was lost for Linda in the figures," said a disappointed Frank Carroll.

Dagmar Lurz of West Germany managed to fight off the challenge of sensational Swiss free skater Denise Biellmann to win the bronze medal. An uninspiring free skater, Lurz won on the basis of her second-place standing in the compulsories. The crowd fell in love with Biellmann, who actually won the free-skate but couldn't overcome her 12th-place finish in the compulsories. She thrilled the fans with her acrobatic finish, in which she twirled with both arms and one leg clasped together high over her head.

Anett Poetzsch

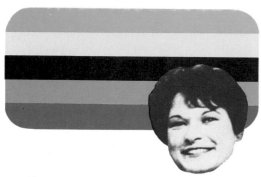

You must fight. You must be strong. You must go for all the jumps. You must win.

—JUTTA MUELLER, Coach

Anett Poetzsch, along with countless other East German students, took her university entrance examinations in the summer of 1980. Unlike her compatriots, however, Anett had already taken a far more demanding test and passed it with flying colors. In February, she had performed before a panel of critics numbering in the millions, triumphing over U.S. rival Linda Fratianne and giving East Germany its first Olympic gold medal in figure skating.

Anett began her figure skating career in 1966, inspired by a champion skater from her own city of Karl-Marx-Stadt. Among the hometown folks eagerly watching their television screens as Gabi Seyfert captured the European title at Bratislava were six-year-old Anett and her mother. "I was so enthusiastic and fascinated that the very next day I went along to the ice stadium and enrolled Anett," Frau Poetzsch later remarked.

It was not a wasted trip. By the time she was 16 Anett had become a champion in her own right. She was East German champion from 1976 to 1979 and a three-time European champion, winning a total of 11 European titles. During these same years Linda Fratianne emerged as her most formidable opponent. In 1977, 1978, and 1979 the two skaters, virtual equals in age, height, and ability, vied for the world championship. Only at the 1978 competition in Ottawa could Anett wrest the title from the American, joining Gabi Seyfert as one of three East German world champions within a decade. The 1978 victory gave Anett the en-

couragement she needed to try for her ultimate goal—a gold medal at the 1980 Olympics. "Although in our sports discipline the atmosphere . . . plays a decisive role, my success [at Ottawa] proved to me that I can also win in strange surroundings," she observed.

But a hard-won victory can also lead to overconfidence and, as Anett's trainer, Jutta Mueller, warned, "in sport you cannot rest on your laurels." Those words were driven home in Vienna the following year when Linda Fratianne recovered the world title. After the defeat, Anett's confidence was balanced by an increased determination to work.

Schooled in the European manner, Anett possesses technical skills as finely honed as her skating blades. But she is no plodding technician. Supplementary ballet training plus a natural sensitivity lend artistry to her performances. Still, knowing that when competition is close a skater's "look" can be the deciding factor, Anett worked to add that extra ingredient to her Lake Placid routines. She slimmed down to 110 pounds to improve her appearance and increase her agility on the ice. Coach Mueller, a stern-seeming woman with surprisingly liberal ideas, geared her student's program to an American audience, incorporating music from *Funny Girl* and *West Side Story*.

And if the pro-Fratianne Lake Placid audience was unwilling to accept her at first, Anett won them over on the last night of the Olympics, during the noncompetitive exhibition skating. Garbed in Gay Nineties costume, complete with feather boa, she skated enchantingly to Louis Armstrong's rendition of "Hello, Dolly." For the moment, at least, national barriers melted away in the warmth of that gesture from East to West.

Anett showed a new technical command in Placid.

Ice Dancing

Ice dancing, very popular in Eastern Europe, is the least glamorous of the figure skating disciplines in the United States. Enormous attention is lavished on the women's and men's competitions, and on the pairs championships, but people habitually confuse ice dancing with pairs skating. They are similar in some aspects, but there is not only no effort by ice dancers to do athletic moves: they are strictly forbidden.

The event was made part of the Olympics in 1976. It is based on ballroom dancing and although it is similar to the freestyle part of the pairs skating, there are three main differences. Lifts are limited to five, and they can be only to the waist. Spins and jumps are prohibited. And couples can separate no more than five times in all.

There are three parts to the ice dancing program. The first sets the skaters three compulsory dances. The skaters are judged for their timing, accuracy, rhythm, style, and placement, and scored on a scale of 0–6 points for each dance. Their total points represent 30% of their final score. Nothing says all three dances must be done in one appearance, and at Lake Placid, two were asked on February 15 and the third on February 17, along with the second part of the program, the original set pattern dance.

For this part the partners create their own choreography. They select their own music, although the International Skating Union dictates the tempo. The original set pattern dance is

Andrey Minenkov and Irina Moiseeva—"Min" and "Mo" to the breezy spectators—added a bronze medal to the silver they won in the 1976 Innsbruck Games.

worth 20% of the total score, and in evaluating it the judges are principally interested in the composition and overall presentation.

The four-minute free dance, equal to half the final score, has no required elements or sequences. The couples choose their own music, determine the tempo, and create their own moves so as to demonstrate ingenuity, ability, and overall style.

From the outset, it was expected that the defending two-time World Champions would stand on the gold level of the awards podium. They did. Starting with the compulsory dances, Natalia Linichuk and Gennadi Karponosov took an early lead, winning first place on the cards of eight of the nine judges. They waltzed away with the top honors in the original set pattern. In that rather lackluster afternoon meet, the most remarked detail was an error of omission by the top American pair, Stacey Smith and John Summers. They left out one of the six required patterns.

The finals evoked spirited comment from the packed stands. Linichuk stumbled once, and she and Karponosov put on a stuffy, traditional free dance. When their marks came up and showed, among others, a pair of 5.9's from the Soviet judge, the crowd of 8,500 booed loudly.

The same judge gave 5.7's to the Hungarian pair, Krisztina Regoczy and Andras Sallay, an outgoing couple who performed a romantic, upbeat program that was enthusiastically cheered. They won the free-skating phase, but their earlier marks did not push them quite into the gold mine.

In third place were Irina Moiseeva and Andrey Minenkov, an attractive couple from the Soviet Union who had been silver medalists in 1976. They, too, were crowd pleasers, and were affectionately called "Min" and "Mo."

After the medals had been handed out, a spectator yelled, "The judges stink!" The crowd echoed accord.

Natalia Linichuk and Gennadi Karponosov, Soviet gold medalists, below, were as stuffy as Hungarian Krisztina Regoczy and Andras Sallay, above, were upbeat.

SCORING

The first thing to understand about figure skating scoring is that it is nearly unintelligible. Points and "ordinals" are awarded, but, under ordinary circumstances, neither actually determines the final order of the athletes.

Scoring of the compulsory figures portion of the women's and men's singles is not done in the public eye, as the short and free-skating portions are, and there is no identifying of a given judge with given marks. In the short and free programs, however, the judges hold up their marks after each performance, and while they are uncriticizable by skaters (and they themselves make no public comment), the judges may come in for candid assessment by the paying audience.

To see how their judging works, take the *pairs* figure skating of couples A and B, for example, in a group of seven couples.

The short program, two minutes' worth of six required moves, is valued at about 30% of the overall event. After each couple skates, the nine judges post two sets of scores. The first is for technical merit—how well they performed their prescribed elements. The second is for composition and style—how well the program looked.

A maximum score in each is 6.0. The two marks of all nine judges—none are dropped—are added together and divided by 2.5. The judges also rank the skaters, leaving room at the top for the expected stronger skaters who are seeded to skate last. These rankings are called ordinals.

After all 14 skaters have performed, the rankings provide an order for the short program. For argument's sake, let's give the top-rated couple, A, 5 first-place votes and 4 seconds, with the next couple, B, picking up the remaining first and second-place votes. Couple A would have 13 ordinals (5 × 1, plus 4 × 2 equal 13), while Couple B would have 14 ordinals (4 × 1, plus 5 × 2 equal 14).

But Couple A would be first, not because of fewer ordinals or more points, but because they had a majority of firsts, 5 of 9. Couple B would be second because of a majority of seconds. *Majority* of ordinals is the key. Theoretically, a couple could have 5 firsts and four 10ths for 45 ordinals, and be first while the couple with 4 firsts and 5 seconds for 14 ordinals would be second.

So what's hard?

Well, suppose no couple nets a majority—of firsts—what then? Then you look for a next greatest majority, and to help find one, you make all first-place votes into seconds, and at the same time keep the second place votes as seconds. Now, whichever couple has the most seconds—provided they total more than five—is the leader.

For the free skating the process is the same, although the scores are worth 70% of the total. If no pair comes up with a majority of ordinals, the couple with the lowest number of total ordinals wins. If that doesn't work, if two couples tie, then the greatest number of points decides the victory.

There is no waiting for decisions, or very little, however it might seem to the nerved-up skaters, because all the separate scores are fed into a computer. It does the searching for majorities and/or points, and spews out the results in whirlaway time.

If you don't like the results, don't kick the machine. It can only digest what the judges feed it.

Charlie Tickner performs compulsory figures, where the emphasis is on precise tracing.

FIGURE SKATING CHRONOLOGY

Olympic Fieldhouse

Friday February 15
In two of the three compulsory dances, Natalia Linichuk and Gennadi Karponosov, the defending champions, take an early lead, although the Hungarian pair show more flair.

To the dismay of the packed house, Randy Gardner falls three times in his warm-up and then the U.S. team is withdrawn. Irina Rodnina and Aleksandr Zaitsev skate imperiously, gaining top marks.

Sunday February 17
Linichuk and Karponosov widen their lead, picking up 9 ordinals and 101.28 points in the third compulsory and the original set pattern dances.

The pairs free skating in the evening, minus the drama of Babilonia and Gardner, gives Rodnina her third gold medal and her partner his second.

Monday February 18
Jan Hoffmann (GDR) moves into first place after the men's compulsory figures, followed by Americans David Santee and Charlie Tickner in second and third. British skater Robin Cousins holds fourth position; world champion Vladimir Kovalev (URS) is said to be ill and withdraws from the competition, having placed fifth in the compulsories.

Tuesday February 19
Jan Hoffmann maintains his overall lead, but Robin Cousins wins the men's short program and leaps from fourth to second spot. Charlie Tickner stumbles on a required jump and sinks to third, weakening his chances for a gold medal.

Although the crowd plainly prefers the upbeat program of the Hungarian dancers, the judges give the gold to Linichuk and Karponosov.

Wednesday February 20
East German Anett Poetzsch places first and Dagmar Lurz (GER) is in second position after the women's compulsory figures. American gold medal hopeful Linda Fratianne places third, leaving herself little margin for error in the next events.

Thursday February 21
Fratianne dominates the women's short program and moves into second place behind Anett Poetzsch, who holds on to her overall lead. In the men's long program, Robin Cousins squeaks past Jan Hoffmann by dint of some spectacular free skating and wins the gold medal. Hoffmann takes the silver and Charlie Tickner the bronze.

Saturday February 23
Anett Poetzsch fights off the challenge of Linda Fratianne and wins the gold medal after the women's long program. Fratianne's vivid performance gives her the silver and Dagmar Lurz takes the bronze, despite a tepid free-skating performance.

MEDAL WINNERS

	Gold	Silver	Bronze
MEN	Robin Cousins (GBR)	Jan Hoffmann (GDR)	Charles Tickner (USA)
WOMEN	Anett Poetzsch (GDR)	Linda Fratianne (USA)	Dagmar Lurz (GER)
PAIRS	Irina Rodnina Aleksandr Zaitsev (URS)	Marina Cherkosova Sergei Shakrai (URS)	Manuela Mager Uwe Bewersdorff (GDR)
ICE DANCING	Natalia Linichuk Gennadi Karponosov (URS)	Krisztina Regoczy Andras Sallay (HUN)	Irina Moiseeva Andrey Minenkov (URS)

With the anxieties of their competitions behind them, Aleksandr and Irina Zaitsev relax with Linda Fratianne.

Ice Hockey

A crowd of 6,000 parents and children had settled in for the Sunday afternoon performance of *Snow White and the Seven Dwarfs* at New York's Radio City Music Hall. Shortly before 2 P.M. curtain time, the stage announcer called for their attention, welcomed them to the show, and passed along the news: the United States Olympic ice hockey team had just defeated Finland, 4-2, to take the gold medal. The crowd rose to its feet cheering, and the orchestra began playing *The Star Spangled Banner*. Six thousand voices joined in.

The success of "The Boys of Winter," as they had become known, was more spellbinding than any fairy tale. For the spectators at Lake Placid it was a time to forget the long, bitter cold hours waiting for buses. For the whole nation it was a welcome relief from the likes of OPEC, Ayatollah Khomeini, and double-digit inflation. With the Summer Games in Moscow under threat of boycott it was a morale booster for the Olympic movement in general. For the players and coaches themselves, it was an outcome they could hardly believe and an experience they would never forget.

"This is just a team of destiny," said defenseman Bill Baker after it was all over. "You just can't explain what happened during this tournament. It just seemed things were supposed to happen this way." Right wing Dave Silk felt the same way: "Sometimes you've got to think fate played a role in all this." In the locker room just before the game against the Soviet Union, Coach Herb Brooks delivered a short pep talk that instilled a sense of destiny. Said Brooks, "You're born to be a player, you're meant to be here. This moment is yours. You're meant to be here at this time. . . ."

If the coach's words had any effect at all, it may have been because they were so out of character. Brooks, an old-fashioned disciplinarian, had been in hockey long enough to realize that miracles are born of hard work. "If you want to play this game effectively," he had often said, "you'd better report with a hard hat and a lunch pail. If not, you better go watch some old guys ice fishing." This was vintage Brooks. His was a simple philosophy expressed in easily remembered aphorisms—easily remembered because he repeated them constantly. In a 16-page booklet entitled *Brooksisms*, several team members recorded for posterity the wit and wisdom of their mentor:

- *Fool me once, shame on you. Fool me twice, shame on me.*
- *Let's be idealistic, but let's also be practical.*
- *You can't be common because the common man goes nowhere. You have to be uncommon.*
- *Gentlemen, you don't have enough talent to win on talent alone.*

If Brooks didn't think his team had the talent to win without

American and Russian teams line up in traditional fashion to exchange congratulations after the stunning U.S. victory over the Soviet Union.

TEAMS OF DESTINY: 1960, 1980

The first and only other time the United States had won an Olympic gold medal in ice hockey was 20 years before, at the VIII Winter Games in Squaw Valley, CA. At Lake Placid in 1980, there were ties with the 1960 team that added a storybook quality to the American triumph.

"When you look at the '60 team and the '80 team, there are so many similarities," said right wing Dave Silk. The strongest link was 20-year-old center David Christian, from Warroad, MN, whose father, Bill, and uncle, Roger, starred on the '60 squad. "My father's gold medal is on an end table in the living room and I've looked at scrapbooks," said the younger Christian.

The other ties were perhaps more tenuous but no less forgotten. Coach Herb Brooks, who did play on the 1964 and 1968 U.S. Olympic teams, was the last player cut from the 1960 gold medal squad. ("They must have cut the right guy," muses Brooks.) Mike Eruzione, the 25-year-old captain of the 1980 team, hails from the Boston suburb of Winthrop, MA, which is less than 10 miles from the Brookline home of 1960 Captain John Kirrane.

If there were reminders of the 1960 team even before the Lake Placid competition got underway, the parallels grew stronger as the tournament progressed. Just as goalie Jack McCartan had become a household name for leading his team to victory after upset victory at Squaw Valley, Jim Craig became America's hero at Lake Placid.

The 1960 team, which included a fireman, a soldier, two carpenters, and two insurance agents, was given little chance for a medal. But the Americans won their first four games, including a 4-0 shutout over a highly favored Czech team. Canada, which had scored 40 goals and given up only three, was the next opponent. The upstart U.S. squad pulled off another upset, 2-1. Just as it would be 20 years hence, the next to the last game was against the Soviet Union, the class of the tournament. In the second period, with the United States trailing, 2-1, Bill Christian took a pass from his brother and tied the score. Then in the third period, Bill Christian scored again for the 3-2 victory.

If on the final day of competition the Americans could again defeat Czechoslovakia, they would take the gold medal. After two periods they trailed 4-3. In a memorable gesture of good will, the captain of the Soviet team, Nikolai Sologubov, came into the U.S. locker room to pass along some advice. Without speaking English he managed to suggest that the Americans inhale oxygen to help their wind at the 6,000-foot elevation. Most of them did. They returned to the ice, racked up six goals, and won easily, 9-4.

Bill Cleary, who scored the last goal and went on to coach at Harvard University, discussed the chances of the 1980 team against the Soviet Union. "When you are home and get that crowd behind you," he said, "it can do great things." He remembered well.

The 1960 team, exultant after winning America's first gold medal in ice hockey.

fate on their side and a blue collar approach to training, he was only being realistic. There was no reason to expect the Americans to finish any better than fifth or sixth. The class of the tournament was the Soviet team, which featured the world's finest passing attack, depth at virtually every position, and a seemingly limitless reserve of determination. The Soviets had won the last four Olympic gold medals and had rolled over the opposition like a red tidal wave in 16 world amateur championships. As a warmup for the 1980 Winter Games, the Russians polished off some of the best teams—including an all-star squad—of the National Hockey League (NHL). Among the players arriving in Lake Placid were such standouts as Vladislav Tretiak, considered by many the best goalie in the world; veteran captain Boris Mikhailov; forward Helmut Balderis, called *Elikritchka*—Electric Train—for his swift, powerful skating; hard-nosed defenseman Valeri Vasiliev; and Viacheslav Fetisov, billed as "the Bobby Orr of Russia."

The team given the best chance of overtaking the Russians was Czechoslovakia's. The Czechs were strong and smart and not far behind the Soviet level of play. They beat them for the world championship at Prague in 1978 and were narrowly defeated, 3-2, in the deciding game of the prestigious Izvestia tournament at Moscow in December 1979. The fine-skating Swedish team, which had stayed away from the 1976 Games to protest the loss of many of its star players to North American professional clubs, looked like a strong contender. Finland's was a solid, hard-checking team, and Canada, fielding its first squad since 1968, was fast improving.

The twelve, 20-man teams in the tournament were divided into two divisions—Red and Blue. Every team played its divisional rivals one time, and the top two teams from each division played the top two teams from the other division in the medal round. The Blue Division comprised the United States, Czechoslovakia, Sweden, West Germany, Norway, and Rumania. The Red Division was made up of the Soviet Union, Finland, Canada, The Netherlands, Poland, and Japan.

Although the Soviet Union was in the other division, the United States would have a formidable task just to make the final four. Czechoslovakia and Sweden posed major obstacles, and West Germany was a perennial problem for U.S. amateur teams. The average age of the U.S. team was only 21, while some of the European players had skated together in world-class competition for more than a decade. The only American player with Olympic experience was forward Buzz Schneider, at 25 the oldest member of the team. About the only things the Americans had going for them were the home ice advantage—although that could backfire by creating undue pressure—and the thorough preparation begun six months before.

From the beginning, Coach Brooks molded a strategy that would take advantage of the 100-foot wide rink used in international hockey. (Professional rinks are only 85 feet wide.) The open space would lend itself to a more deliberate passing style of play. Weaving, soccer-style patterns of offense and long, accurate passes were the keys. It was a system that the Soviets, Czechs, and Swedes had employed successfully for years. Indeed it was the style of play that the Soviets had used to embar-

Jack O'Callahan, just informed that he cannot play because of ligament damage to his left knee, sits disconsolately with reporters. Later, he was put back on the roster and had an assist against Rumania.

Jim Craig, formerly a catcher in baseball, got nervous only when he couldn't see the puck. "I like to lock in on it and follow it," he remarked. "You never know what might happen," said Craig regarding his team's chances. "But you always dream."

rass the NHL. In North America, the traditional style was more static, physical, and confining. A player would shoot the puck into the offensive zone, his teammates would chase after it in set lanes (left wing, center, and right wing), and the object was to muscle the puck away from the defensemen. Passing more deliberately and more often, the European amateurs—and now the American Olympic squad—would be moving all over the ice, exchanging positions, filling in, finding open spaces, and working for the best shot. Brooks:

- *Don't dump the puck in. That went out with short pants.*
- *Throw the puck back and weave, weave, weave. But don't just weave for the sake of weaving.*

Although some of the ideas were borrowed from the Russians, strategist Brooks wanted to preserve the best (most physical) aspects of the North American style. He could not beat the Soviets—or the Czech, Swedes, and others—at their own game. They skated too well, passed too accurately. The Americans would also have to use muscle. They needed close, tough body checking, especially in their defensive zone. Brooks:

- *Boys, in front of the net it's bloody nose alley.*

The U.S. team was selected and trained with Brooks' strategy in mind. Players were chosen on the basis of their skating ability, stick handling skills, and versatility. Selflessness, dedication to a team effort, and the desire to work hard, however, were just as important. The 20 men finally chosen to play at Lake Placid included a large contingent (9) from the University of Minnesota, where Herb Brooks had coached three NCAA championship teams; two others had played at the University of Minnesota at Duluth. Four players, including goalie Jim Craig and captain Mike Eruzione, had performed at Boston University; two players, including Mark Johnson, came via the University of Wisconsin; two had played at Bowling Green University; and one at the University of North Dakota.

The team got down to work immediately—hard hats, lunch pails, and all. "It's been the most demanding training I have ever seen or heard of," Jim Craig would say. "It's hard work, no time off, and no chance to relax." The Russian team that would be going to Lake Placid had already beaten the NHL allstars, 6-0. The U.S. team had six months to learn a whole new style of hockey and develop a strong team bond.

To prepare for the Olympics, the U.S. squad played a full schedule against college and professional teams, foreign Olympic squads, and Soviet club teams. "We had to cram two or three years of experience playing this way into five months of exhibition games," the coach explained.

The outcome was promising. The team won more than two thirds of its exhibition matches, far more than expected. Even more importantly, the team had learned to play good, crisp-passing, patterned, rugged hockey—together. Said defenseman Ken Morrow, "Finally, we feel we've got it down fairly well and we can play at the European level."

If the Americans had got it down at all, it was not apparent in their final exhibition match three days before the Olympics. They took a 10-3 drubbing at the hands of the awesome Soviets at Madison Square Garden. Overconfidence would not be a problem. They entered the tournament seeded seventh.

Divisional Round Robin

The 34-game tournament, expected to be the most competitive in Olympic history, got off to an early start. To allow each team a day's rest between matches, the tournament was begun on Tuesday, February 12, one day before the opening ceremonies of the Games. In round robin divisional competition, three matches were held in the newly-constructed, 8,500-seat Olympic Fieldhouse, while three other matches were being played in the adjoining Olympic Arena, first used for the 1932 Winter Games. Each of the 12 squads would have a day off and then play another team in its division.

The first matchup for the United States was Sweden, and the outcome was crucial. The Swedes were regarded as the second strongest team in the Blue Division and the team to beat for a berth in the medal round. "The biggest game of the tournament," said goalie Jim Craig, "is us against Sweden." Swedish Coach Tommy Sandlin had heard that the Americans were young and spirited but felt that his team had the advantage in ability. "We are the better skaters, so we must try to get into a game with a lot of skating," said Sandlin.

If the Americans were to outskate the Swedes, they would have to do so with only four full-time defensemen. Jack O'Callahan, a backline stalwart, had suffered stretched knee ligaments in the final tuneup against the Soviet Union and would be lost for at least the first two games of the Olympics. Brooks would use Ken Morrow, Mike Ramsey, Bill Baker, and Dave Christian on defense, giving Bob Suter spot duty. "It's a roll of the dice, a calculated risk," he said.

Mark Pavelich (USA) and Sweden's Thomas Eriksson fight for the puck, pursued intently by Sweden's Lars Mohlin (left) and Per Lundqvist, and American Mike Ramsey.

For the first 59 minutes, 33 seconds of the 60-minute match, the risk looked like a bad one. The Swedes had taken a 1-0 lead on a goal by Sture Andersson midway through the first period. Dave Silk tied it up for the Americans with 28 seconds left in the second period, and the small but emotional crowd had something to cheer about for the first time in the XIII Olympic Winter Games. By the third period, the U.S. defensemen were beginning to tire, and at 4:45 Brooks' tactic backfired. Bob Suter, doing spot duty, failed to tie up a Swedish player in front of the net. A pass to Thomas Eriksson left him in perfect scoring position, and he nudged the puck between Craig's legs for the goal.

The Americans rifled shot after shot at Swedish goalie Pelle Lindbergh, but the 20-year-old NHL draftee held them off. Finally, in a desperate last-minute move, Coach Brooks took Craig off the ice and replaced him with an extra skater. This time his strategy paid off. With just 27 seconds remaining in the game, Bill Baker launched a 55-foot blast that whistled past Lindbergh for the tying goal. The tally sent the crowd into a frenzy, and the U.S. bench emptied onto the ice to tackle the last-minute hero.

Brooks breathed a sigh of relief. "Hey, we're happy. The manner in which we got the point—our goalie off the ice, the final minute of play—we were lucky."

The first day's competition saw two more surprises. In a Blue Division contest, 12th-seeded Rumania scored a 6-4 victory over the 6th-seeded West Germany. In the Red Division, Poland knocked off highly favored Finland, 5-4. None of the other scores was nearly so close or unexpected. The Soviet juggernaut rolled over a small, inexperienced Japanese team, 16-0; Czechoslovakia was just as relentless against Norway, beating them 11-0; and Canada shellacked The Netherlands, 10-1. Running up the score was not intended to embarrass the losers; in the case of an eventual tie in the standings, "goal differential" (the difference between goals scored by and goals scored against) could be the deciding factor.

Brooks:
- *You go up to the tiger, spit him in the eye and* then *you shoot him.*

The tiger, in this case, was Czechoslovakia, the next team Brooks' charges would face. The Americans were at an emotional peak coming off their last-minute heroics against Sweden, but it was, after all, only a tie, and Czechoslovakia had been nothing less than awesome in its first appearance. The second-seeded Czechs averaged 27–28 years of age, and many of them had played in the previous Olympics. They were expected to be smarter and stronger than the Swedes, though perhaps not so quick.

Brooks told his players not to stand around in awe. They should not be afraid to make the last fake, the difficult pass, the hard body check. "Go out and use your youth," he told them. "Use your enthusiasm." Their enthusiasm could not have been at a higher pitch. Said Mike Ramsey after the game, "We wanted to win so bad. The feeling in the locker room was unbelievable."

Setting a furious pace in the first period, the Americans ex-

Norwegian player Thor Martinsen topples over the boards during a body check with Czech defenseman Vitezslav Duris. The game between the two Blue Division teams, won by the Czechs, was held on the first day of the hockey competition.

ploited a surprisingly slow Czech defense and delighted the crowd of 7,125. Jim Craig was putting on another fine performance in goal, but the score stood at 2-2 at the end of the period.

Brooks' strategy for the game was to forecheck the Czechs from the top of the face-off circle and clog up the middle of the ice. Close stick checking would frustrate the counterpunching Czech offense. It worked. After Craig stopped a clean breakaway 12 seconds into the second period, it was all the United States. They buzzed around the offensive zone, they bashed into the corners and came away with the puck, and they passed impeccably. The keys, however, were their deft stick checks and thudding body checks. One Czech player was launched headfirst over the boards and into the team bench.

The U.S. scoring barrage picked up at 4:33 of the second period with a remarkable goal by Buzz Schneider off a two-on-one break with Mark Pavelich. That put the Americans in the lead—for good. A goal by Mark Johnson later in the period put them ahead, 4-2, going into the last 20 minutes. Some teams might have pulled back and played defensive hockey, but the roars of U!S!A! U!S!A! and the realization of just how good they could be kept the Americans skating at a feverish pace. Led by the hardworking "Iron Rangers" line of Buzz Schneider, Mark Pavelich, and John Harrington (who came from the Iron Range area in northern Minnesota)—which had three goals and four assists—the upstarts embarrassed the veterans, 7-3. The U.S. hockey team was the toast of the Olympics. People began calling them "The Boys of Winter."

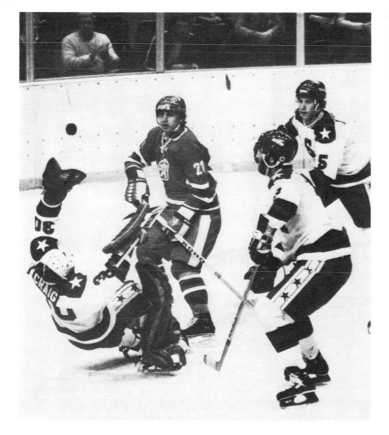

Goalie Jim Craig, attacked by Czech forward Vincent Lukac, grabs for the puck. Dave Silk and Mike Ramsey (5) help out on defense.

Hurling his gloves aside, Rumania's Traian Cazacu goes after Sweden's Bo Berglund in a mid-game melée.

Meanwhile, in other Blue Division play, Sweden rebounded from its disappointment and shut out Rumania, 8-0, while West Germany outclassed Norway, 10-4. In the Red Division, Finland swept Japan, 6-3; Canada remained unbeaten by taking Poland, 5-1; and the relentless Soviets bombed The Netherlands, 17-4. Although it was the Americans who were already being toasted, it was the highly-favored Soviets who had scored 33 goals in only two games. With the United States amassing 3 out of a possible 4 points in its two most difficult divisional games, a medal round confrontation with the USSR grew larger on the horizon.

Nobody was counting his chickens. Sweden had actually overtaken the United States—on the basis of goal differential—in the Blue Division standings, and the Americans still had to show well in their final three division games against Norway, Rumania, and West Germany. Coach Brooks was not one to let his players get cocky. "The next couple of games will be more of a test than the Swedes and Czechs," he said. "A good hockey team has to win some games it's not supposed to win. Now it will be more of a test of our character." While Lake Placid was still celebrating the upset over Czechoslovakia, the players were looking ahead to their next contest with Norway. Said Mike Ramsey, "If we lose to Norway, we'll remember it the rest of our lives."

The Americans would indeed remember the tournament for the rest of their lives, but not for having lost to the Norwegians. After a lackluster start, they battled back to a 5-1 victory. Norway, which had given up 21 goals in its first two games against Sweden and Czechoslovakia, took the ice determined to make a good showing. The United States, meanwhile, was showing signs of an emotional letdown after the Czechoslovakia game. There was an obvious lack of precision and aggressiveness, none of the rhythm or close team play that had brought them so far. "There always seemed to be one of our guys trying to take

on their whole team," said Brooks. "We were expressing ourselves through only one or two people." At the end of the first
period Norway led, 1-0.

Brooks:

> • *Don't let the other team score on you in the first or last
> five minutes of a period, and play them all-out in the mid-
> dle 10.*

If his players had forgotten this bit of hockey wisdom, they
surely were reminded of it in the locker room between periods.
Not only did they keep the Norwegians from scoring, but they
scored three of their five goals in the first and last five minutes
of the second and third periods. Captain Mike Eruzione started
the three-goal, second-period outburst only 41 seconds into the
session. At 4:51 of the period, center Mark Johnson put the
Americans ahead for good.

Johnson, who had suffered a contusion of his right shoulder
from the stick of an overly aggressive Czech defender, was not
even expected to play against Sweden. But even on a team in
which there are supposed to be no individual stars, the 22-year-
old Johnson was the sparkplug. "There's no question he makes
our club go," said Brooks. "You might see Mark get 30 or 40%
of the ice time. We have to get him the puck." The 5'9",
160-pound center from Madison, WI—where as a kid he had
played peewee hockey with Eric Heiden—played brilliantly
throughout the tournament.

*Norwegian defenseman Rune
Molberg, left, and U.S. player Eric
Strobel tangle in front of the
boards during the first period of
the U.S.-Norway game.*

The other goal scorers for the United States were Dave Silk,
Mark Wells, and defenseman Ken Morrow, also playing with a
shoulder injury. Jim Craig again performed remarkably in goal,
stopping 21 shots. After the game, Coach Brooks said the key
to the turnaround was hard work. "We had to become grinders,
so to speak." Insisting that there was "no screaming, no yelling" after first period, he said "We just had to get back our
poise and our patience with the puck."

In another important Blue Division contest, Sweden out-
skated West Germany, 5-2. Czechoslovakia had no problem
with Rumania, winning 7-2. In the Red Division, the Soviet
Union was held to its lowest offensive total by Poland but still
breezed to a lopsided 8-1 victory. Henryk Wojtynek, the Polish
goalie, faced an onslaught of 60 shots, while Vladislav Tretiak,
the Soviet mainstay, faced just 19. In the day's most exciting
match, Finland scored with only 3:05 left, to defeat Canada,
4-3. Hapless Japan and Finland battled to a 3-3 tie.

In the midst of the Olympic playoff competition, it may have
seemed unusual for Herb Brooks—of all people—to give his
players a day off. The coach admitted that they had been less
than fired up for the Norway game and felt that some time off
the ice would do them good. "Sometimes getting away a little
bit helps, and you come back a little fired up," he said.

The Americans came back refreshed for their next game
against Rumania and won impressively, 7-2. Playing patient but
aggressive hockey, they had the capacity crowd of 8,500 (a
ticket to see "The Boys of Winter" was now the hottest item in
town) rising to its feet with every sharp pass and winging shot.

For the first time in four games, the Americans scored first.
At 12:03 of the opening period Buzz Schneider scored off a
give-and-go from fellow "Iron Ranger" Mark Pavelich. Schnei-

Swedish players put pressure on Czech goalie Jiri Kralik on the last day of the round robin. Their 4–2 victory guaranteed the Swedes a place in the medal round.

der had his second two-goal game of the Olympics (the first was against Czechoslovakia), as he scored again in the second period. The "Iron Range" threesome, which began the tournament as only the third line on the squad, led the way as it had against the Czechs. Schneider, Pavelich, and Harrington—also called the "Coneheads"—were once the butt of clubhouse humor because of their lowly status but now were being sent out on the ice at times when the team was struggling.

The victory kept the United States in a first-place tie with Sweden at 3-0-1. But Sweden, which beat Norway 7-1, actually stayed ahead on the basis of goal differential. Czechoslovakia, meanwhile, blasted West Germany, 11-3. With one game remaining in Blue Division competition, the United States needed only a tie against West Germany to guarantee a berth in the medal round. The other qualifier would be the winner of the Sweden-Czechoslovakia contest; in the case of a tie, Sweden would advance.

In the Red Division, the Soviet Union trailed upset-minded Finland, 2-1, with only five minutes remaining in the game. Facing the prospect of their first Olympic defeat since 1968, the Russians came up with three goals—by Vladimir Krutov, Aleksandr Maltsev, and Boris Mikhailov—in a 1:19 span. The victory clinched a spot in the medal round. Japan was blanked again, this time by Canada, 6-0, and The Netherlands bested Poland, 5-3. The second Red Division representative in the medal round would be determined on the basis of Canada's success against the Soviet Union and Finland's fortunes against The Netherlands.

By the time the United States took the ice against West Germany, it didn't even need a tie to reach the final four. Earlier in the day, Sweden had upset Czechoslovakia, 4-2, and the Czechs were eliminated. Sweden, which finished the round robin segment of the tournament with four victories and the 2-2 tie with the United States, capitalized on the first three penalties called against Czechoslovakia. Netminder Pelle Lindbergh contributed another excellent performance, and the Swedes led 3-0 after two periods. Czechoslovakia scored twice in the third session, but Sweden added one more and knocked off the tournament's second seed.

If the United States could beat West Germany by at least seven goals it would take first place in the Blue Division and play Canada or Finland in the first round of medal play and the Soviet Union not until the second. Otherwise, Sweden would hold onto first place, and the United States would have to meet the Soviets first.

"We were talking in the locker room before the game about all those possibilities," said Jack O'Callahan, "and all we decided was that they were confusing." They knew they had to win by as many goals as possible, and they set out to rack up the score. It was the wrong attitude, and they paid a price. The West Germans looked sharp in their red-and-black uniforms and put the Americans at a first period deficit for the fourth time in five games. Jim Craig—struck on the right side of the neck by a slap shot in the pre-game warmup—gave up a 70-foot goal to Horst-Peter Kretschmer and a 58-footer to Udo Kiessling.

The Americans reassessed their strategy. "After a while we said, 'Hey. It's 2-0. We're losing. Let's forget about the goal difference and go at the West Germans. Let's win the game

West German goalie Sigmund Suttner lunges in vain as Rob McClanahan scores the first of his two goals in the U.S. confrontation with West Germany. The goal turned the tide against the West Germans, who led, 2–0, in the first period.

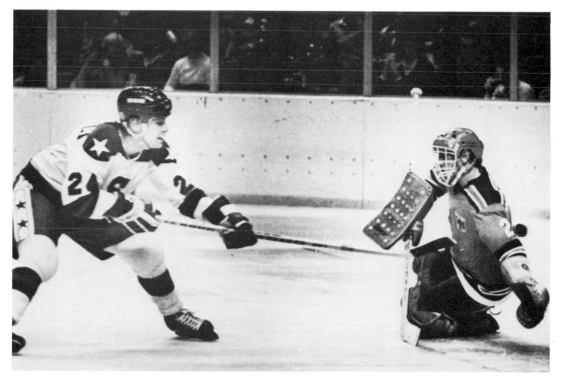

first,' " said Captain Mike Eruzione. "Everyone took this game a little bit lightly and a little bit easy and thought we were going to blow the West Germans out," said Mark Johnson. "But West Germany didn't come here to lay down and die."

The Germans didn't exactly lie down and die for the next two periods, but the come-from-behind Americans took them a little more seriously. Entering the game having outscored their opponents 17-4 in the second and third periods, the U.S. skaters continued the pattern against West Germany. Center Rob McClanahan pulled them within one at 7:40 of the second period off a perfect pass from Dave Christian, who ended up with three assists in the game. Neal Broten tied it up with 1:29 left in the session, bringing the now-familiar roar of U!S!A! U!S!A! from the crowd. As Craig was deflecting every shot by the Germans, McClanahan scored his second goal at 1:17 of the third period, and forward Phil Verchota tipped in a shot by Christian at 4:17. Verchota's tally was the 17th of the 24 U.S. goals in the tournament to be scored in the first or last five minutes of a period. "The Boys of Winter" had followed their coach's strategy to the letter, carried out every assignment far beyond anyone's expectation, and met every challenge that had come down the road to Lake Placid. Their 4-2 victory over West Germany set up a confrontation with the mighty Soviet Union only two days later. A loss to the Russian juggernaut, however, could take nothing away from what Brooks' boys already had achieved.

The Soviets remained undefeated and untied by outlasting Canada, 6-4, in their final Red Division contest, but for the second game in a row they had to come from behind. The Canadians had taken a 3-1 lead on goals by Jim Nill, Randy Gregg, and Brad Pirie before the Soviets got back on track. Ca-

(Continued page 128)

Canadian goalie Paul Pageau is under heavy Soviet pressure in the third period of the Canada-USSR game. Despite the rousing support of the pro-Canadian audience, the Soviets overcame their last Red Division opponents, 6–4. Players are (l-r) Randy Gregg and Stelio Zupancich, from Canada, Russia's Juri Lebedev, and Canada's Daniel D'Alvise.

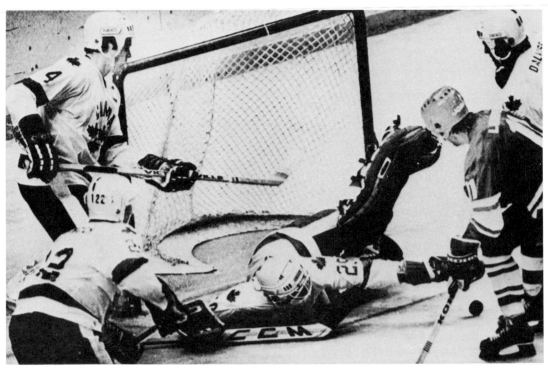

Coach Brooks and "The Boys of Winter"

Throughout his career as an amateur ice hockey player and coach, 42-year-old Herb Brooks has been a winner. The St. Paul, MN, native was one of the best players ever to skate for the University of Minnesota. He was hailed by his own coach, John Mariucci, as "the fastest college hockey player in that era." After being the last player cut from the 1960 Olympic team, Brooks played on virtually every U.S. National and Olympic squad from 1961 to 1970. He was the team captain in 1965, 1967, 1968, and 1970.

Brooks worked as an insurance salesman in St. Paul through the 1960's and became an assistant coach at his alma mater in 1969. When coach Glen Sonmor left the Gophers before the 1972–73 season, Brooks was named as his successor. In his seven years as head coach at the University of Minnesota, Brooks' teams compiled a record of 175–100–20 (an outstanding .636 winning percentage) and won three NCAA championships (1973–74, 1975–76, 1978–79).

On a leave of absence from Minnesota to coach the 1980 U.S. Olympic team, Brooks faced the greatest challenge of his career. Having the final say in player selections, Brooks molded a cohesive team in six months of practice and exhibition games. The final 20-member squad had an average age of 22, making it the youngest team at Lake Placid.

Brooks' staff for the six months of training and at the Games included assistant coach Craig Patrick; goalkeeper coach Warren Strelow; general manager Ken Johannson, who was responsible for the business aspects of the team's preparations; and trainer Gary Smith. Of inestimable value was the advice of Lou Vairo, who sat in the press box high above the ice and reported via walkie-talkie on opposing teams' weaknesses.

Following the Lake Placid Games, Brooks resigned his Minnesota post. After failing to receive a desired bid from a National Hockey League team, he agreed to coach the A.C. Davos team in Switzerland.

BILL BAKER
Defenseman

Born Nov. 29, 1956
6'1", 195 lbs
Grand Rapids, MN

Captained Herb Brooks' 1979 NCAA championship team at University of Minnesota. Holds Minnesota record for most points in a season by a defenseman. Drafted in 1976 by the NHL's Montreal Canadiens but opted for college. Scored tying goal in the U.S.-Sweden game.

NEAL BROTEN
Center

Born Nov. 29, 1959
5'9", 155 lbs
Roseau, MN

Had a record 50 assists at University of Minnesota in 1979. Second-round pick by Minnesota North Stars in 1979. Considered by Brooks as the "best freshman ever to have played at the University of Minnesota." Scored one goal and had one assist in the 1980 Olympics.

DAVE CHRISTIAN
Center

Born May 12, 1959
5'11", 170 lbs
Warroad, MN

Son of Bill Christian and nephew of Roger Christian, both of whom played on 1960 gold medal-winning team. The University of North Dakota star was drafted in the second round by the Winnipeg Jets. Won high-school letters in four sports. Led the U.S. team in assists.

STEVE CHRISTOFF
Center

Born Jan. 23, 1958
6'1", 180 lbs
Richfield, MN

Played three seasons at University of Minnesota, leading the team in scoring twice. Only the third Minnesota player in history to score more than 30 goals in a season. Second-round pick of Minnesota North Stars in 1978. Scored the U.S. team's first goal against Finland.

JIM CRAIG
Goalie

Born May 3, 1957
6'1", 190 lbs
North Easton, MA

Led Boston University to 1978 NCAA championship. Drafted by the Atlanta Flames, and played in first professional game shortly after the Olympics. Perhaps the key to U.S. gold-medal victory. Played without relief in every game, with a goals-against average of 2.14.

MIKE ERUZIONE
Left wing

Born Oct. 25, 1954
5'10", 185 lbs
Winthrop, MA

Second on all-time Boston University scoring list. Played two seasons with Toledo of the International Hockey League (IHL). Olympic team captain. Scored three Olympic goals, including one against Czechoslovakia and the game-winner against the Soviet Union.

JOHN HARRINGTON
Right wing

Born May 24, 1957
5'10", 180 lbs
Virginia, MN

At University of Minnesota-Duluth scored 65 goals in four seasons. Played in five games for Oklahoma City of the Central Hockey League in 1979. The North Stars gained rights to his services. Had two assists against Czechoslovakia and one against Soviet Union.

STEVE JANASZAK
Goalie

Born Jan. 7, 1957
5'8", 160 lbs
White Bear Lake, MN

Most Valuable Player of 1979 NCAA tournament for Brooks' University of Minnesota championship team. Finished the 1978–79 season with a 3.23 goals-against average and recorded a 4.15 goals-against mark for his four-year career. Was only American who did not play.

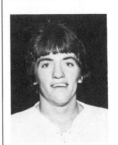

MARK JOHNSON
Center

Born Sept. 22, 1957
5'9", 160 lbs
Madison, WI

Physical education major at the University of Wisconsin, where his father was coach. Collegiate Player of the Year in 1978–79. The two-time All-American joined the NHL's Pittsburgh Penguins after the Olympics. Led U.S. team in scoring with 11 points. Played brilliantly.

ROB McCLANAHAN
Left wing

Born Jan. 9, 1958
5'10", 180 lbs
St. Paul, MN

Played for Brooks at University of Minnesota. Named the school's most determined player for two seasons. Drafted by Buffalo in 1978. Second in U.S. scoring, with five goals and eight points. Scored the winning goal against Finland.

KEN MORROW
Defenseman

Born Oct. 17, 1956
6'4", 210 lbs
Davison, MI

First hockey All-American at Bowling Green University. Played for the Detroit Junior Red Wings. Finished 1979–80 season with New York Islanders. Biggest player on U.S. team, and most recognizable because of his beard. Reliable defenseman who also scored two goals.

JACK O'CALLAHAN
Defenseman

Born July 24, 1957
6'1", 186 lbs
Charlestown, MA

Member of Boston University 1978 NCAA championship team. Voted the tournament's most valuable player. First team All-American in 1979. Majored in American history. Suffered a knee injury in pre-Olympic game against USSR and missed first game.

MARK PAVELICH
Center/Right wing

Born Feb. 28, 1958
5'7", 160 lbs
Eveleth, MN

Three-year regular at University of Minnesota-Duluth. Was third in scoring in the Western College Hockey Association in 1978–79. Led Minnesota-Duluth to its best season in its hockey history, establishing three scoring records. Had two assists against the USSR.

MIKE RAMSEY
Defenseman

Born Dec. 3, 1960
6'3", 190 lbs
Minneapolis, MN

Earned high school letters in hockey, tennis, and football. Played hockey one season at Minnesota. Named to the NCAA all-tournament team. First American to be selected in first round of NHL draft; chosen by Buffalo Sabres. Youngest member of U.S. Olympic team.

BUZZ SCHNEIDER
Left wing

Born Sept. 14, 1954
5'11", 184 lbs
Babbitt, MN

Attended University of Minnesota, and played two seasons with Milwaukee of IHL. Played on four U.S. national teams. Oldest member of U.S. squad and only veteran of 1976 Olympic team. Not known as a goal-scorer but tallied five times, twice against Czechoslovakia.

DAVE SILK
Right wing

Born Jan. 1, 1958
5'11", 190 lbs
Scituate, MA

Scored 70 goals with 73 assists during three seasons at Boston University. Selected to the NCAA all-tournament team in 1977 and 1978. Drafted in fourth round by New York Rangers. Scored two goals in the Olympics. His cousin, Mike Millbury, plays for the Bruins.

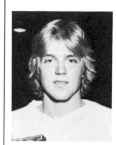

ERIC STROBEL
Right wing

Born June 5, 1958
5'10", 175 lbs
Rochester, MN

Played three seasons at Minnesota for Brooks. Scored 30 tallies for Minnesota in 1978–79. A year of college eligibility remains. Drafted in 8th round by Buffalo in 1978. Scored a goal against Rumania, and had one assist each against Norway and West Germany.

BOB SUTER
Defenseman

Born May 16, 1957
5'9", 178 lbs
Madison, WI

Member of 1977 NCAA championship team at University of Wisconsin. Known as the team's "policeman" for his rugged play. Logged school record for penalty minutes. Fifth-round draftee of Los Angeles Kings in 1976. Played strong defense in the Olympics.

PHIL VERCHOTA
Left wing

Born Dec. 28, 1956
6'2", 195 lbs
Duluth, MN

Four-year player at University of Minnesota. Played on 1976 and 1979 NCAA championship teams. Twice named the team's top student-athlete. Chosen by the North Stars. Scored the tying goal against Finland, and also tallied against Czechoslovakia and West Germany.

MARK WELLS
Center

Born Sept. 18, 1957
5'9", 175 lbs
St. Clair Shores, MI

Scored 77 goals and added 155 assists during four years at Bowling Green University. With Olympic teammate Ken Morrow, led Bowling Green to Central Collegiate Hockey Association titles in 1976, 1978, and 1979. Picked by Montreal. Saw limited ice time in Lake Placid.

nadian athletes had been cheered loudly by the American spectators since the opening ceremonies. Only a few days earlier, the Canadian government had helped rescue several U.S. diplomats from possible capture by Iranian militants in Tehran. Now, against the Soviet Union, whose government had launched troops into Afghanistan and threatened U.S. oil supplies, the Canadian team was spurred by emotional chants of "Go, Canada, go." It wasn't enough. The Soviets scored once in the second period and added four third-period goals—two each by Boris Mikhailov and Aleksandr Golikov—to secure the win. After the final buzzer, the Canadian players waved their sticks to the crowd as a sign of appreciation and received a huge ovation. They still had a chance for the second Red Division spot in the medal round, but The Netherlands would have to upset a strong Finnish squad that night. Finland won easily, 10-3, and athough they wound up with the same 3-2 record as Canada, they advanced on the basis of having beaten Canada in their earlier meeting.

Making their final appearances of the tournament, Norway and Rumania fought to a 3-3 tie, and Poland defeated winless Japan, 5-1.

Medal Round

To determine the Olympic ice hockey medalists for 1980, the four remaining teams—Sweden and the United States from the Blue Division, and the Soviet Union and Finland from the Red Division—would each play two more games, one against each of the teams in the other division. The teams were seeded

Soviet goalie Vladislav Tretiak talks over strategy with an assistant coach prior to the fateful U.S.-USSR game. Political tensions and the awesome reputation of the Soviet team heightened excitement over the impending match.

The American and Soviet flags are silent reminders of underlying nationalistic feelings as the players take to the ice for the pivotal U.S.-USSR hockey game. The underdog American team defeated the Soviets, 4–3.

on the basis of their success in the preliminary tournament against the other medal round representative from their division. Two points were given for a win, one point for a tie, and none for a loss. By virtue of their 2-2 tie, Sweden and United States therefore entered the medal round with one point apiece. Because the USSR had beaten Finland, 4-2, the Soviets were seeded first with two points, while the Finns were seeded fourth with no points.

If the United States could win both its games and the Swedes didn't, it would win the gold medal. If they split, or tied both games, the outcome would depend on Sweden's success against the same opponents. If any two teams ended up with the same point totals after the mini-tournament, the result of their own matchup and the goal differential statistic again would break the deadlock. The possibilities were numerous, the whole system enormously complicated. Even the players were scratching their heads.

"I don't understand it," said Jim Craig. "All I know is that when this thing's over, if I've got some kind of medal hanging around my neck, I'll be happy."

The Americans were not at all confused about the work cut out for them. At 5 P.M. on Friday, February 22, they would be taking on probably the best hockey team in the world. It would be a little more difficult not to be awed by the Soviets than it had been to vilify the Czechs. Two weeks before, the U.S. players gave reverent applause to the Soviet stars when they were introduced before their Madison Square Garden exhibition match. The 10-3 final score did little to raise the confidence of

Steve Christoff attacks the Soviet goal defended by formidable Russian goalie Vladislav Tretiak in the first period of the U.S.-USSR game. Tretiak was thought by many to be the best goalie in the world.

the young American squad. It would take their very best effort even to stay close in the Olympic medal round. "If we play our best and don't make any mistakes, we've got a chance," said assistant coach Craig Patrick. "If we make any mistakes, the Soviets will take us apart."

Herb Brooks thought it would take a miracle of Biblical proportions. "We'll play better than we did at Madison Square Garden, but whether it will be good enough, who knows? It will be David and Goliath, and I just hope we remember to bring our slingshots."

Political tensions between the United States and Soviet Union over the invasion of Afghanistan and the threatened boycott of the Summer Olympics in Moscow contributed to the drama of the Lake Placid confrontation. *Newsweek* magazine called it a "morality play on ice." Seats at center ice sold for $67.20, but scalpers reportedly were getting $150 or more. Standing room was priced at $24.40. It would have been easier to get a ticket for the David vs. Goliath bout.

Herb Brooks delivered his "born to be a player" speech and sent his team out to warm up. Minutes before the 5 o'clock start, the two squads stood facing each other along the blue lines closest to their respective benches. In Olympic tradition, Captain Mike Eruzione skated to center ice and exchanged gifts with his Soviet counterpart, Boris Mikhailov, the legendary Gordie Howe of Gorky Street.

Brooks:
• *Stan Laurel, Stan Laurel, look at Stan Laurel.*

For months Brooks had been telling his players that the Soviet captain looked like Stan Laurel. If a match with the Russians ever came to pass, he didn't want his players to think they were skating against gods or Supermen. "Every time we watched a film of the Russians," said John Harrington, "he'd keep saying, 'Stan Laurel, Stan Laurel, look at Stan Laurel.' "

Both teams came out with more intensity than they had in any of their previous games, and the level of play in the first period was far beyond the normal Olympic fare. Skating, play execution, and checking were sharp. Players flung themselves in front of slap shots. In the early minutes, Soviet forward Valeri Kharlamov—no Stan Laurel—was sandwiched by two American players, lifted in the air, and thrown to the ice.

The U.S. strategy was to maintain possession of the puck as long as possible and to forecheck the Soviet defensemen into mistakes. Easier said than done. At 9:12 of the first period forward Vladimir Krutov, the rising young star of Soviet hockey, deflected a shot by Aleksei Kasatonov past a helpless Jim Craig, making the score 1-0. But the Americans were not about to let things get out of hand, and at 14:03 Buzz Schneider launched a 55-foot slap which whistled over the left shoulder of Soviet goalie Vladislav Tretiak. Later in the period, while the crowd was yelling for a holding penalty against a Russian defenseman, his teammates moved the puck up ice and forward Sergei Makarov knocked it home.

It looked as if the period would end with the Soviets leading, 2-1, but Team Comeback was not quite ready to go into the locker room. With only a few seconds remaining, Ken Morrow streaked down left wing and let fly an 80-foot desperation shot. Tretiak, playing below top form, could not control the puck. It rebounded to an oncoming Mark Johnson, who swatted it in. The red light signaling a goal flashed on, but time apparently had run out. The Russians left the ice thinking the goal did not count, but Referee Karl-Gustav Kaisla of Finland consulted with the other officials and ruled that the puck had gone in with one second remaining. The score counted, and the Soviets were summoned from the locker room to play the last second of the period. Taking the ice was backup goalie Vladimir Myshkin. Tretiak, the best in the world, was gone for the day.

The Soviets came out steaming for the second period and quickly went ahead on a power play goal by Aleksandr Maltsev at 2:18. The Americans then failed on two breakaway opportunities—their only two shots-on-goal for the period—and it looked as if the Soviets would pull away. The Americans continued to skate hard, however, and Jim Craig was no less than spectacular in goal. Late in the period defenseman Ken Morrow nearly came to blows with Soviet forward Juri Lebedev, as Craig lay on the ice after being hit in the mask by a Russian stick. But Craig got up and kept the Americans within striking distance, behind by only one goal as the period came to an end.

John Harrington would later describe how the players felt in the locker room. "We just said, 'Hey. We're going into the third period and we're down one. The last time we played them we were down seven.' We said, 'We're right in the thick of this thing. They're tiring. They've got some older players, and we're going to take advantage of that.' "

They did. At 8:39 of the period, Mark Johnson was five feet to the right of Myshkin when a pass from Dave Silk bounced off the skate of defenseman Sergei Starikov and onto his stick.

Soviet coach Victor Tikhonov, flanked by players Aleksei Kasatonov (7) and Viacheslav Fetisov (2), watches tensely as the last seconds of the U.S.-USSR game tick away.

Johnson rammed the puck pask Myshkin for his second goal of the game and a 3-3 tie. The crowd went crazy.

With the flags still waving and the Olympic Fieldhouse echoing with the chants of U!S!A! U!S!A!, the Americans came back only 1:21 later and scored what would be the game-winning goal. Mike Eruzione, whose name is the Italian word for "eruption," took a Mark Pavelich pass and sent a 25-foot shot past defenseman Vasili Pervukhin and the left leg of Myshkin.

The rest was all Jim Craig, who kicked away shot after shot by the frustrated Russians. As the final seconds ticked away, television audiences saw Herb Brooks looking up at the scoreboard clock near the top of the arena—or else thanking God. The American players already on the ice hoisted their sticks in the air and raced to the goal to mob an ecstatic Jim Craig. Those on the bench leaped over the sideboards and joined the celebration, hugging and tackling each other in sheer joy.

For a change it was the Soviet hockey players who looked on in envy. Downcast, they leaned on their sticks at their blue line awaiting the ceremonial handshake that concludes every international contest. "The first Russian I shook hands with had a smile on his face," Mark Johnson said later. "I couldn't believe it. I still can't believe it. We beat the Russians."

Soviet Coach Vladimir Yurzinov was gracious. His comments after the game also suggested the wisdom of Brooks' forechecking strategy. "I think the victory of the American team was quite fair in tonight's game," he said. "We wanted to play a little more strict in defense, and our expectation was that our forwards would play a better game."

In a dispatch from Lake Placid, the Soviet news agency Tass attributed the defeat mainly to mistakes by the Russian defense and goalies, but also praised the U.S. effort. "Undoubtedly the U.S. hockey players exerted themselves selflessly and boldly," the agency said.

Undoubtedly. The American victory may well have been the most stunning upset in Olympic history, perhaps even in all of sports. In the clamorous U.S. locker room, the team received a phone call from President Jimmy Carter. "The President did call," reported Coach Brooks. "He said we had made the American people very proud. . . ."

"The Boys of Winter" crowd together in elation after a U.S. goal, oblivious of the dejected Soviet goalie standing nearby.

Goalie Jim Craig fends off a goal by a Finnish player in the Americans' final game of the medal round (left). Craig, a constant presence on the ice, played a large role in the U.S. victory.

There were still shouts of ''We beat the Russians!'' and ''Stuff the bear!'' coming from the streets of Lake Placid, when Sweden and Finland took the ice at 8:30 for the second matchup of the medal round. The favored Swedes outshot their opponents 30 to 25 but needed two goals in the last period to come away with a 3-3 tie. Finland was led by forward Mikko Leinonen (two goals) and linemate Jukka Porvari (one goal, two assists).

Thus, at the end of the first round of medal play, the United States was in first place with three points; the Soviets and Swedes had two points each; and Finland trailed with only one point. (In a 1:30 P.M. contest, Czechoslovakia defeated Canada, 6-1, to take fifth place in the overall tournament standings.)

With the United States playing Finland next and Sweden taking on the Soviet Union, the possibilities for gold, silver, and bronze still boggled the mind. The most simple possibility was this: if the Americans could beat Finland in their Sunday morning matchup, the gold would be theirs—no ifs, ands, or buts.

Brooks:

- *Boys, we went to the well again, and the water was colder and the water was deeper.*

Finland's Jari Kurri (17) and U.S. player Dave Christian exchange blows during the first period, while Dave Silk skates in the foreground. The game clinched the gold medal for the Americans.

The coach had used this expression often enough for it to be included in the *Brooksisms* volume, and never did it seem more appropriate than in summing up the win over Russia. But as Brooks fully realized, he would have to lead his team to the well one more time and hope that the pail did not come up dry. ''It scares the hell out of me,'' he said. ''it's rather sobering when you look at all the mathematical possibiliities . . . We can be in fourth place. We can still be out of it. I've tried to impress that on the athletes while they're still in the emotional euphoria of Friday night's victory.''

The athletes didn't need much impressing. From the beginning nobody had expected very much from them, and they had had nothing to lose by playing with youthful abandon. Not any more. ''We all realized what's in front of us, and we're all good enough athletes and good enough hockey players to realize that a win Sunday would give us a dream very few people ever had a chance to do—win a gold medal,'' said Captain Eruzione.

''I can see how the American public would be excited, but I'm sure they'll forget real quick if we don't perform well Sunday,'' thought Jim Craig. ''There's more pressure Sunday. We have something to lose. We have to respect the Finland team. . . .''

In the same spirit of camaraderie that characterized them throughout the competition, the entire American hockey team celebrates atop the winners' podium. Team captain Mike Eruzione had called on his fellow players to join him on the podium after the team received their gold medals.

Brooks hoped his team would not follow their pattern of falling behind early and having to come from behind. But as Mark Johnson said after the game, "That was our team's style." Jim Craig put it in a different way: "These guys, you've got to spot 'em a goal to get 'em going, I guess." At 9:20 of the first period Jukka Porvari, the 26-year-old Finnish captain, beat Craig on a 50-foot slap shot from just inside the U.S. blue line. Porvari, who skated on two shifts, was a constant thorn in the Americans' side. Also giving them fits was goalie Jorma Valtonen, who stopped all 14 U.S. shots in the first period. After 20 minutes, the United States trailed, 1-0.

If at intermission Coach Brooks did not repeat his dictum about the first and last five minutes of each period, it was only because he had said it enough already. At 4:39 of the second session Neal Broten forced a giveaway by a Finnish defenseman, and Steve Christoff captured the puck for a whirling backhander that dribbled between the legs of goaltender Valtonen. But less than two minutes later, with Buzz Schneider in the penalty box for slashing, Mikko Leinonen sneaked behind Mark Johnson, and from a spot 10 feet to the left of Craig, tipped home a shot-pass from the stick of Hanno Haapalainen.

The United States trailed, 2-1, after two periods and looked sluggish in the first moments of the last session. The crowd took time out from its flag waving and foot stamping to sit and be worried. Perhaps the team finally had met the one obstacle—pressure—it couldn't surmount. It was a fear shared by everyone in the arena, except "The Boys of Winter." "We were behind," said Rob McClanahan, "but we played the third period with great confidence." Mark Johnson summed up the effort: "When it got tough, we just sucked it up and did what we had to do."

ICE HOCKEY CHRONOLOGY

Olympic Fieldhouse
Olympic Arena

Tuesday February 12
Blue Division: Czechoslovakia defeats Norway, 11-0; Rumania defeats West Germany, 6-4; United States ties Sweden, 2-2, on a dramatic, last-minute goal.
Red Division: Canada defeats The Netherlands, 10-1; Poland defeats Finland, 5-4; Soviet Union swamps Japan, 16-0.

Thursday February 14
Blue Division: Sweden defeats Rumania, 8-0; West Germany defeats Norway, 10-4; United States upsets Czechoslovakia, 7-3.
Red Division: Soviet Union crushes The Netherlands, 17-4; Canada defeats Poland, 5-1; Finland defeats Japan, 6-3.

Saturday February 16
Blue Division: United States defeats Norway, 5-1; Czechoslovakia defeats Rumania, 7-2; Sweden defeats West Germany, 5-2.
Red Division: Soviet Union defeats Poland, 8-1; Japan and The Netherlands tie, 3-3; Finland defeats Canada, 4-3.

Monday February 18
Blue Division: Sweden defeats Norway, 7-1; United States defeats Rumania, 7-2; Czechoslovakia defeats West Germany, 11-3.

Red Division: Canada defeats Japan, 6-0; The Netherlands defeats Poland, 5-3; Soviet Union defeats Finland, 4-2.

Wednesday February 20
Blue Division: Sweden upsets Czechoslovakia, 4-2, and advances to the medal round; United States defeats West Germany, 4-2, and advances to the medal round; Norway and Rumania tie, 3-3.
Red Division: Soviet Union defeats Canada, 6-4, and advances to the medal round; Finland defeats The Netherlands, 10-3, and advances to the medal round; Poland defeats Japan, 5-1.

Friday February 22
In the first game of the medal round, the United States pulls off a startling upset by defeating the powerful Soviet Union, 4-3. In the second match, Sweden and Finland tie, 3-3. In the consolation game for fifth place, Czechoslovakia defeats Canada, 6-1.

Sunday February 24
The United States clinches the gold medal by defeating Finland, 4-2. The Soviet Union beats Sweden, 9-2, to take the silver. Sweden finishes third in the medal round to win the bronze.

DIVISIONAL ROUND ROBIN
FINAL STANDINGS

Blue Division	W	L	T	Pts	GF	GA
Sweden	4	0	1	9	26	7
United States	4	0	1	9	25	10
Czechoslovakia	3	2	0	6	34	15
West Germany	1	4	0	2	21	30
Rumania	1	3	1	3	13	29
Norway	0	4	1	1	9	36

Red Division	W	L	T	Pts	GF	GA
Soviet Union	5	0	0	10	51	11
Finland	3	2	0	6	26	18
Canada	3	2	0	6	28	12
Poland	2	3	0	4	15	23
The Netherlands	1	3	1	3	16	43
Japan	0	4	1	1	7	36

MEDAL ROUND
FINAL STANDINGS

		W	L	T	Pts*	GF	GA
Gold:	United States	2	0	0	5	8	5
Silver:	Soviet Union	1	1	0	4	12	6
Bronze:	Sweden	0	1	1	2	5	12
	Finland	0	1	1	1	5	7

*Including competition against medal round participants of same division.

First on the agenda was to tie up the score. Taking a pass from Dave Christian, Phil Verchota swept down the left side of the ice and beat Valtonen on a sharp, 15-foot shot. At 2:25 the score was knotted up at 2-2, and the floodgates were open. At 6:05 Rob McClanahan knocked home the go-ahead goal from five feet out, and at 16:25 Mark Johnson added an insurance tally while the United States was killing a penalty to Verchota.

Sensing that the impossible dream was about to come true, the delirious crowd of nearly 10,000 began chanting "We're Number 1! We're Number 1!" Goalie Jim Craig, a standout throughout the tournament, raised his gloved hand high over his head in emphatic agreement.

As time ran out, television commentator Al Michaels had to shout over the din in the Olympic Fieldhouse at Lake Placid, NY: "The impossible dream comes true!" When the buzzer sounded "The Boys of Winter" threw their sticks and gloves into the crowd, and flag-waving fans rushed onto the ice. Their hands upraised, Mike Eruzione and Rob McClanahan took one of the flags and displayed it proudly. After the ceremonial post-game handshake with the Finns, the Americans lined up across the ice, punching the air with their fists and waving to the crowd.

While the other players were hugging each other and saluting the fans, a flag-draped Jim Craig stood alone for a few moments anxiously scanning the crowd for his father. It was something he did after every hockey game. These were hardly usual circumstances, however, and he could not locate his father in the celebrating mob.

What followed in the lives of the 1980 U.S. Olympic ice hockey team would probably take them months to sort out and a lifetime to forget. There were another locker room phone call from President Carter and a trip to the White House the next day. As the Soviet Union was taking out its frustrations against Sweden, clinching the silver medal with a 9-2 victory, the U.S. squad was drinking champagne, holding press conferences, and still trying to figure out how it all happened. "The good Lord works in very strange ways," said Brooks.

There were a triumphant award ceremony, luncheons, interviews, parades, the welcoming cheers of proud families and hometown friends, commercial endorsements, and a dizzying schedule of public appearances. For some there would be lucrative NHL contracts and highly-publicized professional debuts. Herb Brooks would seek offers to coach in the pro ranks, but for the time being would settle for one free beer every day for the rest of his life at a bar in St. Paul, MN. For Mike Eruzione there would be no professional career, just the memory of captaining the Olympic ice hockey champions of 1980. The only thing there would not be was a team, and the players would miss it.

Eruzione: "It was just 20 guys pulling for each other. I'm sorry it's over."

Craig: "I just assumed I'd see them again on the bus and in practice. It's heartbreaking to say goodbye. I hope to run into some of them again."

Brooks:

• *I love this hockey team.*

Team members stand respectfully on the ice during the playing of their national anthem at the awards ceremony. More exuberant celebrations would follow. By defeating Finland, 4–2, the team won America's first Olympic gold medal in ice hockey since 1960.

Luge

Spectators crowd into the luge turns to glimpse a passing two-man sled.

Although Vera Zozulya became the first Russian to win a gold medal in luge at the XIII Winter Games, East German lugers dominated the sport. Since 1964 when luge became part of the Olympic program, Germans had won the top spot in men's and women's singles in three of the four Games and the men's doubles twice. The use of videotapes and other devices of big-time sports was credited with enhancing the German performance at Lake Placid.

The sport of luge, which was developed in Central Europe during the late 1800's, is not widely popular in the United States and Canada. In fact, it was not until 1968 that it became an organized sport in the United States. According to Jim Murray, a former American luger and coach-manager of the 1980 U.S. squad, Americans "really are selling the sport short." However, spectators at the Lake Placid Olympics and television viewers got a fast education in why it has been described as "the single most exciting sport in the Olympic Winter Games." It involves piloting a short, brakeless sled down a twisting course while lying down feet first and steering by shifting weight or tugging on a strap. Lugers easily exceed a speed of 50 miles per hour. The men's singles course at Lake Placid is 1,000 meters long with 14 curves and the men's doubles and the women's run is 749.2 meters with 11 curves. Races are judged by the time accumulated in four runs in the singles events and in two runs in the men's doubles. In the singles, one of the four runs must occur at night.

Although few of the paying public watched any of the practice runs, coaches and advisors of aspiring teams scrutinized both lugers and luge run, noting times, tricky spots, and danger points.

Men's Doubles

East Germany's Hans Rinn and Norbert Hahn have shared a sled since 1968 and on Feb. 19, 1980, they became the first athletes to win consecutive gold medals in men's doubles luge.

Rinn said the victory was made easier by the warm weather which slowed the sleds down, especially in the second and final run down the 749-meter course. Temperatures on Mount Van Hoevenberg rose to 36 degrees during the competition.

"The distance between us and the other sleds wasn't very big after the first run," he explained. "We figured after that they would be going slower, so we knew what we had to do. We went into the last race very calm because we knew we would be going slow, and going slow makes it that much easier. So it was easy for us."

Rinn and Hahn never trailed after making their first run down the icy, twisting course in 39.303 seconds. They followed that with a run of 40.028 seconds that gave them a combined time of 1 minute, 19.33 seconds, .27 second ahead of silver medalists Peter Gschnitzer and Karl Brunner of Italy. Georg Fluckinger and Karl Schrott of Austria finished third.

Richard Healey, the owner of an automobile repair garage in Annandale, NJ, and Walter (Ty) Danco, a Case Western Reserve law student, rode their sled to the best finish ever by American lugers, 11th place, with a combined time of 1:21.34. The two men had been a team for less than three months.

According to Healey, "the track seemed slower for the other nations, but it didn't bother them, probably because they have the knowledge we don't. We don't have the training time to experiment and find out what makes you go slower in the warm weather. If it had been terribly cold out there, it would have been better for us."

A spill during their second run upset the hopes of Soviet lugers Valeri Yakushin and Sergei Danilin (head showing). They righted themselves and finished the course, but they wound up in 17th position overall.

Norbert Hahn-Hans Rinn

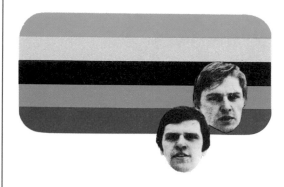

Naturally only one can steer. But both have important jobs to fill. A good start depends in large part on the ability of the backman. And also teamwork during the race is a requirement for that extra hundredth of a second.

—HANS RINN

At Lake Placid on Feb. 19, 1980, Hans Rinn and Norbert Hahn became the first athletes to win consecutive gold medals in the men's double luge competition. The East German team never trailed, as it completed its first run down the icy course in 39.3 seconds and its second run in 40.028 seconds. The team's combined time of 1 minute, 19.33 seconds was .27 second ahead of the runners-up.

With Rinn as driver and Hahn as the backman, the East German team has not only won two Olympic gold medals but also two world championships (1977, 1980) and three European crowns (1973, 1975, 1978). Competing by himself, Rinn took the bronze medal in the luge singles at Innsbruck in 1976, was world singles champion in 1973 and 1977, and captured the European singles title three times (1973, 1974, 1979). Although an entrant in the singles at Lake Placid, he did not start.

Hans Rinn was born on March 19, 1953, in the town of Langewiesen. The gold medalist is now a mechanical engineering student as well as a lieutenant colonel in the National People's Army. Always interested in things mechanical, Rinn took up the luge in the mid-1960's. Over the years his luge competitors have come to admire his fine technique and his willingness to take a chance. At the same time, the 6'1", 190 pound athlete has had to learn to temper his inclinations for unnecessary risk.

Jerzej Piekoczewski, a Polish luger, has called him "an able but extraordinarily cheeky rider." Of himself, Rinn has said that he is "fairly unproblematical, not unfriendly, no more courageous than others but consistent and in love with everything connected with speed."

Norbert Hahn was born on Jan. 6, 1954, in Elbingerode. At an early age, he developed an interest in winter sports at an East German sports center in the Harz Mountains. Following the Lake Placid Olympics, Hahn's goal was to complete his university studies in the field of physical education. He is a lieutenant in the National People's Army.

Unlike his friend Rinn, Hahn has not been particularly successful as a solo racer. In fact he has never finished better than 12th in international singles competition. Hahn takes his role as a member of the winning luge team very seriously. He avoids the suggestion that he is "just along for the ride" and detests being called a "backpack." Together Rinn and Hahn have coached other East Germans and Soviets who are eager to take up the sport.

The 6', 170-pound Hahn is married and the father of a young son. His brothers, Bernd and Ulrich, are also members of the international luge circuit.

Hans Rinn is a hell-for-leather driver.

Men's and Women's Singles

East Germany's Bernhard Glass, the last member of his squad in contention for a medal in men's singles luge, came through Saturday, February 16, to win the gold. On the same day, Vera Zozulya, a 24-year-old student from Soviet Latvia, wrapped up her commanding four-day performance and took the women's event.

Glass, a 22-year-old Army sergeant, crossed the finish line with the best run of the day: 43.48 seconds. Paul Hildgartner of Italy, the last man on the course, took the silver medal in a combined time of 2:55.37, compared with Glass' total of 2:54.79. Anton Winkler of West Germany took the bronze with a strong final run of 44.30, for a total of 2:56.54.

The bumpy, 1,000-meter men's course claimed several top contenders during the four days of runs. Those knocked from medal contention by crashes included the defending Olympic gold medalist, Detlef Guenther of East Germany, and Ernst Haspinger of Italy, the leader after three rounds who spilled in the next-to-last curve in the final run. Guenther, a 25-year-old electrician from Oberwiesenthal and the veteran of more than 1,000 slides a year, finished fourth.

Jeff Tucker of Westport, CT, was 12th, completing the course runs just behind Canada's Bruce Smith. John Fee of Plattsburgh, NY, who compares luging with "riding on a bar of soap," was 14th and Richard Stithem of Sterling, CO, was 20th in the 23-man, final field.

East German Bernhard Glass, gold medalist in the men's singles luge, smiles after his fourth and final run vaulted him into the top spot.

The women's gold medalist, Vera Zozulya, turned in the fastest time in each of the four runs for women as she defeated two-time world champion Melitta Sollman of East Germany by 1.1 seconds. Zozulya totalled 2:36.53 on the 749.2-meter course. Sollmann's total was 2:37.65. Unheralded Ingrida Amantova of the Soviet Union was third, in 2:37.81. Margit Schumann of East Germany, the 1976 gold medalist, was sixth.

U.S. women's champion Debbie Genovese of Rockford, IL, finished 15th and Canada's Carole Keyes was 18th. Prior to the Games, Mrs. Genovese, a dental assistant, credited the clinical sessions the American lugers participated in with improving her mental attitude toward her sport. She said that the sessions helped her with her "relaxation and concentration."

THE LUGE SLED

Constructed according to the same basic principle as the Flexible Flyer, the longtime favorite of children, the luge is now aerodynamically designed to permit maximum speed and endurance. The luge sled, which travels at a speed faster than a thoroughbred, consists of two single runners and a canvas, hammock-style seat on which the lugers lie on their backs, their feet stuck out over the front end. Steering and braking equipment is not permitted; the rubber-suited athletes hold on only to a simple strap.

The weight of the single-seater may not exceed 48.4 pounds and that of the double seater 52.8 pounds, and the maximum width between runners is about 16 inches. The sleds are checked at the finish of each run by a special "weight recorder." If the sled exceeds the weight restrictions, the luger is disqualified. Since the runners are not supposed to be heated, officials check their temperatures at the start and finish of each run.

Austria has long been a prime manufacturer of luge sleds, with the Austrian Gasser enjoying particular popularity. Few sleds are made in the United States. The cost of a sled is about $500.

Austria's Toni Weissnicht, a former official of the International Luge Federation, has noted that athletes "can't make money advertising luge sleds." Weissnicht believes that the luger "competes only for the sport" and that consequently "the Olympic ideal is much more prevalent in luge" than in many other Olympic sports.

Even a small girl looks big for a flimsy luge.

Zozulya pushes off, above. Fittings on her gloves help her grip the ice. Right, Sollmann, Zozulya, and Amantova respond to applause.

LUGE CHRONOLOGY

Mount Van Hoevenberg

Wednesday February 13 Vera Zozulya of the USSR finishes first in the initial run of the women's singles. Later in the evening, Detlef Guenther of East Germany takes an early lead in the first run of the men's singles.

Thursday February 14 Guenther and Zozulya maintain their leads following the second run of the men's and women's singles competition.

Friday February 15 During the third run, Italy's Ernst Haspinger travels through the course in 43.59 seconds to take over first place as Guenther falls from his sled during the final curve. Zozulya has the fastest time in her heat for the third straight day.

Saturday February 16 Bernhard Glass of East Germany wins the men's singles gold medal after Haspinger takes a spill in the next-to-last curve of the final run. Zozulya clinches the women's singles gold medal as she completes the fourth run in 39.121 seconds.

Tuesday February 19 Temperatures on Mount Van Hoevenberg rise to 36 degrees. Hans Rinn and Norbert Hahn never trail and take the gold medal in the men's doubles. The East Germans complete their first run in 39.303 seconds and the second in 40.028 seconds.

MEDAL WINNERS

	Gold	**Silver**	**Bronze**
MEN'S SINGLES	Bernhard Glass (GDR)	Paul Hildgartner (ITA)	Anton Winkler (GER)
MEN'S DOUBLES	GDR (H. Rinn N. Hahn)	ITA (P. Gschnitzer, K. Brunner)	AUT (G. Fluckinger K. Schrott)
WOMEN'S SINGLES	Vera Zozulya (USR)	Melitta Sollmann (GDR)	Ingrida Amantova (URS)

Nordic Skiing

Today's Olympic ski program is divided into two categories, Alpine and Nordic. The Alpine consists of the downhill, the slalom, and the giant slalom, while the Nordic includes various cross-country races as well as ski jumping. To many experts, the jump offers the most sensational skiing competition, the Alpine events are the most dangerous as well as potentially the most graceful, and the cross-country category is considered the most grueling. Since their sport is the most grueling, cross-country skiers must engage in long training sessions. Most top performers begin preparations for the Olympics a good seven months in advance.

The cross-country race occurs over a predetermined distance on a natural terrain that is one third uphill, one third downhill, and one third flat or rolling. The track is divided into three sections—one is the main course, the second for passing, and the third a lane for coaches and officials. No artificial obstacles are permitted on the course. The entrant wears extremely lightweight skis which are fastened to the boots only at the tips of the toes. The cross-country skier alternates between kicking off with one foot and gliding with the other. This technique permits a smooth stride. The skier with the fastest time is the winner.

A marked rise in disposable income and a simultaneous increase in the amount of time available for leisure activity led many individuals to take to the downhill ski slopes during the 1960's. An entirely new subculture of ski fashion soon developed and sections of the North American continent became dotted with new chair lifts, T-bars, rope tows, and après-ski centers to cater to the throng. Before long, many ski enthusiasts became disenchanted with the lengthening lift lines and the generally crowded slopes, the number of hours required to drive to the ski areas, and the expense. They turned to cross-country skiing, and it began to enjoy a new mass popularity in North America during the 1970's.

But by no means is cross-country skiing new. Some form of skis or snowshoes has been used for transportation purposes for centuries. It is known that skis were used in northern Europe and in Asia prior to the Christian era. In fact, skis, dating back to 2500 B.C., have been found in the Altai Mountains of Siberia. By the 13th century A.D. skis were worn in battle.

Ski racing over rolling terrain became a recreational sport during the 19th century. By the 1870's ski carnivals were a feature in many Norwegian towns. Norwegians who immigrated to the United States in the late 1800's introduced the sport to the American soil. As more people took up skiing, the U.S. Ski Association and the Canadian Amateur Ski Association were founded in 1904 and 1921, respectively. The International Skiing Federation, the sport's present governing body, was formed in 1924 with 26 initial members.

Although a clear distinction between Alpine and Nordic skiing did not evolve until the 1930's, Nordic events were part of the first Winter Games in Chamonix, France, in 1924. In that year competition was held in a men's 18-kilometer and 50-kilometer cross-country, a combined (cross-country and jumping), and a 70-meter jump. A 40-kilometer cross-country relay, a 30-kilometer race, and a 90-kilometer jump were added to the Olympic program in 1936, 1956, and 1964, respectively. The

Bill Koch, who had made history in 1976 by becoming the first American to win a medal in cross-country skiing, suffered disappointment at Lake Placid. Although the 24-year-old Vermonter personally did well in the relay, he dropped out of the 30-kilometer race and finished 16th and 13th in the 15- and 50-kilometer races, respectively.

Fellow Soviets Nikolai Zimyatov (left) and Vasili Rochev congratulate one another after finishing first and second in the 30-kilometer cross-country race. Their times were 31.4 seconds apart.

18-kilometer race was reduced to 15 kilometers in 1956. Women began participating in Olympic Nordic events at Oslo in 1952 (10-kilometer cross country). A women's relay and a 5-kilometer cross-country event were introduced in 1956 and 1964, respectively.

The cross-country trails at Mount Van Hoevenberg were constructed in 1968–69 under the direction of J. Vernon Lamb. The courses are said to call for relentless downhill skiing. Long steady uphills caused many athletes to withdraw during the pre-Olympic trials. Juha Mieto, a member of Finland's gold-medal-winning relay team in 1976 and a three-time medalist in the 1980 Games, stated that he "was tremendously impressed with the Lake Placid courses." Prior to the competition, Mieto said, "The big height differences between sections of the courses will cause many problems. The uphills are hard. Overall, I'd rate the courses as very hard."

At Innsbruck in 1976 Bill Koch gave the United States its first Olympic medal ever in Nordic competition. But his hopes—and America's—of adding to that laurel at Lake Placid fell under a Soviet and East German gold rush led by Russia's Nikolai Zimyatov. By winning the 30- and 50-kilometer races and anchoring the gold-medal-winning relay team, the 24-year-old Soviet became the first male to win three gold medals in Nordic events in the same Olympics.

America had pinned its hopes on Koch, the 24-year-old from Guilford, VT, whose silver in the 30-kilometer cross-country at Innsbruck caught the world off guard; on 22-year-old Jim Denney of Duluth, MN; and on 26-year-old Alison Owen-Spencer of Indian, AK. But when the competition ended, the Americans were among the skiers, many of them international favorites, who failed to place among the top six in any of the events they entered.

Norway, known as the cradle of skiing, failed to win a gold medal in Nordic skiing for the first time since the Winter Games started in 1924. Oddvar Braa, the 1979 Nordic World Cup winner and a prime Norwegian contender, was a victim of influenza. He finished 7th, 9th, and 12th in the 50, 15, and 30 kilometers.

Among the women, 24-year-old East German Barbara Petzold helped to break a Soviet sweep by winning the 10 kilometers and anchoring East Germany's quartet to another gold in the relay.

Men's 30-Kilometer Cross-Country

Nikolai Zimyatov, a Soviet cross-country skier, won the first gold medal of the 1980 Winter Olympics on Thursday morning, February 14, when he crossed the finish line of the men's 30-kilometer race in 1 hour, 27 minutes, 2.8 seconds. It was the first Nordic ski race ever run on artificial snow. The win was the USSR's third consecutive victory in the 30-kilometer event.

Vasili Rochev also reaffirmed the Soviet dominance of this event by placing second for a silver medal after a strong finish which brought him up from fourth place halfway through the race. Ivan Lebanov, 23, of Bulgaria, a relatively unknown Nordic skier, placed third after coming almost out of nowhere. The bronze won by Lebanov was Bulgaria's first medal in Olympic Winter Games.

Thomas Wassberg, 23, of Sweden, who raced on the favorable last start number controlling the entire field, placed fourth in 1:28:40.35. The 1978 world champion over 15 kilometers, Jozef Luszczek of Poland, was fifth in 1:29:03.64. Matti Pitkanen was sixth and had the best time of the four Finns who entered the race, 1:29:35.03.

Mount Van Hoevenberg's demanding trails foiled the efforts of Bill Koch. He dropped out after skiing about two thirds of the course when it became clear he was far behind in the field.

"There are no big excuses. The skis were very good. The wax was very good. Things just slipped away and that's it. I can't explain it. That's part of the mystique of this sport," he said. Every time he passed through the ski stadium on one of the three 10-kilometer loops that made up the race, Koch got a strong burst of applause from the mostly American crowd of several hundred people. But while he was among the leaders for the first five kilometers, he gradually fell farther and farther behind. "After 20 kilometers I got the information that I was not anywhere in the running. So I decided I would save energy. That energy will be better used Sunday in the 15-kilometer race," he said.

The three top finishers were drained but happy after their endurance test. "We have been preparing for this competition for a long time," said Zimyatov, who is a student at the Institute of Physical Culture in Moscow. Rochev is a member of the army.

The three other Americans who entered disappointed the home crowd. Stan Dunklee, 25, of Putney, VT, finished 30th in 1:33:48.02—more than six minutes behind the winner. Jim Galanes of Brattleboro, VT, finished 41st in 1:36:15.17 and Doug Peterson, 26, of Hanover, NH, was 45th in 1:38:29.86. No Canadian entered the race.

Of the performance by the U.S. skiers, John Bower, director of the U.S. Nordic ski team, said, "I think an accumulation of pressure got to our guys today. It was the same as in the world championships in 1978. We thought we were ready and we weren't. I don't think it was just the snow and the rocks that caused our low placing."

Women's 5-Kilometer Cross-Country

Raisa Smetanina of the Soviet Union won the second straight gold medal for the Russians in cross-country skiing on February 15, by capturing the women's 5-kilometer race. Her winning time was 15 minutes, 06.92 seconds. The 27-year-old teacher was only five seconds ahead of Hilkka Riihivuori of Finland, who placed second with a time of 15:11.96. Kveta Jeriova, 23, of Czechoslovakia was third in 15:23.44. It was Czechoslovakia's first medal in Olympic ski racing.

Barbara Petzold of East Germany was fourth in 15:23.62. Nina Baldycheva of the Soviet Union was fifth in 15:29.03·and Soviet veteran Galina Kulakova, competing in her fourth Olympics, was sixth in 15:29.58.

Miss Smetanina, who at Innsbruck in 1976 took the gold in the 10-kilometer event, the silver in the 5 kilometers, and a gold as a member of the women's relay team, said, "I'm happy that I won, but I don't know what happened to my teammates. We all used the same wax, and frankly we had expected to do even better than we did." The Russians had expected to score a medal sweep in the event.

Despite being less than one minute behind the winner, Alison Owen-Spencer of Indian, AK, placed only 22nd as the best of 4 Americans among the 38 women entered from 12 countries. Her time was 16:05.04. Beth Paxson, 19, was 26th in 16:20.93, Leslie Bancroft, 20, 33rd in 16:39.71, and Betsy Haines, 19, 37th in 17:27.75. She started first of all the 38 entries.

Canada's four participants in the event—E. Joan Groothuysen, Shirley Firth, Angela Schmidt, and Sharon Firth, Shirley's twin—were 27th, 28th, 29th, and 35th respectively.

Of her victory in the women's 5 kilometers, Raisa Smetanina said, "I'm not better than the others. It just happened to go my way." The Soviet star also participated in the 10 kilometers (above) and was fourth, missing a bronze by approximately 9 seconds.

Men's 15-Kilometer Cross-Country

It was one of the most spectacular duels in the XIII Winter Olympics. And when it was over, less than the tip of a ski separated winner from loser.

On Sunday, February 17, Thomas Wassberg of Sweden nipped Finland's Juha Mieto, the "Scandinavian Giant," by one one-hundredth of a second to win the gold medal in the men's 15-kilometer cross-country ski race. A crowd estimated at 4,000 braved ice-cold temperatures ($-4°F$, $-18°C$) and a stiff western wind to watch the exciting contest. Wassberg's time in the tremendous duel at Mount Van Hoevenberg was 41 minutes, 57.63 seconds. Mieto was clocked in 41:57.64 to win the silver. Ove Aunli of Norway won the bronze medal in 42:28.62.

A late starting position gives a skier the opportunity to learn the intermediate times of the earlier competitors, and the chance

Nikolai Zimyatov

I was ready for it.

—NIKOLAI ZIMYATOV

The best racing skier of the Olympic season was a dark horse. The experts did not mention him among the promising contenders, and in fact he does not look much like a champion of one of the most demanding sports. But as he said after he won the 30-kilometer race (three times around a 10-kilometer course), he was ready for the competition. "I'm used to this kind of course. The ground is like we have at home."

In winning the 30-kilometer race, the first championship—Olympic or world—run on artificial snow, Nikolai Zimyatov took the first gold medal of the XIII Winter Games and put the Soviet Union into the all-time Winter Olympics lead in number of golds won. Six days later he picked up a second gold as the anchor of the victorious relay team, and three days after that he gained his third gold by setting a new Olympic record in the 50-kilometer cross-country.

Of the 50 kilometer, the race that the Scandinavians consider the glamor event of cross-country skiing, America's Bill Koch said, "It's a victory just to finish this race." Zimyatov, who crossed the finish line 2 hours, 27 minutes, and 24 seconds after he started and 7.07 minutes ahead of Koch, modestly said he had no expectation of three gold medals. "I figured I had a chance in the 30 kilometers and the relay." Then, with a smile, he added, "But the hockey players didn't do so well last night [against the U.S. team] so we had to make up for them."

Nikolai Zimyatov at 24 is 5'8" tall, lean and somewhat fragile looking. But what he lacks in heft he makes up in determination. Colds plagued him, causing him to miss almost half of the training season, so he put himself on a toughening schedule that included cold-water bathing.

He has been skiing competitively half his life, having begun in school contests in his village of Rumyantsevo, near Moscow. In 1980 he was in his third year of studies at the Moscow Regional Institute of Physical Culture, where he occupied bachelor quarters. He often returned home to train on the local ski courses and to visit his parents. His mother, a teacher of literature, and his father, a glass-blower of sophisticated equipment for research institutes, were not surprised by the power and speed Nikolai demonstrated. In winning the three cross-country gold medals he became the first man and the second athlete to accomplish the feat in one Winter Olympic meet. In 1972 in Sapporo his countrywoman, Galina Kulakova, had achieved that record.

Zimyatov says he sings while he skis. After Lake Placid he had a lot to sing about.

The name of Nikolai Zimyatov was entered in the record books as an all-time great Nordic skier.

The 15-kilometer race was one of the most exciting in Olympic history. Only one one-hundredth of a second separated the gold and silver medalists, Sweden's Thomas Wassberg (above) and Finland's Juha Mieto (below).

to adjust the pace accordingly. Mieto had the advantage of the 54th position out of 62 drawn by the skiers from 22 countries. As he had in the 30 kilometers, Wassberg drew the last starting position and with it the chance to check his intermediate time against all the field. From start to finish, he led—with Mieto right behind.

Almost as soon as Mieto left the starting gate, it was clear he was setting the fastest pace. At the five-kilometer mark, the 6′5″ Mieto, who had trimmed more than 22 pounds from his frame, was traveling at least eight seconds faster than anyone in front of him. But Wassberg quickly learned what Mieto was up to and managed to ski the first five kilometers five seconds faster than Mieto. Coaches and officials of the competing teams, spread out along the race course, kept in contact by portable radios and passed along timing results as soon as they were known.

"I realized it was going to be a tough fight between me and Mieto, but not until 10 kilometers did I realize it was just me and Mieto," said Wassberg. Mieto meanwhile was getting reports on the sprightly pace of the later-starting Swede. "I'd hear he was a second behind or a second ahead. I knew all the time the condition was very critical," said Mieto.

At the 10-kilometer mark, Wassberg was four seconds in front of Mieto. But the Finn, seemingly oblivious of the bitter cold that was forming icicles on his beard, pushed himself even harder to close the gap in the race's final third. It wasn't enough. As Mieto stood in the stadium, having finished in 41:57.64, Wassberg found the energy for his final push. And when the scoreboard flashed the result figured by the automatic timing device in the finish gate, it read 41:57.63.

Nikolai Zimyatov, who earlier won the 30-kilometer event, placed fourth in 42:33.96 and his fellow Soviet, Evgeni Beliaev, was fifth in 42:46.02. Beliaev had placed second in the 15-kilometer race at Innsbruck four years earlier, when Nikolai Bajukov won the gold medal. Bajukov failed to qualify for the 1980 race.

The best-placing American racer was Bill Koch, who finished 16th in 43:38.56. The Vermonter was among the top ten racers through the first lap before dropping back in the last two tours around the course. He finished sixth in the same race at Innsbruck. Canada did not participate in the race.

Juha Mieto was good-natured when asked about the result. "First, I want to congratulate Thomas Wassberg—and then I'd like to get my revenge in the 50-kilometer race," he said. In return, the winner, who had recovered from a leg injury incurred during an auto accident in 1978, commented, "If I were giving out the medals I'd take a gold one for myself and ask for another one for Juha. He certainly turned in a great race."

Women's 10-Kilometer Cross-Country

Alison Owen-Spencer, the top female U.S. cross-country skier, marveled at her European rivals. "These girls are so fast, it's really almost incomprehensible to me just how fast they go," she said of the East Germans, Scandinavians, and Russians, all of whom easily outpaced her on February 18 in the women's 10-kilometer cross-country race. It was the fourth Olympic cross-country race in which American skiers proved no match for their Russian and European competition.

Barbara Petzold, a 24-year-old medical student from Oberwiesenthal, East Germany, was the surprise gold medalist, turning in a fast time of 30 minutes, 31.54 seconds. The gold was East Germany's first individual win in Olympic cross-country races. Right behind Miss Petzold were two Finnish skiers, Hilkka Riihivuori and Helena Takalo, who earned the silver and bronze medals with times of 30:35.05 and 30:45.25, respectively.

Raisa Smetanina of the Soviet Union, the defending 10-kilometer champion and the 1980 gold medal winner in 5 kilome-

Helena Takalo (left) and Hilkka Riihivuori raise their toy mascots in honor of their bronze and silver medals in the women's 10 kilometers. The two Finnish skiers were runners-up to Barbara Petzold of East Germany.

ters, had to settle for fourth place. Smetanina failed in her efforts to become the fourth woman to win both of the women's individual races.

Down in 22nd and 23rd places were Owen-Spencer and Angela E. Schmidt, the top U.S. and Canadian finishers. Their times were 32:41.33 and 32:56.13, respectively.

"We're just not used to skiing that fast," said John Bower, director of the U.S. Nordic team. "We just don't have that real quick movement in the legs." Bower once again regretted the absence of any major international competition in the month preceding the Olympics. American skiers were unable to pit themselves against the very best skiers and therefore found it difficult to rise above a certain level of performance, Bower said.

But the lack of that tough international competition didn't bother the Scandinavians and Russians a bit. "We have enough competition at home," said a happy Riihivuori after the race. Her silver medal was her second of the 1980 Olympics. She was also the runner-up in the 5 kilometers.

The race took place in 13°F ($-10.5°C$), overcast weather at the Olympic Nordic ski stadium. Race conditions on the artificial snow over the 10-kilometer loop were excellent.

Riihivuori and Takalo attended a post-race news conference with a stuffed bear and a doll which had apparently become the Finnish team's unofficial mascots. They said they bought the toys when they arrived in the United States.

Men's Relay

Anchored by 30-kilometer champion Nikolai Zimyatov, a strong Soviet quartet mastered tricky waxing conditions and won the gold medal in the men's 40-kilometer cross-country relay race on February 20.

The Soviets outclassed nine other national teams, including the United States group, which finished eighth, more than seven minutes behind the winners. Norway placed second and defending champion Finland was third. Juha Mieto proved to be the star of the event. The 31-year-old Finn had the best individual time—28 minutes, 16.64 seconds—of the 40 skiers who represented 10 countries.

It was the third gold medal in Nordic events for the Soviet Union and the third Olympic relay triumph for Russian men since they entered the Winter Games for the first time at Cortina D'Ampezzo, Italy, in 1956.

Finland secured the bronze medal after its anchorman, Mieto, overtook West Germany's 19-year-old Jochem Behle with only 1½ kilometers to go, leaving West Germany in fourth place. Sweden placed fifth and Italy sixth.

"This was the most important victory for the Soviet Union because it represents real team work," said Evgeni Beliaev, who skied the third leg for the Soviets. The Soviet team of Vasili Rochev, Nikolai Bazhukov, Beliaev, and Zimyatov won the race in 1 hour, 57 minutes, 3.46 seconds—a Winter Games re-

Entrants from ten nations began the 40-kilometer cross-country relay at 1:24 on February 20. Following the two-hour contest, Nikolai Zimyatov, the anchorman of the winning Soviet team, was tossed into the air by the other club members, Vasili Rochev, Nikolai Bazhukov, and Evgeni Beliaev. Norwegian and Finnish teams won the silver and bronze.

Barbara Petzold (2), the winner of the women's 10 kilometers, and the other youthful members of the East German relay team were delighted with their victory over such veteran foursomes as those of the Soviet Union and Norway.

cord. Norway was timed in 1:58:45.77 and Finland in 2:00:00.18. West Germany was fourth in 2:00:22.74 for the best West German placing ever in Olympic Nordic cross-country skiing.

Racing into eighth place for the United States were the four Vermont Ski Club team members: Bill Koch, Tim Caldwell, Jim Galanes, and Stan Dunklee. Their time was 2:04:12.17. Koch was third after the first leg but his teammates remained in eighth place throughout the race.

Like some other skiers, the American had problems picking the correct wax for the variable racing conditions. Temperatures during the race changed from below freezing in overcast weather at the 9 A&M& start to 46°F (8°C) and sunny at the finish two hours later.

"I was feeling good. I was really pleased. It's the high point of the Olympics for me so far. It's a lot of fun with the relays. I wish they all were relays," said Koch.

Women's Relay

With a mixture of awe and envy, cross-country skiers and spectators watched as a young, fleet-footed East German team easily outclassed seven other foursomes on Thursday, February 21, to capture the gold medal in the cross-country women's relay. The East German team of Marlies Rostock, Carola Anding, Veronika Hesse, and 10-kilometer champion Barbara Petzold completed the 20-kilometer relay in 1 hour, 2 minutes, 11.1 seconds. The Soviet Union and Norway took silver and bronze medals with times of 1:03:18.3 and 1:04:13.5, respectively. By the end of the second lap, the East Germans had a 26-second lead. Through the next two laps, they simply widened the margin.

"I must compliment my partners. By the time I took over the last leg, we were well ahead already," said Petzold after the race. Despite the big lead, Petzold raced her lap in the second best time of the relay, 15 minutes, 22.71 seconds. Her teammate, Veronika Hesse, had clocked 15:18.28.

After Barbara crossed the finish line, her teammates jubilantly crowded around her and hoisted her onto their shoulders.

For East Germany it was a thunderous triumph of ambition and youthful spirit over the experience and age of the Soviet stars. The average age of the East German quartet was only 22 years, compared with 32 for the Soviet team of Nina Baldicheva, Nina Rocheva, Galina Kulakova, and Raisa Smetanina.

"We expected to win a medal but we did not expect to win the gold," Petzold, who was also a member of East Germany's bronze-winning team in 1976, said after the victory. "It is a good feeling. I'm especially happy for the other members of the team because they had not had any medals and I had already won one race. The conditions were not a problem today. We had fast skis and the waxing was perfect."

The American quartet of Alison Owen-Spencer, Beth Paxson, Leslie Bancroft, and Margaret Spencer remained in seventh place throughout the race and finished in 1:06:55.41, beating only Canada.

"No, I'm not going to continue training until 1984. I've been at this a long time," said Owen-Spencer after the race. But she had some advice for the younger skiers on the U.S. team who are looking toward the next Olympics. "They're going to have to upgrade their training another notch, train harder and faster, and not pansy out," she said. "I think we're going to have to do what the East Germans have started to do. They have a lot of timed workouts so they know exactly what pace they're skiing. Skiing is becoming more like track, where it's done under the clock-watch. In our training so far, we've just been going off with somebody else and skiing against that pace."

Men's 50-Kilometer Cross-Country

Russian cross-country skier Nikolai Zimyatov captured his third gold medal in the XIII Winter Games by winning the men's demanding 50-kilometer cross-country race Saturday, February 23. His winning time of 2 hours, 27 minutes, 24.6 seconds in the premier event in Nordic skiing was an Olympic record for the distance.

Finland's star, Juha Mieto, his beard almost a solid mass of ice, placed second in 2:30:20.52 for his second silver medal.

Aleksandr Zavjalov of the Soviet Union was third for the bronze medal in 2:30:51.52. Of the 43 top world skiers who entered the race, six failed to finish. The ordeal of racing up and down hilly, wooded terrain for some 31 miles simply proved to be too tough.

"Every part of the race was difficult. The whole distance was difficult," said Zimyatov, who looked pale and older than his 24 years after the race.

Norway's Lars Erik Eriksen missed a bronze medal by less than two seconds, placing fourth in 2:30:53.03. Sergei Saveliev of the Soviet Union was fifth in 2:31:15.82 and his countryman Evgeni Beliaev was sixth in 2:31:21.19.

Bill Koch, the best among the American entries, finished in 13th place in 2:34:31.62.

As is evident from the expression on Nikolai Zimyatov's face (above), the men's 50-kilometer cross-country event is one of the most grueling tests in sports. The Soviet student completed the run in Olympic record time for his third gold. Although his beard was covered with ice following the race, Finland's Juha Mieto was pleased to relax with a beverage and to have another silver medal to add to his trophy case.

Ski Jumping

"It is not a jumping sport. It is a flying sport, a lifting sport. You simply take off into the air at the same speed you come down the inrun . . . . You think about being a bird," says Shirley Finberg-Sullivan, a ballet instructor who also trains ski jumpers. Jim Denney, who knows from experience, agrees. "I can fly," he says.

In simple terms, ski jumping can be defined as an attempt to achieve flight. Participants hike to the top of a jump, fasten on skis, and hurtle down sloping "inruns." Reaching speeds of 60 miles per hour, they soar off the ends of the inruns and "fly."

At the Olympics, there are two ski jumping events—the men's 70 meters and the men's 90 meters. These specifications refer to the distance an average jump is likely to cover. A jumper going the average distance or even 20 meters farther will come to earth on the landing hill, the "outrun," below. Beyond the landing hill, the slope flattens out. If a jumper hits a big jump, he could "outjump the hill," which could be very dangerous. It is difficult enough to land safely on one's feet, as is required. But to land on the flat portion is to invite disaster. Strange as it may seem, jumpers are always trying to fly longer distances; the judges are always watching to make sure that no one goes too far and lands on the flat. The officials have the option of shortening the inrun to cut takeoff speeds and thereby reduce distances.

In the 70-meter and 90-meter contests, each athlete jumps twice. He receives points based on his distance and points based on his jumping style, or form. In determining the score for style, judges look for proper body position, steadiness, and boldness. Such mistakes as arms waving, skis crossing, and improper landing cost the jumper points. Total score for the two jumps determines the final standings. Thus it is possible for a competitor to outscore an opponent who has traveled farther.

Although the 70-meter Nordic Combined receives little recognition from the average sports fan, it is probably the most demanding of the various Nordic events. The Olympic combined consists of a 70-meter jumping competition on one day and a 15-kilometer cross-country race the next. The jumping competition is held first to encourage the better cross-country skiers to improve their jumping. As in the two jumping events, total points determine the winner.

Ski jumping developed as a sport by itself during the nineteenth century. Sondre Norheim, a farmer's son from southern

Norway, is considered the father of modern ski jumping. The first ski-jumping contest occurred in Trysil, Norway, in 1862. Following the formation of the Norwegian Ski Association in 1883, cross-country races and ski jumping became separate competitions. Torgus and Mikkel Hemmestvedt of Red Wing, MN, are the first known American ski jumpers. The first American ski jumping contest took place in 1887.

Intervale, the venue of the 1980 Olympic ski jumping, is the oldest sports site at Lake Placid. A crowd of 3,000 persons watched ski jumping there as early as 1921. Until the 1960's when the town of North Elba purchased the land at Intervale, the ski jumps were administered by the Lake Placid Club.

Some critics considered the Intervale ski jumps, which were constructed especially for the 1980 Games, the most exciting pieces of Olympic construction. The jumps are highlighted by two towers of raw concrete shafts that rise above the Lake Placid surroundings. Massive structures curve toward the ground like the famous roller coasters of the world. The larger tower (257') includes an elevator and was built to serve as an observation tower following the Games.

After years of domination by Norwegian and Finnish ski jumpers, no single nation has dominated the jumping and combined competitions at the recent Winter Games. For the most part, this tradition continued at Lake Placid. Of the nine medals, East Germany and Finland captured three each, Austria two, and Japan one.

70 Meters

The wind blew in gusts down the inrun of the 70-meter jump. A crowd of chilled spectators stared up the landing hill, up the inrun, to the top of the 15-story tower. It was early in the afternoon of Sunday, February 17, and shortly, the first of the competitors would come soaring at the crowd through the clear, cold air. And if the harsh Adirondack wind made some of the crowd uncomfortable, it would have reason to make the judges of the competition uncomfortable too. But only after it had taken one jumper on a long, grand ride.

Certain athletic contests have long been subject to the whims of the wind. A fair breeze can blow a would-be home run foul or a field goal attempt wide. And certainly, in a sport where men go launching off of mountains, the effect that the wind can have is obvious.

In the first round of jumping, the ninth man up was American Jeff Davis of Steamboat Springs, CO. The best jump to that point was 83.5 meters, by Alfred Groyer of Austria. Davis came up through the starting gate and began his swift run down the snow-covered slope. The wind at his back, he took off cleanly and sent himself airborne. Leaning out over his skis, he sailed and sailed, gliding through the crisp air as the partisan crowd roared. When Davis finally touched down, he had flown 91 meters, garnered 128.8 points for his grand ride, and taken over first place by a wide margin.

But it was not to be. Davis had never gone so far in previous 70-meter competitions, and he was not highly ranked on the international jumping circuit. The judges felt that if a low ranker like Davis could nearly outjump the hill, when the European and Japanese superstars made their jumps they might land in the dangerous flat portion below the landing hill. The wind was making the inrun too fast. So the judges nullified all jumps to that point, moved the competitors down one starting gate to shorten the inrun by one meter, and began the event all over again. Jeff Davis's jump was wiped off the books.

The crowd yelled in anger, but John Bower, the U.S. team leader, said later that the judges' decision had been correct. "We have certain safety standards in ski jumping. The judges saw Jeff go and evidently thought other jumpers would go farther and it would be dangerous. If they had carried on and there had been trouble, they would have been open to a charge of negligence."

Jeff Davis (left) of Steamboat Springs, CO, thrills the partisan crowd (above) with a leap of 91 meters in the 70-meter special ski jumping event. The judges decided his jump was too good for his ranking and ordered the competition begun again from a lower starting gate. This would reduce speed and keep the jumpers from landing on flat ground. Davis finished 17th with jumps of 80 and 84 meters.

Though at first disappointed, Jeff Davis was later rather elated. His big jump had thrilled him as well as the crowd, and he and his American teammates were pumped up to a higher competitive spirit. Davis's two official jumps measured 80 and 84 meters, good for 17th place. No American placed higher.

As a teenager at the 1976 Innsbruck Games, Austria's Anton Innauer had flown to a silver medal in the 90-meter jump. Even with Intervale's shortened inrun, the 21-year-old Austrian soldier had jumps of 89 and 90 meters, the two best official jumps of the day. Those leaps, along with high scores for jumping style, netted the vegetarian a total of 266.3 points. Innauer was the gold medalist beyond all doubt. No one else broke 250.

But two men came close. So close that at the finish they could not be separated. Manfred Deckert of East Germany jumped a little farther than Hirokazu Yagi of Japan (85 and 88 meters to 87 and 83.5 meters), but Yagi scored a little higher on style points. When the computers had sorted it all out, each had 249.2 total points. Both received silver medals. A bronze was not awarded.

With jumps of 81 and 72 meters, Stephen Collins had 207.7 points for Canada's best finish (28th). Teammates Tauno Kayhko and Horst Bulau had 205.4 and 180.1 points, respectively, and were 30th and 41st.

As for the American team—after Davis's 17th place finish (226.3 points)—Chris McNeill was 23rd (79 meters, 74.5 meters, 212.5 points), Jim Maki was 26th (81, 72, 208.7), and Jim Denney was a disappointing 36th in a field of 48. Denney managed jumps of only 70 and 75 meters for 192.9 points. But team leader Bower was encouraged. After all, Jeff Davis had gone 91 meters, off the books or not.

In the opening ceremony at Intervale before the start of the 90-meter ski jump finals, the U.S. flag bearer stirs up the crowd. Jim Denney, in eighth place, was the top American finisher. Jouko Tormanen of Finland (below) won the gold medal.

90 Meters

No one outjumped the 90-meter hill, but a few men came close, again too close for the judges' comfort. No jumps were nullified this time, though, and the spectators were thrilled by the sight of contestants jumping 110 meters and more.

Finland's Jouko Tormanen rode the winds of Intervale's 90-meter ski jump on Saturday, February 23, to an Olympic gold medal and a future as a national hero.

"I think I had very good winds and good luck, but I don't know if it was exceptional. I managed to jump very well," said the 25-year-old Tormanen. After a 112-meter practice leap, Tormanen used his body as an airfoil to sail 114.5 and 117 meters for 271.0 points and a wide margin over silver medalist Hubert Neuper of Austria, who totaled 262.4.

Jari Puikkonen, another Finn, placed third with 248.5 points after steady leaps of 110.5 and 108.5 meters. Austria's Anton Innauer, who earlier found gold in the 70-meter competition, was fourth at 245.7.

Hans-Joerg Sumi of Switzerland had a 117-meter effort to lead at the halfway break but dropped off to 100 meters the next time around and finished seventh.

Jim Denney was eighth with 239.1 points. "I looked at the progress I had made all week and thought, realistically, that I

SKIS

Like snowshoes, the name by which they were first called in the pioneer American West, skis are basically extensions of the wearer's feet. Their initial use was to make progress possible over deep and immobilizing snow.

The barrel-stave character of those earliest contrivances has scant relationship with modern skis. Whether they are made for touring or downhill skiing or jumping, present-day skis are finely tuned machines. Their planned use determines their weight, length, width, and material; prescribes the boot that the skier must wear; and dictates the attached hardware that will hold boot and ski together.

Skis can be made of a variety of materials—wood, metal, fiberglass, plastic—or combinations of materials. The use the skier has in mind and the performance qualities desired determine which material the skier selects. All come in assorted lengths, to suit the height and the ability of the user, and cost varying sums, depending on their qualities.

Skis are grouped under three broad heads:

Nordic skis, for sport ski touring or cross-country competition, are the lightest and slimmest. They are the same width throughout—two inches or a little less—and are equipped with a binding that firmly holds the toe of the skier's boot, while leaving the heel free to move up and down as it does in normal striding. Like all skis the Nordic curves up at the tip. It is thicker at the midsection, or waist, than at either shovel (fore part) or tail. A groove on the underside helps to keep the ski straight on the downhill. The Nordic ski is waxed to help with going up- as well as downhill.

Nordic ski boots are characteristically flexible, low in cut, and light in weight, and are equipped with a toe fitting which is gripped by the binding fixed to the ski.

Alpine skis are broader than Nordic, and from tip to heel are shaped so that they are narrowest at the waist and broadest in the shovel section. They are equipped with minimal steel edges which give the bottom a sharp, square profile and make it easier for the skier to turn. The steel can be sharpened with either a file or a grinder.

Bindings on Alpine skis are rugged. They hold both toe and heel, since there is no place for striding in Alpine skiing, and there is a device to release the boot when the skier starts to fall, to prevent injury to the skier.

Alpine ski boots can be leather, plastic, rubber, or combinations. Because their prime function is to give the feet and ankles the strength they do not naturally possess, Alpine boots are very stiff and high.

Jumping skis are longer and heavier than Alpine skis. Sometimes called planks by the jumpers, the skis are half again wider than Alpine skis and weigh up to 16 pounds each. They are made of wood, fiberglass, and epoxy, and to hold them straight on the in-run and out-run have 5–6 narrow grooves in their bottom surfaces. An innovation seen in Lake Placid is a flexible tail, like an aileron, on the jumping ski, to aide in flying. Jumping boots have high backs but their soles are flexible. They are held to the skis by a toe attachment and a heel spring binding, which allows the jumper to raise his heels when he leans forward in flying.

The three types of skis are: the Alpine (held by Franz Klammer and Leonhard Stock), the jumping, and the cross-country.

had a chance to be in the top three, but seven (actually 9.4) points out of the bronze is a very small margin in ski jumping. I'm happy with it," said Denney. At a press conference following the competition, Denney announced his retirement from jumping but said he wanted to stay with the sport as an instructor.

Canada's Steve Collins was ninth with 238.4 points. Walter Malmquist of Post Mills, VT, finished 27th, Jeff Davis, 44th, and Reed Zuehlke of Eau Claire, WI, 45th.

Underscoring the danger of soaring off the 250-foot tower at speeds approaching 60 miles per hour, Sweden's Jan Holmlund lost his balance and crashed 75 meters below takeoff on his first leap. Holmlund, 22, was the only one of 50 jumpers to fall during the first of the two leaps that determine the medalists. He was in good form as he left the end of the ramp but tilted too far forward in the air and plunged to the ground. He landed 75 meters below the ramp and was removed from the hill on a stretcher. Holmlund suffered a broken collarbone.

Nordic Combined

On Monday, February 18th, a group of young men climbed to the top of the 70-meter tower for the start of the two-day Nordic Combined competition. The first day they would jump, and the second day they would run. Run and ski, that is, because the second part of the competition would be a 15-kilometer cross-country ski race. It is an odd combination, jumping and cross-country. They have nothing in common, except that each requires skis, but different skis, at that. Not many men are good at both.

If anyone was favored to win, it had to be Ulrich Wehling, a 27-year-old student from East Germany. Wehling was aiming for his third straight gold medal in the Nordic Combined, having won at Sapporo in 1972 and at Innsbruck in 1976. Although he had had a serious knee injury in 1978 and undergone a complicated operation, he had trained himself back into condition and hit top form just in time for the Olympics. Wehling clearly was the man to beat.

Against this two-time Olympic champion the United States sent 23-year-old Walter Malmquist. A fine jumper, Malmquist also qualified for a spot on the U.S. team in the 90-meter special jump. But he was weaker in cross-country, and he knew he'd have the fight of his life to be even in contention for a medal.

In the special jumping competition, each contestant jumps twice. But in the Nordic Combined, each athlete jumps three times, and only his best two leaps are counted toward the scoring.

Wehling, an excellent ski jumper, held true to form. His two best leaps of 80 and 85 meters landed him in first place after the first day, with a total of 227.2 points. But Malmquist was right behind, with jumps of 79.5 and 84 meters, and 221.8 points. A crowd of about 20,000 cheered his efforts. He was in second place. Hubert Schwarz of West Germany was third. Two of Wehling's East German teammates, Uwe Dotzauer and Konrad Winkler, were fourth and fifth. Swiss Karl Lustenberger was

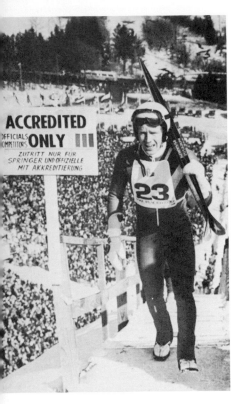

Walter Malmquist of Post Mills, VT, climbs to the top of the 70-meter ski jump for the first part of the Nordic Combined event. To chants of "Walter! Walter!" the personable 23-year-old jumped into second place but wound up 12th overall.

sixth. And in seventh place, waiting impatiently for the cross-country race, was Jouko Karjalainen of Finland.

The scoring of the 15-kilometer race is simple enough. The first finisher gets 220 points. For every minute you come in after the winner, you lose nine points. If you are one minute behind, you get 211 points; two minutes, 202; and so on. On race day, the temperature went up to about the freezing point. The athletes applied warm-weather wax to their skis and took off. Karjalainen sped off along the trails of Mount Van Hoevenberg. He led all the competitiors in, and picked up the most points, 220. But Wehling was no slouch. He was ninth in the race, but only one minute, 40 seconds behind Karjalainen. Wehling scored 205 points for 432.2 overall, and his third consecutive gold medal. Karjalainen's fine race had vaulted him over five men into second place with 429.5 points. He was a silver medalist in his first Olympics. The bronze went to Konrad Winkler, with 425.32 points.

And where was Walter Malmquist? His time for the race was 52 minutes, 54.9 seconds, over 5 minutes behind Karjalainen and 3.5 behind Wehling. He received 173.5 points. "The only reason I didn't do better is that I didn't train enough," said the American. "There are no other excuses."

With two such different disciplines to master, only those who are consistently good in both can hope to win a medal. The top four finishers—Wehling, Karjalainen, Winkler, and Tom Sandberg of Norway—were the only competitors who ranked in the top ten in both jumping and cross-country. Malmquist, by contrast, though second in the jump, was a dismal 27th in the race. However, he wound up 12th overall, with 395.3 points.

Wehling's gold medal made history. He became the first male athlete to win golds in three different Winter Olympics.

Kerry Lynch of Grand Lake, CO, finished 18th with 382.33 points, and Gary Crawford of Steamboat Springs, CO, was 28th among the 29 finishers with 340.18 points. Canadians did not compete in the event.

Coach Jim Page, right, of the U.S. Nordic Combined ski jump team gives instructions during a training session in Lake Placid. Left to right, the jumpers are: Gary Crawford, Kerry Lynch, and Walter Malmquist.

Ulrich Wehling

Inspiration is not enough to win such a tough competition. Years of training are necessary.

—ULRICH WEHLING

Ulrich Wehling could feel comfortably at home as he stood atop the winners' platform to receive his Olympic gold medal. It was the third time the East German skier had taken first place in the Nordic combined event in the Winter Olympics. And it would be the last.

"These Games in Lake Placid are my last Games," said the 27-year-old physical education student. He finished his amateur career gloriously, adding to Olympic history in the process. By winning the combination of 70-meter jumping and 15-kilometer cross-country racing, Wehling became the first man to capture three consecutive Winter Olympic gold medals in the same individual event. Famed Norwegian figure skater Sonja Henie was the only other athlete to have accomplished the feat with her golds in 1928, 1932, and 1936. (Figure skater Gillis Grafström won the gold in three consecutive Olympics, but the first was in the 1920 Games, before the official Winter Games were begun.)

Only two years before, Wehling's career as a top Nordic skier seemed to be over. He suffered a serious knee injury and underwent a complicated operation. But he trained himself back into condition and hit top form just in time for the Olympics. The Nordic combined event, the "crown of skiing," is considered the ultimate test of a skier, and Wehling's comeback victory made him the acknowledged master of his sport.

He did not consider his success a foregone conclusion. "For me the race was not very easy," he said. "I really had a hard time finishing in the time required to win a gold medal."

The challenge of performing two activities equally well first attracted Wehling to the Nordic combination. He has always partaken in several sports at once, and spends his summers bicycling and playing tennis and volleyball.

Life at home in Oberwiesenthal naturally includes athletics. Children Nadja and Tanja will be introduced to sports by Wehling and his wife Eva-Maria, who placed fourth in tobogganing at the 1976 Winter Games. But Wehling also enjoys less physical recreation and can occasionally be found in the kitchen, whipping up a cheesecake.

Following his achievement at Lake Placid, Wehling looked forward to completing his college education and becoming a physical education teacher, or perhaps a coach. He felt that his athletic experience would benefit him in his professional career: "Sport helps one to educate oneself to acquire features which are important in life, for instance determination, courage, willpower, and team spirit." If his mastery of Nordic skiing was any indication, Ulrich Wehling would do very well indeed.

Wehling won his third straight Olympic combined.

NORDIC SKIING CHRONOLOGY

Thursday February 14

Mount Van Hoevenberg Intervale

In the first Olympic cross-country race on artificial snow, Nikolai Zimyatov leads from start to finish in the 30-kilometer race. It is the Soviet Union's third consecutive gold medal in the event. Vasili Rochev finishes second and Ivan Lebanov takes the bronze, becoming the first Bulgarian to win a medal in the Winter Games.

Friday February 15

Raisa Smetanina of the Soviet Union wins her third Olympic gold medal, taking the 5-kilometer cross-country in 15 minutes, 6.92 seconds. Hilkka Riihivuori of Finland captures the silver; by placing third, Kveta Jeriova is the first Czech to win a medal in ski racing.

Sunday February 17

In frigid weather a crowd of 4,000 persons watches Sweden's Thomas Wassberg defeat Finland's Juha Mieto by 1/100th of a second in the 15-kilometer race. With jumps of 89 and 90 meters, Austria's Anton Innauer takes the gold medal in the 70-meter jump.

Monday February 18

Barbara Petzold becomes the first East German to win an individual medal in cross-country skiing. The 24-year-old medical student captures the gold in the 10 kilometers by 3.14 seconds.

In the first stage of the Nordic combined— the 70-meter jump—East Germany's Ulrich Wehling takes the lead. A crowd of 20,000 persons cheers as Walter Malmquist of the United States jumps to second place.

Tuesday February 19

Wehling scores sufficiently well in the 15-kilometer race of the Nordic combined to maintain his lead and win the gold medal. Finland's Jouko Karjalainen, who was seventh in the jumping, is first in the race and takes the silver medal. For the second consecutive Winter Games, East Germany's Konrad Winkler wins the event's bronze medal.

Wednesday February 20

The Soviet Union's men's relay team finds some successful waxing combinations for their skis and wins the 40-kilometer cross-country relay race. Zimyatov, a member of the Soviet team, earns his second gold medal.

Thursday February 21

Four young East German women completely outclass the runners-up Soviet and Norwegian relay teams. The victory is East Germany's first in the women's 20-kilometer relay.

Saturday February 23

Zimyatov is awarded his third gold medal of the 1980 Winter Games as he wins the grueling 50-kilometer race with a time of 2 hours, 27 minutes, 24.6 seconds.

In the 90-meter jump, Jouko Tormanen, a 25-year-old student from Rovaniemi, Finland, totals 271 points (distances of 114.5 and 117 meters) for the gold medal.

MEDAL WINNERS

Men's

	Gold	Silver	Bronze
15-KILOMETER CROSS-COUNTRY	Thomas Wassberg (SWE)	Juha Mieto (FIN)	Ove Aunli (NOR)
30-KILOMETER CROSS-COUNTRY	Nikolai Zimyatov (URS)	Vasili Rochev (URS)	Ivan Lebanov (BUL)
50-KILOMETER CROSS-COUNTRY	Nikolai Zimyatov (URS)	Juha Mieto (FIN)	Aleksandr Zavjalov (URS)
COMBINED	Ulrich Wehling (GDR)	Jouko Karjalainen (FIN)	Konrad Winkler (GDR)
40-KILOMETER CROSS-COUNTRY RELAY	URS (V. Rochev, N. Bazhukov, E. Beliaev, N. Zimyatov)	NOR (L. E. Eriksen, P. K. Aaland, O. Aunli, O. Braa)	FIN (H. Kirvesniemi, P. Teurajarvi, M. Pitkanen, J. Mieto)
70-METER JUMP	Anton Innauer (AUT)	Manfred Deckert (GDR) Hirokazu Yagi (JPN) (tie)	
90-METER JUMP	Jouko Tormanen (FIN)	Hubert Neuper (AUT)	Jari Puikkonen (FIN)

Women's

	Gold	Silver	Bronze
5-KILOMETER CROSS-COUNTRY	Raisa Smetanina (URS)	Hilkka Riihivuori (FIN)	Kveta Jeriova (TCH)
10-KILOMETER CROSS-COUNTRY	Barbara Petzold (GDR)	Hilkka Riihivuori (FIN)	Helena Takalo (FIN)
CROSS-COUNTRY RELAY	GDR (M. Rostock, C. Anding, V. Hesse, B. Petzold)	URS (N. Baldicheva, N. Rocheva, G. Kulakova, R. Smetanina)	NOR (B. Pettersen, A. Boe, M. Myrmael, B. Aunli)

Speed Skating

Speed skating, a European enthusiasm for centuries, has not enjoyed a like popularity in North America. Skating for the joy of moving over the ice on a crisp winter day, yes, and skating as part of a game like hockey. Both have been winter activities in those parts of the country that regularly experience freezing of ponds and lakes, but nothing to match the European interest. In Holland, where the shallow canals remain frozen through long winters, speed skating races long ago achieved the status of the national sport. The Dutch practice of racing in two-man heats (women did not take part) over short, medium, and long courses was adopted elsewhere as the Dutch sport spread to neighboring Germany and France and eventually to other countries.

At a meeting of nations interested in speed skating held in 1892 in The Netherlands, the International Skating Union was founded and races (which had extended over courses of 10, 15, or even 20 miles) were established with lengths between 500 and 10,000 meters, to be known thereafter as the official contests to decide All-Around World Champions. For the next 85 years, until Eric Heiden won it in 1977, the world championship was a European property.

Until a 400-meter oval was built in Lake Placid for the XIII Winter Olympic Games, there was only one refrigerated competition site in the United States where aspiring skaters could train. One result of that fact is that the U.S. speed skaters have usually been a very close group. Close and successful. In spite of the low level of popularity among the general public, this small band of ardent athletes managed to contribute 32 of the total of 94 medals won by U.S. Olympians between the 1924 and the 1980 Winter Games—more than any other sport has accounted for.

Women's 1,500 Meters

There had been hockey before the opening ceremonies at Lake Placid, and some luge running in the evening of opening day, but it was the women's 1,500 on Valentine's Day that began the show for the individual athletic matches of these Winter Games. The 1,500 proved to hold as many surprises as a Mexican piñata. One name, Beth Heiden's, had rung through the pre-Olympic talk about women's speed skating. Not without reason. The petite (5'2") blonde had fixed her green eyes on the 1979 world title, and swept the card. From women of greater experience, whose sturdiness made her look frail, she had taken the 500, 1,000, 1,500, and 3,000 races. A month before the Lake Placid meet, she had finished second overall in the same races. So it did not seem unfitting to hear her described as per-

Competitive speed skating demands long, lonely hours of training. Only two days before the opening of competition at Lake Placid, an Olympic hopeful pushes himself around the oval as the sun begins to set.

Skating in the first heat, Beth Heiden of Madison, WI, speeds through a thick snow to an Olympic record in the women's 1,500 meters. The record didn't last long, however, as six other skaters beat Heiden's time. The highly-touted American took one bronze medal at Lake Placid.

haps the best woman speed skater in the world, or unrealistic to expect to see her in the medal groups for the longer races.

The morning of the 14th was cold, with big, blotchy snow filling the air. There was wind across the 400-meter oval, but not strong enough to prevent new records. Great expectations fairly crackled among the 1,500 or more spectators as Beth Heiden and Sylvia Burka of Canada, who had drawn the first heat, moved to their places. On the inside lane Beth was visibly nerved up; when retired Admiral George O'Connell raised his starting pistol, she jumped the gun.

Both girls hurled themselves down the ice when the gun went off, while the crowd roared. Heiden finished in 2 minutes 13.10 seconds, Burka in 2 minutes 14.65. Both had broken the 1976 Olympic record set by Galina Stepanskaya of the Soviet Union. The crowd was delighted, and the "Bet on Beth" contingent invited attention to their prescience. It was a brief glory. As pair succeeded pair, astonishments multiplied. No fewer than 19 of the 31 women entered completed the 500 meters in less than the old record time of 2:16.58.

When all the times were in, Beth Heiden was in seventh place. She stoutheartedly said the rank was no great surprise to her. "To tell the truth," she told reporters later in the day, "I'm pretty much where I thought I would be. . . . I thought I'd be up there about sixth." The words were faithful to the sporting ideals, but they were not universally convincing. A U.S. teammate, Dr. Mike Woods, said that before the race Beth "looked like Frankenstein."

If the Heiden performance surprised her fans, Natalia Petruseva left hers in total confusion. Only a month earlier she had walked away from the women's world championships with three of the four titles. In Lake Placid she had gone off like a rocket, setting the best performance in the first 300 meters. Up to almost the halfway mark she looked like a sure winner. Then she began to fade, and when she reached the finish line her time was 2:14.15, behind Heiden's, but more importantly, behind that of her paired competitor, Ria Visser of The Netherlands. With three pairs finished, Visser's 2:12.35 was the best time.

The excitement at the track began to abate when Heiden was displaced as number one, first by Visser and then by Bjoerg Eva Jensen, the Norwegian who drew the fourth pair with Sarah Docter (USA). No press promotion had given anyone else the kind of play that creates fan clubs and star gazers. As pair number five skated into position, some of the crowd began to drift off. They missed the biggest surprise of the event.

Those who stayed saw the gold medal won by an unheralded Dutch nurse named Annie Borckink. It was a classic case of the unexpected performed by an unknown. Skating may have had its beginnings in Holland, but no Dutch woman had ever taken a gold medal for speed and it was as plain as a pikestaff that even the Dutch considered Borckink unlikely to do so. Not only had she never won a championship, but her best placing ever in the 1,500 had been a fourth in the world championships. Moreover, anyone might have been forgiven who called her a has-been. She herself was afraid that was true when, in the summer of 1979, she strained her ankle so badly that she had to wear a cast. It cost her a late start in training. "Maybe," said Dick

de Vroomen, the leader of the Dutch team,"that's the secret."

The reddish-haired nurse, at 28 a full decade older than her silver-winning teammate, Ria Visser, had been told after the January world championships that her ninth place showing in the 1,500 was not good enough to qualify her for a Lake Placid spot. But it was going to take more than official discouragement to sideline Annie. Within the month, in Switzerland, she clocked 2:11.35 in the 1,500, handling their "not good enough" back to the Dutch Olympic committee. For her determination she had an Olympic record time of 2:10.95 and a medal. It was the first gold medal of the 1980 games, but far more exciting, it was the first for a Dutch woman speed skater.

Beth Heiden said it for most everyone. "I'm really surprised at the Dutch girls' results. To see Ria Visser and Annie Borckink right up there is a real surprise." Dianne Holum, coach of the U.S. speed skaters and herself the 1972 gold medalist in the 1,500, had counted on the psychological boost to be gained by getting the team off to a great start. That hope was blown.

If the Dutch girls' showing was a surprise, so was Silvia Albrecht's. In the unofficial time trials run in Lake Placid on the weekend before the Games, the East German girl had clocked 2:11.88 in the 1,500, the best time for the distance. Her Placid official time of 2:14.27 put her in ninth place.

Ria Visser clocked 2:12.35, three hundredths of a second better than Sabine Becker of East Germany, who won the bronze medal.

Canada, China, East Germany, The Netherlands, the Soviet Union, and the United States each entered 3 skaters; Great Britain, Japan, Korea, Norway, and Sweden had 2 each; and Finland, West Germany, and Poland had 1 skater apiece. Perhaps the roughest going was experienced by the skaters from China, which was participating in the Winter Games for the first time. Two of them finished 27th and 29th and the third, after being fouled by a Briton, who was disqualified, came in 30th.

Annie Borckink of The Netherlands (above, left) had the best race of her life for a surprise victory in the 1,500. Teammate Ria Visser was second, and Sabine Becker of East Germany (below) was third.

Borckink's best of all possible Valentine's days had proven to be one of the worst for the American women. Even Leah Poulos Mueller, who had Olympic experience to sustain her, felt the emotional letdown. Everyone, she said, was just in awe. "Nobody thought that the Dutch girls would come in one-two, least of all themselves. But things like that happen in the Olympics."

Women's 500 Meters

Nearly half of the hopefuls on the ice oval during the beautiful, sunny morning meet of the women sprint skaters had also been there the day before in the 1,500. Again, there were 31 contestants, again the old Olympic record fell not once but several times, and again a good many fortune tellers were proved to be misreading the cards.

The first couple to race the clock, Ann-Sofie Jarnstrom of Sweden and Makiko Nagaya of Japan, set times of 42.47 and 42.70 seconds, respectively. Both were fractions faster than the

SPEED, HOCKEY, AND FIGURE SKATES

Racing skates say speed by their design, the most obvious feature of which is the very long, thin blade that extends well beyond the toe and heel of the boot. The blade itself is 16–17½″ in length and is set in steel tubing which reenforces it. The long blade gives the racer more push on the ice as the skate is brought down on it at an angle of about 10°. The racer rolls on the blades from the inside to the outside edge. Blades are sharpened daily. The boot of a modern racing skate is very different from the higher-cut sort seen in the first Winter Games. It is cut low on the ankle and to give the needed support must fit like a hand-made shoe.

Hockey skates are much less exotic, and easier to find. The blade curves up in front to join the toe of the boot, and does not stick out behind the heel. The chunky-looking blade bespeaks sturdiness rather than speed. The boot is cut high enough to cover the ankle, and give support.

Skates made for figure skaters and ice dancers are also short-bladed and curved up in front to join the toe of the boot. They extend behind the heel an inch or more. As with hockey skates, blade and boot join without the intermediary of tubing. Both blades and shoes are lighter in weight than hockey skates. Boots are higher cut, extending well up above the ankle. Figure skating blades are sharpened so that the inside and outside edges are distinct.

Karin Enke (left), an 18-year-old East German, won the women's 500 meters by nearly one half of a second. Below, Beth Heiden seems to be leading Natalia Petruseva in the 500, but looks are deceiving on a speed skating oval. The Soviet took third place in the event, Heiden seventh.

time (42.76) that had won Sheila Young (USA) the gold medal in Innsbruck in 1976. Then came the thrill only a dark-horse can provide. Karin Enke, a long-legged 18-year-old student from a sports high school in Dresden, East Germany, cut around the oval so deftly that the clock stopped at 41.78, almost a full second better than the 1976 record.

After she won the championship in the 1980 World Sprint speed skating in West Allis, WI, racing buffs had begun to expect Enke to give a good account of herself. Associated Press sports writer Mike O'Brien called her a sensation in the world sprints who had surprised even herself. Until shortly before she had been concentrating on distance racing. So it was not very surprising that even the German journalists were not predicting just where Enke, who made the East German team in Wisconsin only as an alternate, might show well. She was so new to the sport that she did not have a specialty. Even the East German Olympics officials did not perceive the challenge in the tall (5'9"), powerful teenager. What they knew was that she had taken up the sport after illness and injury had caused her to end a not very promising performance as a figure skater. They saw that, like many beginners, she had trouble with her stance; she skated too upright. And she had trouble changing lanes.

Not so in the 500 in Lake Placid. She had it all together. When the 500 was done, the East German team, which in the past few years has emerged as the greatest challenger to Soviet domination of the Winter Games, collected its first gold medal.

"I'm not fully aware of what's happened to me," the bubbly medalist said through an interpreter. "I feel I will be aware of it only in a few days."

Leah Poulos Mueller brought cheers from the home crowd for her second-place finishes in the women's 500 and 1,000 meters. Her two silver medals brought to four the number of Olympic medals on display at the Mueller household in Dousman, WI. Husband Peter, who did not fare so well at Lake Placid, took a gold in the men's 1,000 at Innsbruck in 1976, where Leah won a silver at the same distance.

The third pair out started Beth Heiden in the inside lane and Natalia Petruseva (USSR) in the outside. Petruseva finished in 42.42, plucky Beth in 43.18.

Petruseva's time won the bronze and Beth's put her in seventh place when all the marks were in. After all the media clamor about the gold-mining Heiden siblings, it was inevitable that comment and question would arise. American coach Dianne Holum said that Beth's middling times were not unexpected and endeavored to establish some perspective.

"First of all, I think people expected a little too much of her. Second, she had to skate the first pair yesterday (the 1,500 meters)—the first pair of the entire competition. And third, she wasn't off the medal by very much." It sounded hollow, somehow.

Pair number four in the draw matched Leah Poulos Mueller (USA) and Cornelia Jacob (East Germany). With 21 years of skating behind her Leah Mueller wasn't expected to have beginner's nerves. Nevertheless, she was keyed up, and with reason. First, she had almost missed the Games because of work. When she got the chance to skate, she couldn't get used to her new team uniform. Now she had two bad starts in her first race of these Games. In fact, her race had to be restarted four times because of two bad starts by each girl. It was a tense situation—a competitor is disqualified after three.

Leah had the confidence and the time in practice to beat Enke, she said, but the false starts broke concentration. "The Games are hard to predict. They happen every four years and you get one shot at each race," said Mueller. "I went to the starting line with the idea I had to wait for the gun and not anticipate it. I was relaxed and ready to go. The starter was consistent. There was a pause between the command and the gun," she said.

The first false start was counted against Jacob.

"From there it was all downhill for awhile. You start to get picky after that, thinking you're doing this wrong and that. Your concentration isn't as good as you want it to be. You don't want to get another false start. And when you do it's nerve-wracking. It's hard to maintain concentration when each of you has two.

"Then we got going and I came on strongest after the first 100 meters."

Her finish was 48 one-hundredths of a second behind Enke's Olympic record-setting performance.

It was the third Winter Olympics for Mueller. In Sapporo in 1972, competing as Leah Poulos, she came in 17th in the 3,000-meter. Then in Innsbruck she won a silver medal in the 1,000-meter, and finished fourth in the 500 and sixth in the 1,500.

In 1978 she retired from skating to work to support her husband, teammate Peter Mueller, whom she married after the '76 Games. She quit skating to become a secretary, saying it was simple economics: the family budget wouldn't support two Olympic training programs.

"I had no thoughts of competing at Lake Placid," she said. "There was no way."

Then she heard of the United States Olympic Job Opportunity Program under which Olympic hopefuls could hold full-time positions with time off to train. She got a job in marketing

with Coca Cola, and sharpened her skates. Leah hadn't lost her winning style. She took the 1979 Women's World Sprint Speed Skating, beating Beth Heiden.

Leah had the distinction of being the first U.S. medalist of the XIII Winter Games.

"I feel privileged, very honored, and I feel very pleased that I was the first to win a medal, especially a silver medal," said Leah. "I like silver," she quipped afterward, beaming.

When all the times were posted—30 of the 31 women slated to race completed the course—there was only 5.47 seconds' spread between the first and the last. Fifteen nations were represented. Again, Annie Borckink skated for The Netherlands, but this time she ranked 22nd. As Leah Mueller observed on day 4 of the program: "There have been so many surprises already."

The medalists in the women's 500 meters—Karin Enke (center), Leah Mueller (left), and Natalia Petruseva—raise their arms in triumph at the award ceremony on Mirror Lake. After confusion at the first medal ceremony the night before, things went more smoothly the second time around, so Olympic officials, too, had something to celebrate.

Men's 500 Meters

As his sister Beth had in her first race, the chance of the draw in his first race gave Eric Heiden what neither like, the first pairing. Being first is being the mark all subsequent skaters shoot at.

In speed skating, as even the tots know, the competitors race in pairs against the clock. And the pairs are determined by the luck of the draw. On occasion, the pairing works out so that the best are together, and that promises great sport. The faster the other person in the pair, the faster both times are likely to prove.

Pair number one had been identified by the crowd at the skating oval; the excitement was all but palpable: Eric Heiden, the American super skater entered in all five men's speed events, and Yevgeni Kulikov from the Soviet Union, the Olympic and world record holder in this event. It was something like having Secretariat racing head-to-head against Affirmed.

They did not speak as they took their places, but each was glad that the other was there. Both had trouble with false starts, but thereafter it went well.

Kulikov got ahead after 100 meters. Heiden caught up on the backstretch. Stride for stride the two dueled for the lead. Gradually the Russian inched ahead toward the last curve. Then came the break. Kulikov slipped slightly, righting himself instantly with his arm. But with a few swift glides, Heiden was ahead—for good. It's just possible that it was by the grace of Kulikov's overeagerness that Heiden was able to gratify the crowd, who were chanting "Err*ric*! Err*ric*! Err*ric*!"

"Those last three strokes coming out of the turn really did it," the 21-year-old American sensation said after he had clocked 38.03 seconds—a new Olympic record—against Kulikov's 38.87. "It was nice to race with him. Throughout the race, you know where you stand with him. I expected him to be one of the toughest."

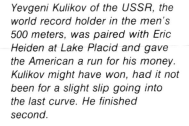

Yevgeni Kulikov of the USSR, the world record holder in the men's 500 meters, was paired with Eric Heiden at Lake Placid and gave the American a run for his money. Kulikov might have won, had it not been for a slight slip going into the last curve. He finished second.

Heiden was obviously happy to have the 500 successfully behind him. He is not considered a pure sprinter, and in the World Speed Skating Sprint Championship a week earlier, Tom Plant, of West Allis, WI, an Olympic teammate (who did not qualify for the 500 in the Olympics) had upset Heiden, winning the 500 by three hundredths of a second. Heiden and Peter Mueller of Dousman, WI, tied for second place. "I was worried about the 500," Heiden said in the days between the Wisconsin meet and Lake Placid, "and still am. A lot of skaters are within a couple of hundredths of a second of me. Weather conditions will be a big factor in the (Lake Placid) 500." Plant said of the World Sprint race, "Any time you beat Eric in anything, you're surprised. The coaches have made us peak for this meet and the Olympics, but I'm still surprised."

Yet another threat to Heiden's peace of mind had appeared in Lake Placid the weekend prior to the Olympics' opening. In the pre-Games time trials Yong Ha Lee of Korea, who deliberately passed up the World Sprint Championships at West Allis, won the men's 500-meter race in 38.56 seconds. That was 0.10 second faster than Tom Plant's World Sprints time.

Kulikov, who still holds the world mark of 37 seconds flat, said he had slipped simply because he was going too fast, not because there was anything wrong with the ice. The mishap marred his concentration.

"I think I would have won if I had been working with my head instead of my feet," the 29-year-old student from Leningrad said.

Twelve of the 36 men who finished the race beat the previous Olympic record of 39.17 seconds for a distance roughly equal to five football fields end to end. All that separated the last from the first were one and 12 hundredths seconds! Eighteen nations were represented, including Mongolia, whose contingent arrived unannounced and so late that the IOC officials in Lake Placid had to scramble to complete their formalities. But the top competition that had been predicted from Canada's Gaetan Boucher, Norway's Froede Roenning, Japan's Kazauke Ishimura, and the Soviet Union's Sergei Khlebnikov had not come up to expectations.

Eric Heiden stood on the awards podium to receive the first gold medal won by a U.S. athlete. At the same time, Yevgeni Kulikov (USSR) accepted the silver, and the bronze was hung around the neck of Lieuwe De Boer of The Netherlands.

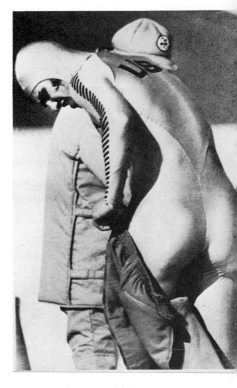

After crossing the finish line in the 500 meters, Heiden went straight for his warmup suit. The thin, nylon racing "skin" cuts wind resistance but does little to keep out the cold.

Men's 5,000 Meters

The 5,000 is a grueling race—even more so than the 10,000, according to some racers—because of the necessity of pacing oneself for 12 laps and the difficulty that entails. The 10,000 is considered by most to be more relaxed. It had been one of Irving Jaffee's triumphs when the Games were held in Lake Placid the first time. Jaffee's time had been 9:40.08, in a competition that had all the hopefuls on the ice at one time, racing each other rather than the clock. Europeans had no liking at all for that untidy American fashion, and their taste had long since prevailed.

Fred Anton Maier did the 5,000 in 7:22.04 in 1968 in Grenoble, and no one had been able to better it in the two succeeding Olympics. When the 5,000 meet began in Lake Placid, Maier's was the oldest standing Olympic record for speed skating.

It was retired on Saturday, February 16—not once, but 17 times! The conditions were not ideal—snow fell steadily and an erratic wind blew—but the track was fast. Officials had to sweep it clear at the turns with every lap of the races. The temperature hovered around 12°F (−11°C). The biting cold made the 12 laps a long chill for each pair of skaters.

Tom Erik Oxholm of Norway and Sweden's Tomas Gustafson were the first pair out. They clocked 7:05.59 and 7:16.85, respectively, both beating the old record.

The second heat paired Eric Heiden with Hilbert Van Der Duim of The Netherlands. The heat began with Heiden on the inside lane, but in or out, it made no difference: Van Der Duim trailed throughout.

As his bent-over form completed each lap, Heiden's eye was on his coach who was on the sidelines computing his times and signaling him either to slow down or speed up. His trust in her judgment was total.

"Dianne has been my trainer for a long time," he said. "She knows how I skate and how I do under different conditions, when I need to be faster or slower. On a longer race that's important."

"It is crucial for a racer to pace himself exactly, to hold his lap time," said Holum. "If a racer is going too slow you hold your hand with your fingers pointing up, each finger representing a second. If he's going too fast you hold your fingers down. That way he knows exactly where he is at all times in the race," the coach explained.

Eric Heiden, center, receives the second of his five gold medals, this one for the 5,000 meters. He is flanked by Kai Arne Stenshjemmet, left, and Tom Erik Oxholm, both of Norway, who won the silver and bronze medals, respectively.

His easy manner, boyish good looks, and five Olympic triumphs made Eric Heiden an all-American hero.

Heiden said he felt neither the cold nor the wind—he was too busy concentrating. He did so to such good purpose that the clock reached 7:02.29—no more. It had helped to have Oxholm go first.

At the middle of his race Heiden was a full four seconds behind Oxholm's time at the same distance. But he picked up almost a full second with each succeeding lap, skating steadily and smoothly, and was out of trouble with about three laps to go.

"We knew Oxholm would give us a good indication of the time we had to shoot for," said Holum. "We weren't worried when Eric was running four seconds behind him. Oxholm had started awfully fast. When you do that you're going to pay in the end for it."

And on the final laps, Heiden—slowly, methodically, without breaking stride—made up the precious seconds to pull out in front and stay there.

In all, 29 skaters gave it their best shots. Many skated better than they had before, and more than half of them beat the long-standing Olympic record. But they were paced by Heiden, and as his seventh-place teammate, Dr. Mike Woods put it, "Eric is a little weird. He can do anything."

At the finish, he pulled off the hood of his gold uniform, and coasted around the oval. He raised his hands several times to acknowledge the roars of the spectators, but he scarcely looked up at them. When he got off the ice, Heiden was asked by a reporter if he thought much about the talk of a sweep of all the skating events.

"It goes in one ear and out the other," he said. "I want to skate well. If I give 100 percent and someone beats me, I'm still happy. I know I've done as well as I can."

While many of the competitors Saturday seemed to suffer after their runs, Heiden appeared in good shape, if tired.

"I didn't feel tired until about five laps to go. Even though it was cold, about 12°F, I didn't feel it. It was kind of nice," he said. "On the last lap, I gave it everything I had at the end."

Then he donned his warmer clothes and his now familiar multicolored cap and continued to circle the inner part of the track.

"My girlfriend gave me the cap. I think she'd probably get mad if I didn't wear it all the time," he said. His girlfriend, reportedly a Norwegian, is named Cecelia. He would not divulge her last name to reporters.

With a time of 7:03.28—99 hundredths of a second behind Heiden's time—Kai Arne Stenshjemmet of Norway, who skated brilliantly, had the silver medal. The 26-year-old public relations man from Lillistrom, Norway, in 1977 set the World record for the 5,000-meter race: 6:56.90. That was in the Soviet Union at Medeo, where the ice and wind conditions are as nearly perfect as can be. Stenshjemmet said he had mixed feelings about his medal.

"I am satisfied, but disappointed," Stenshjemmet said through an interpreter. "I was so close to Heiden. I got tired, that's all. I used my arms one lap too early. I tried to beat the man and I didn't do it. He's No. 1 and I'm No. 2."

The bronze also went to Norway, for Oxholm's 7:05.59.

Women's 1,000 Meters

In little more than an hour on a partly cloudy morning, February 17, 37 women whipped around the 400 meter oval 2½ times, each wanting first to clock a time lower than any other skater there, and then to better the old Olympic record. Only one could accomplish both objects—Natalia Petruseva of the Soviet Union—but no fewer than 10 others finished in less than the old record time. Earlier, one of the U.S. coaches, Peter Schotting, had expressed doubts about the ice oval. Skaters, who are gliders rather than runners, do not like soft ice, which makes gliding difficult. As it turned out, the ice was very fast. But wind was a constant concern, and skaters soon learned to study the direction and force of wind. For the women's 1,000 it fluctuated between 5-10 miles per hour at the start, and 6-11 mph at the end.

Petruseva and Leah Mueller of the United States were the second pair out and they finished in 1:24.10 and 1:24.41, respectively. Silvia Albrecht (GDR), paired in the third heat with Makiko Nagaya (JPN), ranked third, with 1:26.46. Karin Enke

Leah Poulos Mueller struggles to stay ahead of Natalia Petruseva in the 1,000 meters. She couldn't. The Soviet would wear gold, the American silver.

Chilled and winded after giving her all in the 1,000, Beth Heiden still manages a smile as she glides away from the finish line. She took fifth place.

was fourth, Beth Heiden fifth, and undiscourageable Annie Borckink sixth.

Natalia Petruseva, a 24-year-old graduate student in a Soviet sports college, had won the world championship in Norway in January. She arrived in Lake Placid under a cloud of rumors that she had failed a test for illegal drugs after the world championships. Officials of the Norwegian meet denied the reports. But the speculation resumed after her race Sunday when she did not immediately appear at a press conference. Asked to explain what had happened in the testing in January, Petruseva reddened but smiled broadly and replied at length in Russian.

"I had been preparing for the world championships very long and very hard. You can imagine that I was very surprised that I beat Beth Heiden. . . . I was so excited that it took me very much longer than it did for the others to do what the officials wanted me to."

She was referring to the requirement that competitors selected for testing must yield a urine sample.

Petruseva, one of the Soviet Union's top female skaters, is trained by her husband, Anatoly. She began to be a factor in speed skating only after taking time from training to care for her son, Alex.

Leah Mueller also is trained by her husband, Peter, himself a top U.S. team member. The silver medal Leah won in the 1,000, her second in the 1980 Games and the third of her Olympic career, obviously pleased her, but it also made her a little wistful, because it marked the finish of her Olympic career.

Natalia Petruseva brought with her to Lake Placid the women's world championship, which she had taken from Beth Heiden in Norway the month before, amid rumors that she had been aided by illegal drugs. She left with undisputed gold and silver medals in the 1,000 and 500 meters.

After more than two decades of competitive skating, she was going back to private life, perhaps to rearing children "before I get too old to run after them."

Her two events in Lake Placid tested her championship caliber and competitive spirit. In the first, everything seemed to go wrong. Two early starts left her rattled. Then she got off slowly and lost time on the first 100 meters round the ice oval.

In the second event it was just the opposite—everything seemed to go right. She was relaxed. In fact, the night before she went to the movies and watched *Superman*. On the ice, the strong Russian, Petruseva, was an added incentive to do well. "I know she skates really strong races, the way I like to race," Mueller said.

Would she swap her two silvers for a gold? "In my 1,000-meter I would not swap. Natalia said she knew she had it with her race. I knew it, too. In my 500-meter I would have exchanged my first 100 meters, but I can't tell if that would have meant gold or not," she said.

The other American who had been much discussed in relation to the 1,000—Beth Heiden—clocked 1:27.01. It was faster than the 1976 record, but it disproved another of the assumptions that had surrounded the Heidens when it was known that both would enter every speed race in their categories. The reputation that had begun to gather around her brother had so generally transferred to her that she had been touted to parallel him.

It was in vain that she and her teammates said it was wrong to expect her to be a surefire medalist, that she had been caught unfairly in the swirl of acclaim for her older brother.

"If I could have, I would have changed my name last spring when both Heidens became well known in this country," Beth said, laughing, after the 1,000 was over. "The pressure has been really good for my brother. He really knows how to handle it. It's a new experience for me. It kind of bothers me, but what can I say? There's nothing I can do about it."

Beth was not the only one to know that the hopes of the individual athlete and the hopes of that athlete's teammates can translate into impairing pressure. After starring in the 500, Karin Enke began repeating to herself, "I must. I must." Her first trip to the winners' platform was her last.

Men's 1,000 Meters

The race began on the warmest morning (about 32°F, or 0°C) since the competitions started. Before it was done it was both warmer and somewhat windier—up to 21 mph—which gave the later contestants an added struggle in battling the clock. In spite of that, right through the 20th pair to skate, contestants were breaking the 1976 Olympic record set by Peter Mueller. Sixteen in all, Mueller among them, did better than the 1:19.32 set in 1976 when the distance was first made part of the Games. As Denny Allen, the man in charge of making and maintaining the ice on the oval, observed, the skaters were great. Without question, all of them, from all over the world, are better trained than ever. Most of them work with weights, run sprints and distances, and work carefully with coaches.

But the terrific times were due also in large part to the ice itself. It was very fast, and the chance of rain held the prospect that it would become faster by acquiring a glassy surface.

The key in speed skating is to reduce friction. At the 400-meter oval, the one-inch thick ice was made with local water which is low in calcium, according to Allen, and makes fairly low-friction ice. The latest machinery was used to make and

Gaetan Boucher of Canada skated against Eric Heiden in the men's 1,000 and was pushed to a silver medal-winning pace. While others hoped Heiden would retire after the Games, Boucher wanted another chance to beat him.

groom the ice. Compressors raised or reduced ice temperature to compensate for weather conditions.

There was a considerable criticism when the oval here was used for the first time, because of the unpredictable gusts whipping around it. There were also problems with ruts in the ice and dust on the surface. The ice problems were solved, but the oval was in the wind, when wind blew, and that went a long way to explain why world records did not fall along with the Olympic ones. Most of the world marks were set at Medeo.

Gaetan Boucher of Canada skated with Eric Heiden in the first pair out. Boucher achieved 1:16.68, which proved good enough to take the silver medal. It was 1.50 seconds behind Heiden, whose 1:15.18 hung a third gold medal around his neck. Froede Roenning of Norway, skating in the third pair, and Soviet Vladimir Lobanov, in the fourth pair, clocked identical 1:16.91 times, to share the bronze-medal rank.

When the event was over and Heiden was assessing his performance, he was candid, as always.

"It's getting harder and harder to get prepared for each race," he said. "Today I didn't think I was as psyched up as I should have been."

He had paced himself well through the race, and at both the 200 and the 600 meter points his coach's hand signals told him that he was precisely on his planned schedule. On the last backstretch, he seemed to falter slightly, but charged on to a record finish. He had kicked himself in the heel with the blade of his other skate.

On top of three straight victories in the World Championships, Heiden's dominance was so great that other skaters were

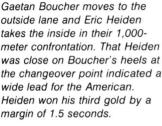

Gaetan Boucher moves to the outside lane and Eric Heiden takes the inside in their 1,000-meter confrontation. That Heiden was close on Boucher's heels at the changeover point indicated a wide lead for the American. Heiden won his third gold by a margin of 1.5 seconds.

Vladimir Lobanov of the Soviet Union (left) and Froede Roenning of Norway recorded identical times of 1:16.91 to share the bronze medal for the men's 1,000.

heard to wish he would hurry up and push off for other things, as he talked of doing.

"That's what we're waiting for," said Froede Roenning. "There's no excitement to racing now. The medals are delivered before the races are run."

But Boucher said he wasn't so eager for Heiden to go away. "I'd like to see him keep skating a few years," he said. "Personally, I want him to keep skating because I'd like to beat him."

The gold for a U.S. skater in the 1,000 marked only the third time since 1952 that the American team had acquired three gold medals in individual events in the Winter Games. For Heiden himself it was another milestone, putting him on a par with three other men speed skaters. In 1936 Ivar Balangrud of Norway took the 500, 5,000, and 10,000 meters—a virtuoso display of sprinting and enduring. Then, in 1952, Hjalmar Andersen took home to Norway the top awards for the 1,500, 5,000, and 10,000. Five Olympiads later, Holland's powerful Ard Schenk repeated Andersen's feat.

Women's 3,000 Meters

A week after the speed skating events began, the 3,000 meters was run. With a temperature near 40°F (4°C) the ice on the oval was glassy and slick, and there was almost no wind. In all, 29 women raced, and a round dozen bettered the Olympic record of 4:45.19 that the Soviets' Tatiana Averina racked up in 1976. Fastest of the dozen was Bjoerg Eva Jensen of Norway, who finished in 4 minutes 32.13 seconds. Only 66 hundredths of a second separated Sabine Becker (GDR) from Jensen, and only 98 hundredths of a second separated Beth Heiden from Becker. Within no more than 10.45 seconds of the medalist rank were Andrea Mitscherlich (GDR), Erwina Rys-Ferens (POL), Mary and Sarah Docter (USA), Natalia Petruseva and Olga Pleshkova (URS), and Brenda Webster and Sylvia Burka (CAN)—all faster than the old record. After she had crossed the finish line, 15-year-old Sarah Docter fell to her knees and crashed into the boards surrounding the oval. Ria Visser (HOL), the silver medalist in the 1,500 meters, fell, crashed into the boards, and could not finish.

Eleven of the skaters' numbers were very familiar. They had competed in all four of the women's contests: Rys-Ferens, Sarah Docter, Petruseva, Burka, Holland's Annie Borckink and Sijtje Van De Lende, Sweden's Sylvia Filipsson and Annette Karlsson, Finland's Anneli Repola, West Germany's Sigrid Smuda and Beth Heiden.

Beth's bronze ended a week of frustration. Before the Olympics convened, the advance publicity had made it all seem so sweet and wholesome and wonderful, this brother and sister who were supposed to cart off all the gold medals in speed skating. There they were, look-alikes in their sleek nylon racing suits, skating out at the nation from the covers of national magazines.

Except for the fact that he is as tall as she is tiny, they did seem a lot alike, with a strong facial resemblance, golden brown hair, and bright, wide smiles.

At 6-foot-1, 21-year-old Eric had earned the description of the best male skater in the world. In three successive weeks in 1977 he had dazzled the skating world by winning the world championship, then the world junior (under 20) championship, and finally the world sprint title—the first person ever to sweep the three championship performance.

Bjoerg Eva Jensen was the fastest of the fast in the women's 3,000 meters. No less than twelve racers broke the old Olympic record of 4:45.19. Sabine Becker of East Germany was a close second to Jensen, and Beth Heiden finished third.

With media pressure and public expectation a heavy burden in each and every event, Beth Heiden should have been proud—and was—of her bronze medal. "She's a tough competitor," said coach Dianne Holum.

At 5-foot-2, Beth was one of the best women in the sport, a former world champion in her own right. But she is not the dominant skater that Eric is. And no matter how nice it was that people had assumed she was, and even though she finally won a medal, the XIII Winter Games were not much fun for the tiny athlete.

After a week of coming up short in the chase for medals Beth tried to seem chipper, laughing as she fielded questions about the sort of pressure she and Eric endured after winning the 1979 world championships. But when Bjoerg Eva Jensen observed, after the 3,000, in which she and Heiden were the first pair, that Beth did not seem to compete with the same fervor that won her the world championship, Beth was candid. "I would agree . . . that I don't have the same fighting spirit; I like to skate for myself. This year, I sort of had the feeling I had to skate for the press, you know." She laughed—but her cheeks were flushed and her eyes moist.

"It got in the way of our family. That's what really got me mad." Pushed for specifics, she began to reply, but her eyes welled with tears; she jerked away suddenly and left the room.

The next day her generally unbreached poise was restored. "There were so many emotions at once," she explained. "I was so happy to be all done and win a bronze."

Eric Heiden signals his fourth gold medal after winning the 1,500 meters. One more would make a handful.

Men's 1,500 Meters

Jan Egil Storholt (NOR), part of the first pair on the ice, knocked down his own 1976 Olympic record, 1:59.32, with a time of 1:57.95. In rapid succession, under a light rain and with a little wind, skaters of pairs 2, 3, 4, 5, 6, and 8 did the same thing. Pair number 4 started Kai Arne Stenshjemmet and Eric Heiden together, but Heiden finished 1.37 seconds sooner than the Norwegian. After 10 pairs had skated, a half hour delay was required to resurface the ice. When the 16 others had had their chance, none had bettered Heiden and Stenshjemmet. Another Norwegian, Terje Andersen, came closest; his 1:56.92 secured the bronze medal.

The powerful, steady strokes of the casual Wisconsin racer had won him an unprecedented fourth gold medal, although it had looked for a moment as though his gold rush would end disastrously in midrace when he slipped on the third turn. He had run over a rut and the ice cracked under him. But he put down his arm and quickly righted himself. And with less than 400 meters to go, he produced a slingshot kick on the next-to-last turn to propel him to the best time.

"I knew somewhere along the line he would have a slip or fall," said Beth, who watched from a ramp near the scoreboard. "He had me a little worried, but I have a lot of confidence in my brother."

Before the race, Heiden was concerned about it, "because you have to get prepared to really suffer. When you're done it hurts a lot." It hurts because it requires a skater to go at the sprinter's pace of the 500, and it is three times as long. The lactic acid that builds up in the skater's legs numbs sensation. Just staying on one's legs can be difficult. In spite of that, and in spite of being up against skaters who were rested, Eric could report afterward:

"It was not as hard as I thought it would be. To tell you the truth, I really feel pretty good."

Before the fourth gold medal was won by Heiden, only one other speed skater had achieved a like feat. In 1964, Lidia Skoblikova, a school teacher from Soviet Siberia, took all four women's events.

Men's 10,000 Meters

Seven thousand fans jammed the bleachers, hundreds without tickets pressed against the chain link fence around the rink, a couple of dozen huddled on top of the portable latrine. They had converged on the oval for the running of the last, the longest, and the most punishing event on the Olympic speed skating card. The best in the distance were entered: Piet Kleine, the Dutch postman who set the Olympic record in 1976; Norway's Tom Erik Oxholm, the European champion; Viktor Leskin of the Soviet Union, the holder of the world record. But the focus

Even in practice, Heiden led the pack. In a workout for the 10,000 meters, his teammate, Dr. Mike Woods, and Masahiko Yamamoto of Japan keep pace. In the main event, Woods was a respectable fourth and Yamamoto seventeenth.

of all eyes was the gold-suited athlete with the easy smile and the chance at a history-making fifth medal.

He had already handed the fans an unprecedented performance—victory in sprints and distance alike. They adored him; their chanting and their hand-lettered banners made that plain. And yet, on this last day of skating competition, he stood in the comfortless position of the absolute beginner who must prove his worth. If, to a success no man had matched, he did not add still another, he would leave the XIII Winter Games a failure.

This race is above all a test of endurance. The 10,000 is more than six miles long and, as Heiden says, "You hurt all over. Your legs have to support you on the turns, the breathing is rough, you're bent over and the last couple of laps it's a struggle to keep your balance." Besides preparing himself for the rigorous physical demands, the racer has to hone himself mentally, thinking out his strategy, his pairing, the possible track conditions.

Heiden had said repeatedly that skating well was his interest, whatever the outcome. But it was clear that he was concerned that he did not match in experience the best competitors at this distance. He had used the day before to rest from the wearing pace of four earlier events and to think hard about the one ahead. He had not wanted to start first, and he didn't have to. The luck of the draw gave him the inside lane in the second pair. First skaters on the rink are, in a sense, guinea pigs. They have to do the most guessing about track conditions. And they have no competitive time to race against.

(Continued page 194)

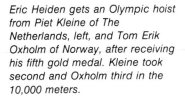

Eric Heiden gets an Olympic hoist from Piet Kleine of The Netherlands, left, and Tom Erik Oxholm of Norway, after receiving his fifth gold medal. Kleine took second and Oxholm third in the 10,000 meters.

Eric Heiden

"It really doesn't matter whether I win or lose, just so long as I do my best."

—ERIC HEIDEN

On the first day, the 500-meter sprint was scheduled, and on the very next day the 5,000 meters, a distance race. Not bad planning, really, since different classes of skaters would be involved. On day 5, there was the 1,000, a longer sprint, and on day 7 the 1,500, the longest sprint. But there was time between those two for the skaters to rest up. On day 9, the last of the speed events, the 10,000 meters was posted—a racking 6-mile endurance race that numbs a skater's legs and makes him wonder if he will ever be able to straighten his bent back. Still, there was plenty of recuperation time between the different sprints and the different distance races.

Plenty, that is, unless you are a skater entered in all five races; then the difficulties multiply. Besides the physical drain, the mental effort to plan each race is taxing. Such an athlete is, in effect, an unrelieved player, facing a fresh team on each occasion.

That he did it, that he won each race, and that he made it all seem so reasonable to expect of him gives the measure of the man inside the gold uniform. No skater has ever before so dominated the sport. By the noon of Saturday, February 23, Eric Heiden had rewritten the Olympic book and shown himself the absolute master of speed skating.

At 6'1" and 185 pounds, with a boyish grin and a gentle, engaging manner, the 21-year-old from Madison, WI, conveys an impression of amiable strength. On the ice, sleeked into his skating skin and poised for the starting gun, his 29" thighs suggesting immense frogs legs, he is a figure of truly formidable power. Enormous strides move him in seconds from standing to speeds close to those of thoroughbreds, speeds his superb physique permits him to maintain.

The golden machine pumps to victory in the 500 meters, establishing a new Olympic record and the pattern of the next four races. Heiden's awesome precision faltered only once: a rut in the ice brought him close to a fall in the 1,500-meter race, but he surged to a gold medal with less than a second's delay.

Eric and Beth Heiden were not brought up to be just Olympians. Says their mother Nancy, "It galls us all that people assume we've raised our children with the sole thought of winning gold medals. . . . Do we really want to idolize people that one-dimensional? Our children are not impressed by the word 'Olympics' or by themselves." Below, nine-year-old Eric poses with his trophy after winning the boys' Pony Division in the 1968 Silver Skates Derbies in Chicago.

He comes explicably by his interest in sports: it's an interest his whole family shares. He was born and grew up in Madison, where his grandfather was the University of Wisconsin ice hockey coach. His father Jack, an orthopedic surgeon, is a champion senior cyclist and his mother Nancy plays competition tennis and skis and skates.

There were those who wondered at the press predictions of success for the U.S. skaters that sounded a steady drum roll of confidence in the days before the Games commenced. Dianne Holum, understandably high on the team she had coached, counted up to 18 medals as good possibilities. "We should get a sweep in the 500, at least two in the 1,000, maybe one in the 1,500, two in the 3,000." Such great expectations fed an eager and growing public appetite. But there were those who thought them exaggerated, and who felt that, like the gold color chosen for the U.S. suit, they were presumptuous.

In Eric's case, neither prediction nor color was in error. He was the champion other cham-

For the whole two weeks at Lake Placid, Heiden seemed never to be without his stocking cap and wide, honest smile, Left, the affable American relaxes with Soviet skater Anatoly Medennikov as they meet during practice.

pions could not catch. Training, at which he was relentless, was a principal reason. While he is obviously an excellent athlete, it was hard work and perseverance, said his coach, rather than sheer natural athletic ability, that made the difference. He is a child of the work ethic, as he says. "I guess I'm kind of weird, but I enjoy being tired. I enjoy knowing I've worked hard."

Skating, as Dianne Holum knew from experience, takes both strength and skill. "A lot of great natural athletes don't want to put out the effort it takes to excel as a skater. Besides the conditioning, it's very technical. You can be very strong, but you can waste energy. Everything has to be perfect—pushing right, where you put your blades, using centrifugal force on the turns."

In terms of its strenuous conditions, the training Heiden and the other skaters of the U.S. Olympic team underwent is not much different from that of a professional football preseason camp. But unlike the pro footballers' six weeks, the skaters generally put in almost a year. Heiden began his regime in May 1979. He worked out 3–4 hours a day five days a week through June. Thereafter, it was two workouts six days a week and one on the seventh. The exercise involved running, cycling, simulated skating, jogging, duck walking, and weight lifting. "There are 30 to 40 repetitions of things," Heiden said. "There are maybe 12 sprints at 400 meters. There is an eight to 15-mile endurance run once a week. I lift 220-pound weights in repetitions until I just can't do them anymore."

After a summer of hard work Heiden and the other Olympic hopefuls met in Colorado for an

intense two-week training camp under Holum's direction. "That was very valuable because we could see exactly where everybody stood," Holum said. "We worked very hard and were able to prescribe what kind of conditioning each individual should have before we could go on ice about the beginning of October."

Lake Placid and the nonstop television concentrated on the athletes there had the effect of making them all larger than life. None more so than Eric Heiden, which was an irony not lost on him. A few weeks earlier, very few of his countrymen knew him or what he does. Speed skating ranks near the bottom of the U.S. sports spectrum in terms of participation and fan interest. Whereas there are 11 Olympic standard 400-meter rinks in The Netherlands and nine in Japan, there are only two refrigerated rinks in North America—one built in 1965 in suburban West Allis, WI, and one in Lake Placid, NY, made for the 1980 Winter Olympics.

An estimated 500,000 speed skaters are trained—many of them with government subsidies—in the Soviet Union. There are only about 4,000 speed skaters in the United States and, says Heiden, "only about 100 are into it seriously."

In Norway, where speed skating has an intensely interested following, a biography of Heiden was published when he became the first American world champion in the twentieth century. The acclaim helped to accustom him to public attention. Between the time he began skating, at 13, and the XIII Winter Olympic Games, Eric had learned how to keep his balance in the glare of adulation. At 17 it had been a great lark to enter the 1976 Olympics, and creditable enough when he finished 7th in the 1,500- and 19th in the 5,000-meter races. He was competing against men who had years more competitive experience. Then, to general disbelief, including his own, the very next year he

Heiden is one exhausted speed skater after his fifth race in eight days, the grueling 10,000 meters. His time of 14:28.13 shattered the world record, and admiring Tom Erik Oxholm of Norway, the bronze medalist, gives a sporting pat on the back.

won the all-around World Championship. And the proof that it was no fluke came the next year, when he again took the championship. He repeated again in 1979, and added the World sprint championship.

Somehow along the route he had learned self control so nearly total that when the pressure seems greatest, he seems coolest.

He never takes anything for granted. "I think about skating the perfect race. I find out about the lane and who I'm paired with. I think over the strategy." Under pressure, says coach Holum, "he's amazingly strong. Pressure helps him concentrate." At the same time that he has learned to deal with the pressure he has acquired considerable practice with the down home one-liners and the good-humored rebuffs reporters love.

His trust in Dianne Holum is complete. His trainer since he was 14, she encouraged him, showed him movies of premier skaters, drew on her own gold-winning experience to develop his potential.

"If it wasn't for Dianne," Heiden says, "I'd probably be playing hockey somewhere. She knows what I can take. I let her select my times. I believe in her."

Even before he reached Lake Placid the clamor of would-be exploiters was growing, and his parents, who worried that their children might be overwhelmed by the hucksters, hired an agent to screen them from the people whose only interest was to turn them into commercial "properties." Both Eric and Beth had taken leave from college, and both said they intended to return, Beth to pursue civil engineering, Eric sports medicine. He said he would like to become a serious cyclist, and to play hockey. And he would *not* like to go commercial, as Mark Spitz and Bruce Jenner had done. "I don't think those guys really thought about it very much," he said.

Before he left Lake Placid for Washington and lunch at the White House with Jimmy Carter, Eric said that at the end of the season he would stop competitive skating. Thereafter, skating would be for his own fun. As to the adulation, "It can be a drag," Heiden says, "I really prefer being obscure. I like to be myself and do what I like without being watched—or even being noticed. Maybe, if things had stayed the way they were and I could still be obscure in an obscure sport, I might want to keep skating. I really liked it best when I was a nobody."

Having reached the top in speed skating, Heiden began the pursuit of excellence in other areas—medicine and bicycle racing.

Heiden's chief threat was Tom Erik Oxholm, who chased him in the 5,000-meter event and finished third for a bronze. He also was wary of his teammate, Mike Woods. Oxholm and Woods were the opening pair, which meant Heiden knew their times before he raced—a help in pacing as he stroked the laps.

Heiden and Leskin were pair number two. Dianne Holum had advised Eric to skate the first 12 laps at about 34½ seconds each, dropping to 35 thereafter. But Oxholm and Woods posted times that jolted him.

"I didn't expect the times to be as fast as they were, but after seeing Woods and Oxholm skate, God, I was scared!" he said. "I just had to go out and go for it."

In the first lap, Leskin was behind by 10 hundredths of a second. Then he gained, and for the next 11 laps his times were better than Heiden's. On the 13th lap Heiden began to gain, his times bettering Leskin's by 16 hundredths of a second, then 80 hundredths, then 1.55 seconds, until the 16th lap showed 7.76 seconds' difference between them. Leskin was vanquished. Holum began signaling Eric to slow down, telling him that he was racing ahead of his own schedule. Heiden just kept gaining.

He crossed the finish lane, and went around another lap, still crouched over, obviously in pain. "I kept thinking how nice it was going to be to stand up again," he said. When he did, it was to the tumultuous cheers of the crowd. With the clock at 14:28.13 the new Olympic record, set only minutes before by Tom Erik Oxholm, and the world record were both in the dust. The only skater in the men's events who competed in all five events had, with his steady, powerhouse stroke, turned the speed skating into a one-man event.

At the White House welcoming ceremony for the U.S. Winter Olympic team, President Jimmy Carter put Heiden's achievement in the proper perspective: "Eric Heiden will take his place in Olympic history along with greats like Jim Thorpe, Jesse Owens, Mark Spitz, Nadia Comaneci, Jean-Claude Killy, and others who have distinguished themselves in an extraordinary way."

The silver medalist, Piet Kleine, had gone into the race thinking he could beat Heiden. "I tried but I just couldn't. I did my best. In the last eight rounds I came a little too short," he said. "At this moment I don't think there is anybody who can do the 500 and 10,000 to catch Heiden."

Twice, in the 5,000 and then in the 10,000, Tom Erik Oxholm had thought *he* could beat Heiden. Both times he finished third, for bronze medals.

Besides the three medalists, Mike Woods in fourth place, Oeyvind Tveter (NOR) in fifth, and Hilbert Van Der Duim (HOL) in sixth broke the 1976 Olympic record. They merited greater acclaim than they received at the moment from the wildly cheering fans. In the blaze of Heiden's triumph, it was hard to distinguish lesser lights.

SPEED SKATING CHRONOLOGY

Lake Placid High School Oval

Thursday February 14 Annie Borckink and Ria Visser of The Netherlands set the first, second times in the women's 1,500-meter event. East Germany's Sabine Becker is third, among 30 contestants, 19 of whom better the old Olympic record. All three Dutch, Soviet, and American entrants are among the record breakers.

Friday February 15 The women's 500, begun at 10:30 A.M., ends with a surprise gold medalist in Karin Enke of East Germany. Leah Mueller captures the silver, giving the United States its first medal of the Games.
Within two hours, Eric Heiden gets the second U.S. medal and first gold, setting a new Olympic record in the men's 500.

Saturday February 16 For the first time in 48 years an American wins the 5,000, again at Lake Placid, where Irving Jaffee triumphed in 1932. This time the champ skates the clock, rather than the pack.

Sunday February 17 Two women who had interrupted their skating for family reasons, and who were paired in the 1,000 meters, come in 1, 2 in the awards: Natalia Petruseva (URS)

and Leah Mueller (USA). The old Olympic record is tumbled not once but 11 times.

Tuesday February 19 Heiden takes his third gold medal in as many races; this time it is the 1,000 meters. Afterward he remarks that it's getting harder to prepare for each race. His competitors hope it is.

Wednesday February 20 In the women's longest race, stouthearted, oversold Beth Heiden gets a bronze, bringing to three the number of medals won by U.S. women skaters.

Thursday February 21 In light snow Eric Heiden wins the 1,500 meters, sets a new Olympic record, becomes the first male skater to win four different distances and the first man to win four golds in the same Winter Olympics, and gives the United States its best showing ever in the Winter Games.

Saturday February 23 Heiden, the golden lightning bolt, strikes a fifth time, breaking both Olympic and world records for the 10,000-meter race, so powerful that his last 3 laps are successively faster. Membership in his class: 1.

MEDAL WINNERS

Men	Gold	Silver	Bronze
500 METER	Eric Heiden (USA)	Yevgeni Kulikov (URS)	Lieuwe De Boer (HOL)
1,000 METER	Eric Heiden (USA)	Gaetan Boucher (CAN)	Froede Roenning (NOR)
			Vladimir Lobanov (URS)
1,500 METER	Eric Heiden (USA)	Kai Arne Stenshjemmet (NOR)	Terje Andersen (NOR)
5,000 METER	Eric Heiden (USA)	Kai Arne Stenshjemmet (NOR)	Tom Erik Oxholm (NOR)
10,000 METER	Eric Heiden (USA)	Piet Kleine (HOL)	Tom Erik Oxholm (NOR)
Women			
500 METER	Karin Enke (GDR)	Leah Mueller (USA)	Natalia Petruseva (URS)
1,000 METER	Natalia Petruseva (URS)	Leah Mueller (USA)	Silvia Albrecht (GDR)
1,500 METER	Annie Borckink (HOL)	Ria Visser (HOL)	Sabine Becker (GDR)
3,000 METER	Bjoerg Eva Jensen (NOR)	Sabine Becker (GDR)	Beth Heiden (USA)

Arts Festival

"Slalom racing," a 41″ × 29″ work by B. Fuchs, was exhibited at the 1980 Olympic arts festival.

Poetry readings and jazz concerts do not spring to mind as Olympic events, and athletic rather than aesthetic achievement is certainly the focus of the Games. However, while the average Olympic enthusiast did not travel to Lake Placid to stroll through an art exhibit or attend the premiere of a new play, these events were part of the 1980 Olympic festivities. Through the efforts of the National Fine Arts Committee of the LPOOC, Lake Placid was the scene of the largest Olympic arts festival ever presented in the United States.

"The Olympic Movement is intended to bring together in a radiant union, all the qualities of mankind which guide him to perfection." So declared Baron Pierre de Coubertin, prime mover in the establishment of the modern Olympic Games. Coubertin was inspired by the ancient Greeks, who sought a perfect union of mind and body and placed the artist on equal footing with the athlete. Competitions in music, poetry, and drama were often included during the gatherings at Olympia, and winners in these categories, too, were awarded the coveted olive wreath.

The arts played a key role in honoring victorious athletes; statues carved by such renowned sculptors as Phidias commemorated the champions, and odes composed by distinguished poets were spoken at victory feasts. The odes, such as those written by the great lyricist Pindar, celebrated the athlete and his family in an operalike combination of poetry, music, and dance. Thronging spectators at the games were addressed by orators like Gorgias and Isocrates, who seized the opportunity to reach an audience gathered from the entire Hellenic world. It is believed that the historian Herodotus read from his great work at Olympia.

To emulate the Greek celebration as closely as possible the founders of the modern Games decreed that fine arts should be part of the Olympics. The 1912 meet in Stockholm was the first to have a fine arts program. In that year, competitions were held in Design for Town Planning, Architectural Design, Sculpture, Painting and Graphic Arts, Literature, and Music. In later Olympics Medal Design; Drawing and Water Coloring; Posters, Diplomas, Stamps, and Seals; Wood and Copperplate Engraving; Etching; Lithographs; Lyrics, Drama, Novels, and Epics; and Music for voice, for one instrument, and for orchestra were all endeavors for which medals were to be awarded. Not surprisingly, the prizes went to efforts that idealized sport, planned new sport stadia and arenas, or hymned athletic perfection.

The contests ended after the 1948 Games and the responsibility for a fine arts program was left to the host country. According to International Olympic Committee rules, the Organizing Committee must arrange exhibitions and demonstrations of architecture, literature, music, painting, and sport philately.

Preston Brooks and Joanna Merlin were featured in Nancy Donohue's romantic comedy, "The Beach House." The play, presented by the Long Wharf Theatre, was part of an ambitious performing arts program at Lake Placid that included music, drama, dance, and mime.

In addition, theatrical, ballet, and opera performances, and symphony concerts may be included in the program.

The arts had been ignored at the two previous Winter Games held in the United States, in 1932 at Lake Placid and in 1960 at Squaw Valley, CA. The Lake Placid Fine Arts Committee was determined to make up for that neglect. Committee chairwoman Carolyn Hopkins anticipated that the 1980 Games would ''bring together the leading artists of our nation and the athletic talent of the world in an exciting festival of sports and art which has never before been experienced in this country.'' Funded by federal, state, and private donations, the program was an ambitious one, encompassing many facets of the performing and visual arts.

Lake Placid and the surrounding area were peppered with displays and events intended to echo the excitement generated by the athletic competitions. Special exhibitions were held at the nearby communities of Saranac Lake and Tupper Lake, and at Plattsburgh, 47 miles northeast of Lake Placid. In Lake Placid, the Center for Music, Drama and Art (CMDA) and the Agora Theatre housed many of the program's indoor events.

Four original works were performed for the first time at the 1980 Olympics. The Long Wharf Theatre of New Haven, CT, one of America's leading repertory theaters, performed *Beach House,* a new play by Nancy Donohue. The Long Wharf is famous for its discovery and promotion of important new American plays. Acclaimed violinist Yehudi Menuhin, honorary chairman of the National Fine Arts Committee, joined the Cantilena Chamber Players to premiere a work by composer Lukas Foss. The composition, entitled ''Round a Common Centre,'' was deemed abstruse and overly complex by some listeners, but virtuoso performances by Mr. Menuhin and the Adirondack-based Cantilena Players captivated the audience. New works were also introduced by the Los Angeles Chamber Orchestra and the Pilobolus Dance Theatre. The Los Angeles group, one of the few chamber orchestras in the United States, featured Mikhail Pletnyov, winner of the Tchaikovsky Piano Competition, as soloist. Pilobolus, an innovative group that incorporates acrobatics into its dance routines, emphasized the link between art and athletics that was an underlying theme of the arts festival. The uniquely American sound of jazz throbbed over Lake Placid, courtesy of the versatile Jazzmobile. This group, headed by pianist Dr. Billy Taylor, has spread the message of jazz across the country through numerous outdoor concerts, lectures, and workshops.

''Interaction artists'' brought the festivities outdoors, scattering throughout the village and onto the ski slopes and bobsled runs. Entertaining passersby with their impromptu performances were storyteller Jay O'Callahan, magician Craig Collis, and an assortment of mimes and street performers.

The visual arts, too, spilled out into the streets and environs of Lake Placid. Colorful banners designed by local children dotted Olympic routes, and environmental art offered new perspectives on local landscapes. Notable in the latter category was Richard Fleischner's ''Covered Fence and Fence,'' located in a meadow across from the Intervale ski jumps. The wooden frame structure, reminiscent of a racecourse starting gate, repeated the rectilinear form of a nearby row of cedar trees, invit-

Several of the 25 musicians of Jazzmobile entertain a Lake Placid audience. Jazz, indigenous to the United States, was a fitting addition to the arts program, which showcased American talent.

ing a fresh interpretation of the natural scene. Two murals and four outdoor sculptures were commissioned to enhance the Olympic site and will remain as enduring tributes to the 1980 Games. In addition, an ''all-weather'' fountain dedicated to figure skating champion Sonja Henie was created by Norwegian artist Carl Nesjar. The shimmering drops of water that spray from the fountain in warm weather freeze in winter, creating an entirely different visual effect. The aluminum fountain is situated in front of the Olympic Ice Center.

Displays of American artistic talent sprouted inside the sports-dominated Olympic centers and arenas, and in more traditional gallery settings. Included were American Indian art, American crafts, fine arts photography, and the works of twelve American painters who, according to the committee, ''are expected to make a major impact during the '80's.'' More obviously pertinent to the Olympic Games was the exhibit by television sports director Robert Riger. Entitled ''The Athlete: An Influence on American Life,'' it employed photographs and slow-motion videotapes, set to music, to trace 25 years of sports in America.

Children's art added sparkle, starting with the bright banners created to herald the Games. In addition, a display called ''My Neighbor and My Neighborhood,'' presented by UNICEF, featured the artistic efforts of children from 135 countries. Other works of international children's art were sponsored by the Ewing Museum of Illinois State University and the New York State Education Department.

Stamp collectors were delighted by the exhibition of Olympic philately, which included an international collection of stamps, early postcards, and the first commemorative stamp.

All events, excepting the stage and musical performances, were available free to Olympic athletes and officials, Olympic event ticket holders, and area residents.

Inevitably, and in spite of the months of meticulous preparation, the arts were subordinate to the sporting events. Transportation problems and insufficient publicity hurt attendance at many performances, causing artists to complain of neglect and shabby treatment. The biggest upset occurred when the Los Angeles Chamber Orchestra, citing a salary dispute and poor lodging conditions, canceled a second performance and left town. Yet, forcing a way past all the traffic snarls, disappointments, and bureaucratic gaffes, artistic creativity bloomed in the frigid air of Lake Placid, leaving little doubt that the Winter Olympics were indeed a festival for the whole person.

Nancy Holt's ''30 Below'' (above), a 30-foot tall tower of red brick, was sited according to the points of the compass and aligned with the North Star. It was a striking contribution to the environmental art at Lake Placid. Yehudi Menuhin (left), violinist and humanitarian, lent his immense prestige to the performing arts program.

199

The Closing Ceremony

The flags of all participating nations were brought in by their athlete bearers.

The XIII Winter Games stepped into history on Sunday night, February 24, after thirteen days that belonged to Eric Heiden and to hockey. Perhaps most to hockey. Heiden had been expected to do well, but the hockey players, a faceless team of college boys and minor leaguers, seeded seventh in a rank of twelve, had not. Their startling success had caught up the whole of America in elation, and had taken away much of the sour taste that problems of transportation and politics had engendered in Lake Placid. In the prior months there hadn't been much to cheer about. Iran held 50 diplomatic persons hostage. Détente was cracking up. Energy was sapping everyone's pocketbook, and inflation was heading for the moon. In Lake Placid there were grumblings about the accommodations when the athletes got there, and bursts of angry criticism when the ticket-holding public did not. The Games touted as the "Olympics in Perspective" gave promise of being one more in Uncle Sam's eye.

And then it changed, for two principal reasons: a gold-suited skater kept tearing around the ice, setting record after record; and a patchwork bunch of scrappy, never-say-die players, together less than six months, licked the Big Red Machine that had ground up pros and amateurs alike.

Purists like to remind us that there is no room for nationalism in the Games: they are built on the concept of individual competition, in which winning is unimportant. Forget the anthems, the flags, the medal standings; the main thing is to compete. That's the ideal.

From its tower where it had flamed, day and dark, throughout the Games, a portion of the Olympic fire was taken into the Fieldhouse, where spectators crammed every possible space.

Just so. But that's not the way it is. The Olympic Games are contests among human beings, with human desires, prides, jealousies, and loyalties. By their very nature, the team sports especially are a square-off of ideologies. Nationalistic feeling runs high, as Jesse Owens understood. "If there were no national pride, flags and anthems, and desire to win, you might as well hold the Games in somebody's backyard."

George Christian Ortloff, the 30-year-old native of Lake Placid charged with organizing ceremonies that, within the restrictions of IOC rules, would be interesting as well as simple and dignified, had labored mightily to meet the challenge. Given the joyous mood of the final-night spectators in the Olympic Fieldhouse it would have been hard to fail.

The prescribed ceremony was delayed more than 30 minutes by yet another muddle. The crowd that had gathered to watch a figure skating exhibition collided with the ticket holders for the closing ceremony, causing mass confusion. Falling snow and temperatures, delay, confusion—nothing could dampen the spirits of the sellout crowd of 8,500, or shake their certainty that the show was worth waiting for.

They watched the maneuvers and listened to the fanfare played by the Fort Ticonderoga Corps of Drums. John Curry of Great Britain and Dorothy Hamill of the United States, the figure skating gold medalists in 1976 at Innsbruck, put on exhibitions of the skill and grace that won their honors.

The athletes and flagbearers trooped into the arena, mingling without formal distinction of nationality. The flagbearers formed a semicircle behind the rostrum where Lord Killanin, the president of the International Olympic Committee, took his place beneath the flags of Greece, the United States, and Yugoslavia. The president's closing speech is a set piece, by tradition. Kil-

The bearers of Olympia's flame, above, joined the massed athletes on the ice, where Lord Killanin waited to give the farewell.

lanin pronounced it, as prescribed, through to its concluding call "upon the youth of all countries to assemble four years from now at Sarajevo, Yugoslavia, to celebrate with us the XIV Olympic Winter Games."

Then, in a departure from tradition, Killanin made an impromptu speech.

"I feel these Games have proved that we can do something to contribute to mutual understanding in the world—an understanding which is without race, creed, or color, [that emphasizes] what we have in common and not what our differences are. If we can all come together it will be for a better world, and we can perhaps avoid the holocaust which will be upon us if we are not careful."

The keyed-up crowd cheered Killanin wildly.

As a fanfare was sounded, torchbearers brought in the Olympic flame, which was extinguished for another four years. To the strains of the Olympic hymn, the Olympic flags in the fieldhouse and on the horseshoe grounds were lowered simultaneously. Five aerial salutes were set off at the speed skating oval, the scene of Heiden's quintuple triumph.

At the end of the ceremony children skated on to the ice and presented flowers to the athletes, who tossed blossoms into the cheering crowd. Then folk dancers in the costumes of the last century joined dancers in traditional Yugoslav dress in a symbolic representation of the passing of the Winter Games from America to Yugoslavia.

Outside, in a night of gripping cold, the celebrators who would not quit enjoyed a last display of fireworks. Within hours Olympic Lake Placid would be gone—like Brigadoon, vanished from the world's sight. But—like Brigadoon—never to be forgotten by any who saw it.

Indoors and out, the flame was extinguished. The Games were done. At once, children sped onto the ice, to begin a final pageant.

Who's Who at the 1980 Winter Olympics

MONIQUE BERLIOUX

As director of the International Olympic Committee (IOC), 54-year-old Monique Berlioux is one of the world's most influential sports administrators. With all of the crises that the Olympic movement faced in 1980 —the boycott of the Summer Games in Moscow, the debate over the participation of Taiwan in the Winter Games, and problems at Lake Placid ranging from transportation to protocol—she was also one of the most assailed.

Often caught in the eye of the storm, Berlioux presided over news conferences and briefings with toughness and self-assurance. Although critics of the IOC characterize her as stiff, crusty, and shrewd, Madame B., as she is known, sought above all to resolve these Olympic-size problems fairly and in good faith. F. Don Miller, the executive director of the U.S. Olympic Committee (USOC), described Berlioux—the only female voice on the 89-member IOC and its only salaried constituent—as strong, tough, and fair. Berlioux attributes these qualities to her experience as an amateur athlete. "Sport teaches you to fight, but you have to last a little longer to win," she says. "And you have to be fair.

Otherwise, people won't trust you. It's easier to tell the truth."

Born Dec. 22, 1925, in Metz, France, Monique Berlioux received her bachelor and master of arts degrees at the Sorbonne. As a young swimmer she won more than 40 titles, set numerous national records in France, and reached the semifinals at the 1948 London Olympics. Before going to work at the IOC offices in Lausanne, Switzerland, in 1967, Berlioux was a reporter for several French newspapers. She had been a television producer and director and had worked for the French Ministry for Youth and Sports.

Feb. 29, 1980, marked the 24th anniversary of her marriage to Serge Groussard, the French writer. "We have an anniversary every four years," jokes Berlioux.

GAETAN BOUCHER

In the years to come Canada's Gaetan Boucher can always say that he was one of four speed skaters to finish in a runner-up spot to the five-time gold medalist Eric Heiden at the 1980 Winter Olympics. (Norway's speed skater Kai Arne Stenshjemmet did it twice, and earned two silvers.)

On February 19, Boucher, a 21-year-old clerk from Charlesbourg, Quebec, completed the 1,000-meter race 1.5 seconds behind Heiden. For that, he won a silver medal, the only Canadian to do so at Lake Placid. He and Heiden were the first pair to skate in the 1,000-meter event. He also competed in the 500 and 1,500 meters, where he was not even close to a medal, finishing 8th and 15th, respectively.

The Olympics were not new to Gaetan Boucher in 1980. At Innsbruck in 1976 he had placed 6th in the 1,000 meters and 14th in both the 500 and 1,500 meters. And he was far from unaccustomed to international contests. He was first in the 1977 World Indoor Championship.

After finishing second at the 1979 World Championship and at the World Sprint and sixth at the World Indoor, he was named Ca-

Monique Berlioux is director of the IOC.

Gaetan Boucher won Canada's only silver.

nadian speed skater of the year for 1978–79. He took first place in the 1,000 meters at the Madonna Di Campiglio International in 1980.

After Heiden won his third gold medal, Norwegian skater Froede Roenning said the other skaters wished Eric would hurry along with career plans, so others could win some races. But Boucher expressed another view: he wanted Heiden to continue competing, so he could beat him.

ART DEVLIN

Perhaps Lake Placid's most famous native son, Art Devlin distinguished himself as a World War II bomber pilot, a ski jumper, and a color commentator for ABC-TV's *Wide World of Sports*. Active in community affairs for his whole adult life, he worked for 17 years to help bring the Olympics back to Lake Placid. For the XIII Winter Games, Devlin served as vice president of the Lake Placid Olympic Organizing Committee (LPOOC), as well as a member of the LPOOC Executive Committee and the Marketing and Television Committee.

As a boy, his first love was ski jumping. Art and a friend once built a ski jump with a takeoff point on the roof of the Main Street movie theater and a landing area in a vacant lot across the street. Although he never won an Olympic medal, Devlin jumped in the Winter Games of 1948, 1952, and 1956, as well as countless other national and international competitions. He was U.S. Eastern Ski Jumping Champion in 1942, 1946, 1949, and 1950; North American Ski Jumping Champion in

1949, 1950, and 1954; set the North American distance record of 307 feet in 1950; and set the world ski flying record of 436 feet at Obertsdorf, Germany, in 1952. In 1963 he was elected to the U.S. Ski Hall of Fame.

Devlin attended Syracuse University prior to his military service in the European Theater of Operations. He has been involved with the Olympics as a commentator since 1964 and has appeared in two movies, *Red River Valley* and *Northside 777*.

Art Devlin is married and has three children. He still lives in the house in which he was born and operates the Art Devlin Olympic Motor Inn in Lake Placid. A display case in the lobby contains his many jumping medals and trophies, along with his Distinguished Flying Cross and Purple Heart earned as a pilot.

KEN DRYDEN

After eight years of throwing his body in front of hard, fast-flying hockey pucks, Montreal Canadiens goaltender Ken Dryden decided to pack away his skates, bid adieu to the rough-and-tumble world of the National Hockey League (NHL), and pursue the more peaceful career of an attorney-at-law. Hired by ABC to give expert commentary on the 1980 Olympic ice hockey tournament, the multi-talented Dryden made millions of sports fans wish that he might someday hang his barrister's wig alongside his goalie's mask and plant himself permanently behind the microphone.

In his first television appearance as an announcer, Dryden teamed with veteran sportscaster Al Michaels (who hadn't done a hockey game in 8 years) in providing incisive, well-informed, and refreshingly candid commentary on the most-watched sport of the 1980 Winter Games. Having played against the Soviet National team several times in the Challenge Cup series against the NHL, Dryden was able to enlighten viewers on the nuances in style of international amateur hockey, the strengths and weaknesses of individual players, and the execution of team strategies. What made his commentary all the more impressive was that it was part of a juggling act. At the same time that he was preparing for his on-the-air debut, Dryden was also studying for the Ontario provincial bar examination. After announcing the games on Thursday night, February 14, he drove to Ottawa for two five-hour parts of the test and returned to Lake Placid for the matches on Saturday.

Kenneth Wayne Dryden was born on Aug. 8, 1947, at Islington, Ont., Canada. A small, serious-minded boy growing up in a Toronto suburb, Dryden imagined a way of life that would combine goaltending and scholarship. At Cornell University he distinguished himself in both areas, winning All-American honors three times and compiling a high-B average in the field of government. In his eight years with the Montreal Canadiens, the 6'4", 210-lb goalie won the Calder Trophy (rookie of the year) in 1971–72 and won or shared the Vezina Trophy (best goalie) five times (1972–73, 1975–76, 1976–77, 1977–78, and 1978–79). He also led the Canadiens to five Stanley Cup championships. When he was not stopping slapshots, Dryden was studying at the McGill University Law School in Montreal and working with Ralph Nader's "Raiders" as an expert on water pollution litigation.

THE REV. J. BERNARD FELL

The Rev. J. Bernard Fell, a 57-year-old Methodist minister, served as president of the Lake Placid Olympic Organizing Committee (LPOOC). As such, his objective was "to stage the finest Winter Games possible in keeping with the objective of an 'Olympics in Perspective!' "

Unfortunately, an inadequate and poorly organized ground transportation system marred the Games' Opening Ceremony and the early days of competition. Fell's irritated suggestion of a solution to the crisis—hold the competition without spectators—subjected him to some ridicule.

The Rev. Fell was selected as president of the LPOOC on Jan. 17, 1979, following the death of Ronald M. MacKenzie. A longtime winter sports enthusiast, Fell had served as the executive director of the committee since its formation in 1974 and had been executive director of the Lake Placid Sports Council since 1964. Of his service to the Lake Placid Games, he said, "It's been a long six years and we have had our difficulties, but I have just loved the whole thing."

Prior to his ordination as minister of the Methodist Church in 1970, Fell had spent 20 years as a member of the Lake Placid police force, was the community's fire chief, and had been a town councilman and the first president of the Lake Placid Junior Chamber of Commerce.

Following his ordination, the Rev. Fell became pastor of the United Methodist Church in Bloomingdale, NY, 16 miles from Lake Placid, a post he still holds. According to Fell, "it's a little church, with great people. They were all involved in the Winter Games in some way or other."

A cross-country skier and a world luge judge, Fell is a native of Lake Placid. He and his wife, Doris, have two children.

LINDA FRATIANNE

Linda Fratianne's Olympic medal didn't glitter with gold, but its luster mirrored the years of effort that led to her outstanding performance at Lake Placid.

Winning an Olympic medal had been Linda's goal for nearly half her life. She has been at home on ice ever since, at age nine, she found her first pair of skates lying under the Christmas tree. Before long, the petite skater from Northridge, CA, was executing complicated jumps and spins in whirlwind style—

Figure skater Linda Fratianne was a silver medalist.

and carving a name for herself in international competitions.

She finished eighth in the 1976 Olympics at Innsbruck and followed Dorothy Hamill as U.S. champion the next year. She won the world championship in 1977, but lost it to Anett Poetzsch of East Germany in 1978. One year later, tempering her athleticism with a more expressive style, Fratianne regained the title.

To prepare for her Olympic challenge, Fratianne sought to improve her image. A new hairdo and a medical and cosmetic operation on her nose helped her on-ice confidence. "I was pretty shy and within myself," she said. "Now I'm not as timid." Coach Frank Carroll also worked on Linda's skating personality, occasionally drawing criticism for being too manipulative. He aimed for a "sexier" image, as indicated by his choice of a brilliant red costume and Spanish music for his student's Olympic routines.

In skating, the glamor of the final performance belies the drudgery of the daily routine. Six days a week, Linda was up by 5 A.M., to be taken to the rink by her mother for practice. After a two-hour break, she went to another rink, 40 miles away, for an afternoon session. Her practice also included gym workouts and twice-a-week ballet classes. Bob Fratianne, a judge with five children to support, estimates the skating expenses of his third child at $12,000 a year.

At the climax of all this intense preparation, Linda Fratianne came in second. Although her mother and her coach complained of biased judging, Linda accepted her silver medal with good humor. "I didn't think I could have skated any better," she said.

SCOTT HAMILTON

Scott Hamilton, a 21-year-old figure skater from Haverford, PA, had the honor of carrying the American flag and leading the U.S. team during the Opening Ceremonies at the XIII Winter Olympics. The popular performer said that he was "really proud" to carry the flag but that it was "tough to describe" his exact feelings about the honor. Calling himself the patriotic sort, Hamilton went on to say that when he thinks about it he gets a big lump in his throat.

Scott was in the Olympic Village watching the movie *Close Encounters of the Third Kind*

Scott Hamilton was honored to carry the U.S. flag.

when he learned that the captains of the different U.S. Olympic teams had unanimously selected him to carry the flag. Hamilton was picked not because he was expected to win medals but because of his medical past.

Scott Hamilton was born on Aug. 28, 1958, in Toledo, OH. At the age of 5 the future Olympian suffered from a rare ailment which was identified as Schwachman's Disease. It is an illness similar to cystic fibrosis that paralyzed Hamilton's intestines and completely halted his growth. "I wasn't processing my food properly," he said. "I'd become bloated. I had a big stomach and skinny little legs."

He spent the next four years as a patient in hospitals in Ohio, Michigan, and Massachusetts. "I would hear things like I was going to die from it, but that was always in the far future," he said.

Hamilton had taken an interest in figure skating when he went to the rink near his home in Bowling Green, OH, with his sister. He was the one in the wheelchair. He said he wanted to skate "and everyone looked at him like he was crazy," said his coach, Donald Laws.

One day, the 9-year-old Hamilton left his

wheelchair at home and joined his doctors' kids at the local rink. He tried skating and liked it. Not only that, it was good for his health. "The more I skated, the more muscles I got. I started growing again and absorbing my food.

"It's kind of funny. I went to all these specialists, and I ended up curing myself."

Hamilton began making up for lost time. In one year, he grew seven inches. "I went from tiny to small," he said.

He also quickly rose in the competitive figure skating ranks, placing third at the 1978 nationals. In January 1980 in Atlanta, he grabbed the bronze medal behind four-time U.S. champion Charlie Tickner and David Santee to qualify for the final spot on the Olympic figure skating team.

At the Olympics, the appealing 5'3" skater finished eighth in the compulsory figures but still managed to capture 5th place overall, just behind teammates Tickner and Santee.

DIANNE HOLUM

Dianne Holum became an international oddity: the only female coach of a national speed skating team and, in the XIII Olympic Winter Games, mentor, counselor, and house mother to the greatest male speed skater ever.

Eric Heiden refused to find it either unique or uncomfortable. And in the wings, always, was Dianne Holum, a petite young lady of 28, who learned the sport in her hometown of Northbrook, IL, and put into practice what she learned, with considerable effect. In 1968 in Grenoble, she won a silver medal in a dead heat with two other American girls, Jenny Fish and Mary Meyers. In 1972, at Sapporo, she took the 1,500-meters gold, setting a new Olympic record, and the silver in the 3,000 meters. She earned a degree in physical education at the University of Wisconsin after the 1972 Games, then took a high school teaching position in Madison, where she volunteered to coach members of the Madison skate club. In 1976 she was a coach on the U.S. Olympic team.

In Lake Placid she announced, "This will be my last year."

It is ironic that Dianne chose as her valedictory the moment of her greatest triumph as a coach. She could have the speed skating world at her fingertips.

"I must seek a life of my own while I am still young," she said, emphasizing that the World Speed Skating Championships in Holland early in March 1980 would be her farewell to the sport.

"I am tired of traveling—airports, packing and unpacking suitcases, the long periods of training, endless demands. I must settle down to something less hectic. I probably will get into teaching."

Attired in the official red, white, and blue snowsuit, her long dark hair hanging to her shoulders from beneath a stocking hat, she was a striking figure at rinkside, guiding Heiden and her other protégés around the track with the precision of an airplane navigator.

She lived with a stop watch in one hand. As a skater glided over the track, she gave hand signals to regulate the speed. Once the race was run—and won—Dianne appeared uncomfortable with the traditional requisites that follow—the TV interviews, the formal press conference, the mass of squealing teenage admirers, and other distractions.

Her blue eyes coldly assess every questioner. She appears austere and aloof. It is a deceptive picture. Outside her official cocoon, she is bright, personable, sensitive.

"You can't crack the whip with these kids," she says. "You have to keep them fresh and interested. I find Europeans who train constantly tend to get jaded. At West Allis, WI, we can't start training until November.

"So we find fun things to do in the summer—camping, biking, and canoeing—things to build strength and stamina without getting bored."

When she is asked about her pupil of seven years, she is characteristically to the point. "Eric is a jewel. His superb physical assets are just a part of his success. He is a thinker. And I've never seen anyone so good at producing that one dynamic effort when it is needed."

ROBERT KANE

In mid-April 1980, after the U.S. Olympic Committee (USOC) House of Delegates had voted overwhelmingly to support President Jimmy Carter's call to boycott the Moscow Summer Games, USOC President Bob Kane summarized his feelings to the press: "I am satisfied it was a completely right decision, while feeling desperately sorry for the athletes who have been hurt by it."

Robert Kane is president of the USOC.

Kane, at 67, knew all too well how the athletes felt. In 1936, while a student at Cornell Law School, he wanted to try out for the U.S. Olympic track team. (His best time in the 200-meter dash, 21.1 seconds, stood as a Cornell record from 1933 to 1977.) After three semesters in the law school, Kane had run out of money and was forced to coach the freshman track team in exchange for tuition. Olympic officials ruled that he was a professional and could not compete in the Games.

Kane spent the next 40 years at Cornell. In 1939 he became the assistant athletic director, in 1940 the acting athletic director, in 1943 the athletic director, and in 1971 the dean of athletics and assistant to the university president. At the same time he had an abiding interest in the Olympics. His first involvement was in 1952, when he was the manager of the U.S. track team. A year later he became a member of the USOC's board of directors.

"I went into the Olympic movement because of my frustration at not making the team in 1936," he said. "In 1934 I competed with an American team in seven European countries. I experienced what athletics can do. I felt that international sport was a great factor in

bringing about understanding and good will in the world."

In 1960 Bob Kane was elected USOC secretary, in 1968 second vice-president, and in 1972 first vice-president. In 1976 he was voted president of the U.S. Olympic Committee. (They were all unsalaried positions.) Under Kane's leadership, the role of the committee expanded enormously. Its budget grew from $13 million to $43 million; it established two national training centers and planned several more; it created the annual National Sports Festival; it contributed millions of dollars to athletic development and sports medicine research; and it has helped numerous athletes in training to find jobs with major companies.

Mr. Kane lives with his wife, Ruth Brosmer, in a small house in his hometown of Ithaca, NY. His office is provided by Cornell University and maintained by the USOC. The Kanes have a son and a daughter.

LORD KILLANIN

At the closing ceremony of the Winter Games, IOC president Lord Killanin cast protocol aside and urged that the Olympics be used to achieve world peace and understanding. Killanin went out of his way to make a longer speech than usual. The Olympic Charter directs that the president simply thank the host country and city and call upon the youth of all nations to meet again at the next Games in four years' time. Though he made no reference to President Carter, or to the 1980 Summer Games, Killanin's remarks obviously alluded to the threatened U.S. boycott of the Moscow Games.

On February 12, the IOC had reaffirmed Moscow as the site of the Summer Games, despite a U.S. request for a postponement or change of venue. Killanin viewed the intrusion of politics and nationalism into the Games as a threat to the Olympic ideal. Of the possibility of an American boycott, the Irish peer said, "The athletes come first, and in no way should be prevented from competing in international competition by political, racial, or religious discrimination."

Michael Morris, 3rd Baron Killanin, commenced an eight-year term as IOC president in September 1972. A member of the House of Lords of the United Kingdom, Killanin began his nearly 30 years of involvement in the Olympics when he became Ireland's representative to the IOC in 1952. He was made chief of protocol in 1966 and an IOC vice-president in 1968.

A former journalist, Killanin is more moderate than his predecessor, Avery Brundage, whose rigid stand on amateurism was considered unrealistic by many athletes. Killanin has tempered the IOC's standards of amateurism by expanding the amount and kind of financial help an athlete may receive. His most important job, in his own eyes, is to keep the Olympics in existence: "If the 1984 Games are firmly programmed when I leave the presidency in 1980, I'll have preserved the physical shape of the Olympics. Don't forget that they have clearly been in danger."

In 1980, the impending boycott posed the greatest danger to the Olympics. As more countries appeared to support the United States in its decision to stay away, Lord Killanin and the IOC struggled to prevent nationalism from splintering the Olympic movement. Proposals considered by the committee to salvage the Moscow Games included allowing athletes to compete as individuals, without the trappings of national flags and anthems. For future Games, Lord Killanin began to investigate the feasibility of a permanent site near historic Olympia, Greece.

Terry McDermott took the oath for all the judges.

TERRY McDERMOTT

As part of the opening ceremonies of any Olympic Winter or Summer Games, a judge from the host country mounts the rostrum and takes the oath on behalf of all judges and officials: "In the name of all the judges and officials, I promise that we shall officiate in these Olympic Games with complete impartiality, respecting and abiding by the rules which govern them, in the true spirit of sportsmanship."

In the 1980 Winter Games at Lake Placid the oath was taken by Terry McDermott, a former speed skater who had won the only U.S. gold medal at the 1964 Innsbruck Games. Now a skating judge, McDermott's love for the Olympics and dedication to its ideals made him a good choice to take the oath. His success as a speed skater was a victory for pure amateurism. Going into the 1964 Games, the 23-year-old apprentice barber from Essexville, MI, was a decided underdog against Yevgeni Grishin, the USSR's two-time defending champion, and other foreign skaters who trained year-round under expert supervision.

Taking little time off from the barber shop, McDermott prepared almost casually—a month of three one-hour workouts a week, followed by a month of daily two-hour drills—and went on to win the gold medal in the 500 meters with an Olympic record time of 40.1 seconds.

After the Games, McDermott returned to chair No. 3 at Bunny's Barber Shop in Bay City, MI, and continued to live in a four-room house in Essexville with his wife of four months, Virginia. Before long he moved to a suburb of Detroit and became a sales representative, selling die castings and plastics to automobile companies. By 1968 the chunky 5'9", 170-pound McDermott was ready for another Olympics, where he tied for second in the 500 meters with a time of 40.5 seconds.

Richard Terrance McDermott was born on Sept. 20, 1940, the seventh child of Joseph and Exora McDermott. None of his six older sisters was athletically inclined, but one of them, Marilyn, married a speed skating coach, Richard Somalski. Somalski asked young Terry, age 7, if he would like to learn to skate. The boy agreed, and a year later he won the Michigan cradle-division championship. Mc-

Dermott went to St. John's High School in Essexville, where he played halfback on the football team and met his future wife, Virginia Vermeesch. He then attended Michigan Tech for two years, before leaving to become a barber in the shop owned by his uncle Harvey (Bunny) Herbert.

Pleasant and modest, the brown-eyed, curly-haired McDermott runs to keep in shape and likes golf and bowling for recreation. He also keeps up with his first love—Olympic speed skating. He is vice-president of the United States Speed Skating Association.

JIM McKAY

In the 13 eventful days of ABC's Olympic coverage, there was one constant: Jim McKay. The seasoned sportscaster served as anchorman, besides joining Dick Button for figure skating commentary. McKay's solid presence seemed to hold together the wide-ranging reports on competitions, personalities, and background that added up to more than 50 hours of programming.

For many viewers, McKay was a more familiar figure than any of the athletes. Since 1960, not one Olympic year had gone by without Jim McKay on the scene, explaining the intricacies of the Games to a receptive American audience.

In 1968, McKay became the first sportscaster in the history of television to win an Emmy; he had received six more by the time the 1980 Games were held. Two were awarded for his coverage of the 1972 Olympics in Munich—one for his sports commentary and the other for his reporting of the tragedy that befell the Games when Arab terrorists attacked the Olympic Village. Staying on the air for more than 15 hours, McKay turned newsman to keep American viewers posted on the events that culminated in the deaths of the Israeli hostages and several of their captors. His muted observations accurately reflected the sadness and disillusionment that everyone felt upon hearing the story.

Ironically, these unhappy circumstances gave McKay the recognition he deserved. He had previously labored in relative obscurity, performing his job so well that his abilities were taken for granted. After Munich, McKay was recognized as a consummate professional: competent, informative, and articulate. "He's like an offensive right guard," an ABC official remarked at the time. "He's always there. He always does the job. Maybe you could say he's the decathlon man of our business."

McKay's interest in public speaking and journalism originated in his high school years and continued through college, where he was an announcer at varsity basketball games. After a stint in the Navy during World War II, he was hired as a reporter for *The Baltimore Sun*. When the *Sun* acquired a television station in 1948, McKay was recruited as a combination reporter-interviewer-variety show host. He worked for CBS from 1950 to 1960, and in 1961 was offered the job of hosting ABC's *Wide World of Sports*. This unique program was the first to emphasize off-beat sports and McKay has traveled throughout the world covering such athletic events as log rolling, water skiing, and arm wrestling.

At the Lake Placid Olympics, however, McKay was confined to the studio. "I see my job as trying to present an overview," he said concerning his responsibilities as host. "I try to anticipate what the personality of a particular Games will be, and then convey that to the audience. Sometimes the personality changes during the course of the Games—and you have to sense such changes and make the audience aware of them."

He is the author of *My Wide World*, which was published in 1973.

Jim McKay explained the Games to TV viewers.

Chuck Mangione composed the Olympic theme music.

CHUCK MANGIONE

Chuck Mangione took on a challenging assignment for the 1980 Winter Olympics. The Grammy-winning musician was commissioned to compose a theme for the ABC telecasts of the Games.

Mangione had a tough act to follow. Since 1964, ABC's Olympic programs had been heralded by a majestic trumpet fanfare, termed "the most identifiable theme on television" by one ABC executive. The network had no intention of retiring its Olympic trademark (which is entitled "Bugler's Dream"), but planned to include a special theme for the Lake Placid Games.

Mangione could provide a distinctly American sound. His music is a fluid jazz-pop blend, featuring catchy melodies played on the flügel-horn. Jazz by Mangione is always upbeat—and smooth enough to appeal to popular tastes. Mangione reached his widest audience with the album *Feels So Good*, released in the fall of 1977. Despite the initial reluctance of disc jockeys to play a jazz instrumental on AM radio, the buoyant title tune was an immediate success, hitting the top ten on the pop charts.

Mangione was introduced to music at an early age, often accompanying his father to jazz clubs located in his home town of Rochester, NY. Sometimes the elder Mangione would invite the musicians home; more than once Chuck and his older brother found themselves jamming with Dizzy Gillespie and other jazz greats.

Mangione pragmatically earned a degree in music education from the Eastman School of Music in Rochester. But his goal was to be a performer, and, having taught for one year, he formed his own group and began touring. After several punishing years on the road his music finally began to catch on; in 1976 Mangione received a Grammy for the title song of his album *Bellavia*. With the success of *Feels So Good* and the Grammy-winning album *Children of Sanchez* (1978), the ebullient musician, who usually sports a distinctive felt hat and a wide grin, became a household figure.

For his Olympic assignment, Mangione viewed films of all the sporting events and tried to capture the spirit of the competitions in his music. The result was an appealing jazz-flavored tune entitled "Give It All You Got." The theme was played at different tempos to convey the mood of different events.

F. DON MILLER

A retired U.S. Army colonel, Francis Don Miller has served as executive director of the United States Olympic Committee (USOC) since 1973. In 1980 Miller worked closely with USOC President Robert Kane in formulating and promoting the committee's position regarding the boycott of the Summer Games in Moscow.

It was thankless work. Miller and Kane met repeatedly with representatives of the Carter administration and U.S. State Department and carried the administration's message to an adamant International Olympic Committee, hundreds of disappointed American athletes, the USOC body, and the press. Miller and the USOC were in a double bind. They could not express opposition to the boycott without coming under attack by the government for interfering with U.S. foreign policy; they could not favor the boycott without incurring the disfavor of the nation's amateur athletes and all their supporters. Either way, they risked jeopardizing the Olympic movement.

The first official USOC reaction after President Carter announced the boycott in his January State of the Union Message was negative. On January 6, Miller issued a statement expressing the committee's opposition: "I am saddened and deeply regret that our government did find it necessary to consider the use of the Olympic movement as a vehicle in international politics. It would appear to me that this possible consideration is counter-productive and we would be punishing ourselves in using our dedicated American athletes as pawns in this international political struggle."

Under increasing government pressure, however, Miller and Kane reluctantly supported the boycott, feeling it was in the best national interest. On April 12, after the USOC House of Delegates voted by a margin of more than 2-to-1 to support the boycott, Miller made the following comments: "I'm confident we made the best informed decision in the history of the United States Olympic Committee. There has been political interference with the Olympic movement for years. But there is a difference between political interference and dictatorship."

Miller was born April 9, 1920, in Racine, WI. He received his bachelor of science degree in physical education at the University of Wisconsin in 1943, and joined the army the same year. He was an infantry commander in Europe from 1943 to 1945 and stayed on in the military after the war. Miller advanced through the ranks and became a colonel in 1966. He was senior instructor of sports at the Special Services School in Fort Monmouth, NJ, 1947–49; administrator of the army sports program, 1949–52; chairman of the Inter-service Sports Council, 1967–1968; and director of the Army Education and Morale Support Directorate, 1968–69. After retiring from the military in 1969, Miller served as assistant executive director of fund raising for the USOC in New York City, and was elected executive director of the committee in 1973.

F. Don Miller has been married for 33 years to Katherine Rose Julian and has two children, Patricia Ann and Donna Louise. The Millers reside in Yorktown Heights, NY, but spend much of their time in Colorado Springs, CO, home of the USOC.

LEAH POULOS MUELLER

In Lake Placid Leah Poulos Mueller performed better than was immediately apparent. Much was made of the fact that in the 500-meter women's sprint she lost the first place that she had gained, late in 1979, by besting Beth Heiden in the World Sprints Championship. Karin Enke took the sprint gold, and Leah got the silver. In doing so, it was worthwhile to note, she broke the old Olympic record. Her time was only 48 one-hundredths of a second longer than Enke's, a skater a full decade Leah's junior. In the 1,000-meter race, where she was also the silver medalist, Mueller trailed Natalia Petruseva—by 1.31 seconds. Again, an old Olympic record was beaten. Again, the winner was a younger woman, by four years.

When she was asked about her performance, Leah said that she was pleased with the way she had skated. It was a characteristically calm and judicious assessment. She knows what suits her technique—"I like to glide because I'm not a runner. I try to conserve strength"—and she knows when she has skated well, medals or no medals.

Leah Poulos Mueller was a two-time silver medalist.

Lake Placid was her third Olympic meet. She had begun by competing in the longest races in Sapporo, but the results were disappointing: 17th in the 3,000 meters and 24th in the 1,500. Four years later, in Innsbruck, where she did not do the 3,000, she moved up to 6th in the 1,500, took the silver in the 1,000, and came in 4th in the 500. In 1980, in what she said was her last Olympics, she concentrated on the 1,000 and 500 races, and she held her own in the one and moved up in the other.

Leah Poulos was born in Berwyn, not far from Chicago, IL, in 1951. "I came from a skating family," she said. "I learned the basic principles by trial and error—falling down and getting up." At the age of seven she began to skate competitively. After high schooling in northern Illinois she attended the University of Wisconsin. Following the 1976 Games she married her teammate, Peter Mueller, the gold-medal victor of the first running of the men's 1,000-meter race. They made their home in tiny Dousman, in a farming area west of Milwaukee. Two years before the Placid Games Leah gave up skating for a time, taking various jobs to support her husband's chance to go on in competition. She planned to complete college after Placid.

STEVE PODBORSKI

At the 1980 Winter Olympics Steve Podborski had the honor of becoming the first Canadian to win an Olympic medal in Alpine skiing. The 23-year-old from Don Mills, Ont., finished third in the men's downhill. His time was 1 minute, 46.62 seconds, .5 second behind silver medalist Peter Wirnsberger of Austria and 1.12 seconds behind Austria's Stock.

Of his medal, Podborski said, "Stock raced too well for me to beat him. . . . I just skied the best I could. When I looked up at my time I thought, ah, that's too slow, but it was fast enough for third." The bronze medalist also pointed out that he "made some mistakes, but bronze is good for me."

Together with Ken Read, David Irwin, and David Murray, Steve Podborski is a member of Canada's Kamikaze Kids. The group is considered one of the world's best skiing teams. The fact that Ken Read lost a ski during the downhill and consequently lost his chance to win an Olympic medal was one of the major surprises of the 1980 Games.

Canadian skier Steve Podborski received a bronze.

Steve Podborski, who enjoyed a first place finish in the downhill in the 1979 World Cup, was seventh in the 1978 World Championship downhill event. It was Canada's best standing.

With regard to training, Podborski believes that "if you go too fast in training, you miss things. You have to work into it, tighten your line gradually."

Steve Podborski is a competitive road cyclist. He enjoys windsurfing and target shooting. Reading is also a favorite pastime.

PETR SPURNEY

"What you have here has been designed with the years after the Olympics in mind. There are no white elephants here." Petr Spurney's opinion, reassuring to the Lake Placid Olympic Organizing Committee, carried weight. He had the experience to know.

Close to the time for Lake Placid to be ready to greet the world's athletes, the LPOOC sought out Spurney to act as its general manager in staging a successful XIII Olympic Winter Games—in his words "to put all the pieces together in a workable and economic format." For his $100,000 manager's fee the LPOOC was buying a known quantity.

At 43, Petr Spurney, of Chevy Chase, MD, had already achieved national standing as a manager of big and complex projects. After being graduated by Cornell University with a B.S. in mechanical engineering and serving in the U.S. Naval Reserve, he worked, both in the United States and abroad, as a manager and marketing executive. As a consultant to the federal Department of Transportation for the U.S. International Transportation Exhibition, he contributed to the success of TRANSPO '72.

In 1973, when Spokane's Expo 1974, with only seven months to get ready for opening, was so plagued with what seemed like insurmountable problems that postponement or cancellation was rumored, Spurney was named general manager and chief executive officer (CEO). He and his staff not only got the fair open on schedule, they made it so attractive that the expected 4.2 million visitors proved to number 5.1 million.

In 1975 he became chairman, president, and CEO of the American Freedom Train Foundation. Under his direction the nation's most widely shared Bicentennial show—The Freedom Train–traveled more than 25,000 miles to 138 cities, where it was visited by nearly seven million people. Thereafter, as a special consultant to the National Museum of Canada, he helped to plan and develop The Discovery Train, a traveling exhibit featuring Canadian history and culture.

Spurney was awarded the American Advertising Federation's Annual Advertising Silver Medal in 1974.

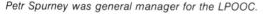

Petr Spurney was general manager for the LPOOC.

CHARLES TICKNER

At an age when most champion figure skaters have either signed on with a touring ice show or hung up their skates altogether, 26-year-old Charles Tickner of Littleton, CO, still had his sights set on an Olympic medal in Lake Placid. The three-time U.S. men's singles champion (1977, 1978, 1979) and former world champion (1978) was touted by many to win the gold, but Tickner knew his work was cut out for him. "I've got to skate the best I can," he said. "I have to be very aggressive. I'd be happy with any medal—gold, silver, bronze. I am the one I have to beat."

A classic free skater, the 5'10", 140-lb Tickner performed well in the compulsory figures, taking second place. In fine shape going into the short program, Tickner stumbled on the required jump combination, a triple Salchow double loop, and lost valuable points. He fell to third place, and despite a strong showing in the free skate could not pass Jan Hoffmann of East Germany or gold-medalist Robin Cousins of Great Britain. Tickner said he was "very honored" to win a bronze.

The road to Lake Placid had been long and difficult. A native of California, Tickner was graduated from Acalanes High School in Lafayette in 1971 and then attended college for one year. At 19, living in San Francisco, Tickner was filled with frustration at his lack of progress on the ice. His parents urged him to quit. It was at that time, however, that he met coach Norma Sahlin. Although Sahlin recognized his "great raw talent," it seemed a little late to begin the formal training usually given to promising 13-year-olds. Still, Tickner moved to Denver, where Sahlin lived, and made figure skating his job. "Before I came to Denver," he said, "I didn't know what it meant to train."

Hitting the ice at 6:20 A.M. six days a week, Tickner would do four hours of school figures, three hours of jumping and spinning, and additional time on the "belt"—a safety harness for practicing difficult jumps—before leaving at about 5 o'clock. At once an elegant and powerful skater, Tickner still had a problem with self-confidence, poise, and concentration. Sahlin urged him to learn self-hypnosis to master the psychological aspects of the sport, and the results were all he needed to become a world-class skater. "It kind of rejuvenated me," said Tickner. "It made me feel like I could do anything."

Disorganized and poorly equipped, Afghan rebels fought stubbornly against the tens of thousands of invading Soviet troops. Located primarily in northern regions, the insurgent tribesmen had the advantage of familiarity with the mountainous terrain. The Soviet incursion and continued presence in Afghanistan brought economic sanctions from the United States and a boycott of the 1980 Olympic Games in Moscow.

The Boycott

On Dec. 27, 1979, President Hafizullah Amin of Afghanistan was ousted from power, executed, and replaced by exiled former Deputy Premier Babrak Karmal. The overthrow was engineered by the Soviet Union, which had airlifted thousands of troops into Afghanistan in the preceding days. Soviet forces continued to arrive after the coup. An estimated 30,000 had entered the country by December 29 and a reported 100,000 within a few short weeks. Early 1980 saw increasingly violent insurgency by Afghan Muslim tribesmen and heard protests from around the world against the brazen Soviet maneuver.

In a nationally televised address on Jan. 4, 1980, U.S. President Jimmy Carter denounced the Soviet intervention as "an extremely serious threat to peace. . . .

"The world simply cannot stand by and permit the Soviet Union to commit this act with impunity," he went on. Carter then announced several retaliatory measures against the Kremlin: grain sales would be sharply curtailed; the sale of high technology equipment would be suspended; fishing privileges in

U.S. waters would be restricted; and finally, if the "aggressive action" continued, the United States would consider boycotting the 1980 Summer Olympic Games, scheduled to be held in Moscow during July and August. On January 20, Carter formally proposed that the Games be moved from Moscow, postponed, or canceled unless all Soviet troops were removed from Afghanistan in one month. On the television news program *Meet the Press* and in a letter to United States Olympic Committee (USOC) President Robert Kane, Carter said that if none of these changes were effected an international boycott should be organized.

Sympathy with the U.S. proposal was not long in coming. Canadian Prime Minister Joe Clark publicly called for moving the Games from the Soviet capital. British Prime Minister Margaret Thatcher also declared her government's support for moving the Games from Moscow. Although participation in an actual boycott would have to be determined by the National Olympic Committee of each country, the U.S. position found growing support. Whatever the reaction of the rest of the world, President Carter was firm. "Regardless of what other nations might do," he emphasized on *Meet the Press*, "I would not favor the sending of an American Olympic team to Moscow while the Soviet invasion troops are in Afghanistan."

The moral reasons for staying away from Moscow were put in a nutshell by Nelson Ledsky, head of the Olympic Task Force of the U.S. State Department. "There is something repellent," said Ledsky, "about Soviet troops being in Afghanistan at the same time flights of doves are being let loose in Moscow."

Carter and the State Department realized full well that a disruption of the Moscow Games would also have a devastating political and social effect on the Soviet Union. It was perhaps the most damaging weapon in Carter's diplomatic arsenal. In his

President Carter's proposal to boycott the Games found wide and vocal support among the U.S. public. Below, Ukrainian-Americans demonstrate against Soviet domination of their homeland and for the boycott.

The buildings at Red Square (above) and all around Moscow were cleaned and their domes gilded in anticipation of the influx of visitors. The symbol of the 1980 Games appeared everywhere.

January 20 letter to Kane, President Carter noted "the desirability of keeping Government policy out of the Olympics," but argued that "the Soviet Government attaches enormous political importance to holding the 1980 Olympic Games in Moscow, and if the Olympics are not held in Moscow because of Soviet military aggression in Afghanistan, this powerful signal of world outrage cannot be hidden from the Soviet people, and will reverberate around the globe."

The XXII Olympic Summer Games were keenly anticipated by the Soviet Union. For the first time a socialist country would play host to the Games, and Moscow organizers predicted they would be nothing less than "a major event in human history." The 1980 Olympics would be the culmination of a long political and social process, giving a stamp of legitimacy to the whole Soviet system. The Bolshevik state would come of age in the eyes of the world. Soviet citizenry would be at the center of global attention, its way of life showcased in all the pomp and glamor of this venerable institution.

The high place accorded to sports and physical education in their way of life would make the plaudits of the world ever more rewarding—and legitimizing—to the Russian people. The Communist leadership had long recognized the value of athletics as a political instrument and had made it one of its highest national priorities. In terms of international relations it was an opportunity first to gain equal standing with the West and then to demonstrate the superiority of Soviet ways. For the masses it had long been a source of unity and pride. Article 41 of the Soviet

Constitution establishes "mass development of sport" as a right of the citizenry. Unlike the United States and other Western nations, where an athlete's development depends primarily on his or her own initiative and where the benefit of professional coaching does not become available until the athlete is relatively accomplished, the Soviet Union begins formal training for promising athletes as soon as they begin school. The education is intensive and for the most part restricted to sports, the training rigorous from the beginning. The best prospects are winnowed out in regional competitions, and the elite are guaranteed a life of comfort and privilege. It is a no-nonsense, production-line approach which many Westerners consider grim. To the Soviets, however, every gold medal is a vindication of socialist ideology. The great Soviet spawning ground of champions and an harmonious citizenry would be on display in Moscow, and the Olympics would cast all of it in the light of brotherhood.

The 1980 Games would also be the first major exposure of the socialist bloc to Western culture. The responsibilities of ordinary Muscovites in meeting Westerners were laid out, more than a year before the Games were to open, in a speech by Viktor Grishin, the head of the Moscow party committee and a member of the nation's ruling Politburo. Said Grishin: "It is necessary to ensure that, in relations with foreigners, residents of the capital show cordiality and hospitality, stress the advantages of the Soviet way of life and the achievements of our society, and at the same time repulse the propaganda of alien ideas

(Continued page 225)

Among the new facilities built for the Summer Games was the Central Sports Hall (above), planned site of the gymnastics events. Misha the Bear (below) was the official mascot.

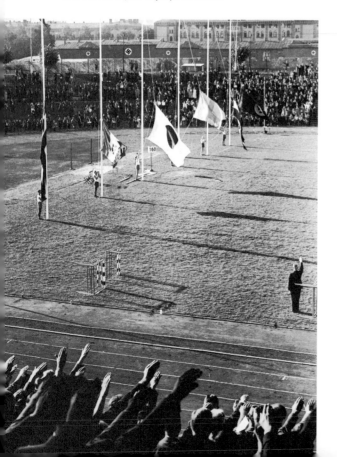

Germany staged the 1936 Games to publicize Nazism and enthusiastically welcomed the nation's 101 medals. Below, Germans salute as the flags are lowered at a pre-Olympics meet.

POLITICS AND PAST OLYMPICS

In 1935, amid fierce debate over a proposed boycott of the 1936 Berlin Games, Avery Brundage, then president of the United States Olympic Committee (USOC), dismissed as irrelevant the question of anti-Semitism in Hitler's Germany and took the traditional view that political disputes must not interfere with the Olympic movement. "Frankly," he said, "I don't think we have any business to meddle in this question. We are a sports group, organized and pledged to promote clean competition and sportsmanship. When we let politics, racial questions, or social disputes into our actions, we're in for trouble." The boycott movement was defeated, and Nazi propaganda chief, Joseph Goebbels, spared no expense in making the Games a showcase for Hitler's National Socialism. The Berlin Olympics were the most overtly politicized Games in the history of the movement.

In 1980, supporters of U.S. President Jimmy Carter's call for a boycott of the Moscow Olympics drew an analogy to the situation prior to the 1936 Games. The political and moral responsibility to protest the Soviet invasion of Afghanistan, they argued, was more important than any athletic competition, however lofty its ideals. The Moscow organizers were constructing a 1936-like showcase for the Soviet system, and participation would be tantamount to approval of political repression and an expansionist foreign policy. With a Moscow boycott in mind, Rolf Pauls, the West German representative to NATO, reflected on the 1936 Games: "If the world had boycotted Hitler's Olympics," he said, "the course of history might have been different." Vladimir Popov, vice president of the Soviet Olympic Organizing Committee, did not think the analogy was fair: "As part of a nation that lost 20 million people in a war against fascism, I put aside the question completely."

However valid the parallel, everyone could safely put aside, once and for all, Brundage's creed that "sports transcends all political and racial situations." Although the Russians, the International Olympic Committee (IOC), and other opponents of the boycott urged that the Games be kept free of politics, none of them could deny that the Olympic movement had been very deeply affected by this and other international disputes. Even IOC President Lord Killanin admitted, "I have never denied or ignored the intrusion of politics into the Olympic movement." The apolitical sanctity of the Olympic Games was a pipe dream from the very beginning. A detailed history of the modern Games chronicles the major international political disputes of the twentieth century.

The 1912 Games in Stockholm were the most efficiently organized and run Olympics up to that time. Their success would prove vital to the perpetuation of the whole movement, because mounting German militarism and political turmoil throughout Europe threatened war and the possible cancellation of the VI Olympiad in 1916. Berlin, Budapest, and Alexandria were the prime candidates to host the 1916 Games. The IOC voted unanimously for Berlin because it thought the Games might divert Germany's attention from political issues and help avoid war. Even as the Kaiser was building up his armies and as war became imminent, preparations for the Games went on, and IOC President Pierre de Coubertin would hear of no other arrangements. The outbreak of World War I in August 1914 forced the cancellation of the 1916 Olympics.

Again demonstrating a lack of foresight as to international political affairs, the IOC voted to hold the 1940 Summer Games in Tokyo and the Winter Games in Sapporo. But when the second Sino-Japanese war broke out in July 1937, the Japanese government ordered a halt to the preparations. Helsinki was selected as the alternate site for the Summer Games, and St. Moritz was to host the Winter Games. But the XII Olympiad was canceled altogether with the outbreak of World War II. The 1944 Games were to be held in London and Cortina d'Ampezzo, Italy, but they, too, were canceled because of the war.

Since the revival of the Olympics after World War II, no Games have been wholly free of international political interference. The history is one of exclusions, boycotts, and dis-

Twenty years after "Hitler's Olympics," politics again had a profound influence on the Olympic movement. After Soviet tanks quelled a rebellion by Hungarian "Freedom Fighters," several European nations boycotted the Melbourne Games. Tension between Hungarian and Soviet athletes was particularly strong during a water polo match, which led to a riot.

Egypt, Lebanon, and Iraq
boycotted the 1956 Summer
Games after Anglo-French troops
seized and blocked the Suez
Canal.

putes. Germany and Japan, the Axis aggressors, were barred from participating in the 1948 Winter Games at St. Moritz and the Summer Games in London. Israel, which had gained independence in May of that year, was declared by the IOC to be ineligible on a technicality, thereby averting a boycott by Egypt and other Arab countries.

In 1952 the Cold War was at its peak, and the hostilities in Korea were still in full swing. The Soviet Union, which had sent only observers to London in 1948, fielded a full complement of athletes for the XV Games in Helsinki. For whatever reasons, the Soviets insisted that their athletes, as well as those of other Iron Curtain countries—Bulgaria, Czechoslovakia, Hungary, Poland, and Rumania—be quartered in their own village. For the first time in the history of the Olympics, athletes were segregated along political lines. The IOC, in spite of its rules, tolerated the split.

The 1956 Games in Melbourne were more affected by the international political scene than any Olympics since Berlin. The circumstances were in many ways similar to those of 1980. In the autumn of 1956, an uprising by Hungarian "Freedom Fighters" was put down by a wave of tanks sent into Budapest by the Soviet Union. The Netherlands, Spain, and Switzerland refused to compete against Soviet athletes and boycotted the Games in protest. The Hungarian Olympians were on board a Soviet vessel en route to Melbourne when the rebellion began. They decided to take part in the Games but flew the flag of Free Hungary in the Olympic Village and wore black arm bands to mourn their countrymen killed in the uprising. The tension in Melbourne came to a head in the semifinal water polo match between the Soviet Union and Hungary. A butt by a Soviet player opened a cut over the eye of a Hungarian, and the sight of blood led to a riot by his countrymen in the stands. Numerous Hungarian athletes took asylum in Australia after the Games.

Events in the Middle East also affected the 1956 Games. In July of that year Egypt announced it was nationalizing the Suez Canal. Israel launched a campaign in the Sinai Peninsula in October, giving France and Great Britain, the canal's "legitimate owners," the occasion to replace futile negotiations in the United Nations with military force. Anglo-French troops seized control of the canal in early November and, later that month, Egypt, Lebanon, and Iraq boycotted the Olympics in protest. As if that were not enough, the team from Communist China walked out when someone raised the Taiwanese flag in the Olympic Village. The Communists called it a "scheme of artificially splitting China." The participation of Taiwan and the absence of Communist China was a turnaround from four years earlier, when Nationalist China boycotted to protest the participation of the Communists. East and West Germany sent a single team in 1956, four years after East Germany stayed away because it had been denied recognition as a separate state.

The China issue arose again in 1964, as it would in the next several Olympiads. Only days before the opening ceremonies in Tokyo, North Korea and Indonesia called home their teams over a controversy stemming from a 1963 international athletic event in Jakarta. North Korea withdrew because six of its athletes had been denied reinstatement by the IOC after being suspended for taking part in the November 1963 Games of the New Emerging Forces (GANEFO) in Jakarta. Indonesia had organized GANEFO after being suspended by the IOC for sponsoring the 1962 Asian Games, which had excluded Taiwan and Israel but had invited mainland China. Indonesia withdrew from the 1964 Games shortly after North Korea.

Another recurring problem that arose before the 1964 Games was that of South Africa. In June the IOC decided to ban that nation from the Tokyo Olympics unless by August 16 it modified its racial apartheid policy. The changes were not made, and South Africa was excluded.

The controversy over South Africa flared again at the close of the 1968 Winter Games in Grenoble. President Avery Brundage and the other IOC officers accepted a committee report recommending the reinstatement of South Africa for the Summer Games in Mexico City. Angry black African nations threatened to boycott, and the IOC reversed its stand three months later. The Mexico City Games still were not without major political incidents. Student riots over the plight of Mexico's poor and other social and political issues left 30 persons dead, 100 injured, and 300 jailed in Mexico City just prior to the opening Games.

Never was the question of politics in the Olympics more hotly debated than at the 1968 Games. The issue was forced by two U.S. runners, Tommie Smith and John Carlos, who finished first and third, respectively, in the 200-meter dash. The two blacks had attended San Jose State College, where Harry Edwards, a sociology instructor, had tried to organize a black boycott of the Games to protest racial discrimination. The boycott did not come to pass, but Smith and Carlos were set on making their own gesture. At the medal ceremony for the 200-meters, both mounted the victory stand with their pants rolled up, revealing long black socks like those common in Negro ghet-

toes, and wearing black gloves. During the playing of the national anthem, Smith and Carlos bowed their heads and raised their gloved fists in a black power salute. Under pressure of the IOC, the USOC issued an official apology, reprimanded the two athletes, and finally expelled them from the team.

The 1972 Olympiad will be remembered for the Munich Massacre. Nations had grown very far removed from the practices of ancient Greece, when wars were called to a halt for the quadrennial celebration of the Olympiad. In 1972 the Olympics were made a stage on which political terrorists could play out their mindless hatreds. Early in the morning of September 5, eight militant Arabs of the Black September group made their way into the dormitory of the Israeli Olympic team. Several Israelis escaped through windows, but two were shot dead and nine were taken hostage. Negotiations for the release of the hostages were unsuccessful, and an attempted rescue by West German police left all nine of the Israelis and one policeman dead. Several of the terrorists escaped. Strong representations were made to cancel the remaining events, and many athletes left for home. But Avery Brundage, at the end

Although the Israeli flag was carried proudly at the opening, the 1972 Games were tragic for Israel.

of 20 years as IOC president, felt the Olympics should not be compromised. After a memorial service on the morning of September 6, the Games were resumed.

On the eve of the 1972 Games, the IOC, as it had in the past, avoided a boycott by the black African countries. The Supreme Council for Sport in Africa threatened to lead a massive walkout over the participation of Rhodesia, whose white minority government it regarded as racist. The Africans got their way. The IOC voted narrowly to withdraw the invitation to Rhodesia. Brundage was angered by the decision. He felt that the committee had bowed to political pressure.

Four years later at Montreal, the African countries got involved in another dispute, this time over a New Zealand rugby team that had toured South Africa. The 28-nation bloc demanded that New Zealand be thrown out of the Games and staged a boycott when the IOC refused. The Taiwanese team, which was barred from competing under the banner of the Republic of China because the Canadian government officially recognized the People's Republic of China, also withdrew from the Games.

At its 1977 session in Prague, the IOC amended its charter and took measures to suspend or otherwise discipline any National Olympic Committee which enters its athletes in the Olympic Games and then withdraws them for political reasons. The gesture represented another attempt by the IOC to keep politics from interfering with the Olympics.

It was tilting at windmills. Beyond even the boycotts, exclusions, withdrawals, propaganda displays, and terrorist assaults, the modern Olympics are inherently political. Their nationalistic character was established even by their founder, Baron Pierre de Coubertin, who sought to enhance the pride and prestige of his native France by holding the first modern Games there in 1896. Instead they were held in Greece, where Crown Prince Constantine escorted his victorious countryman, Spyridon Louis, across the finish line of the marathon. Hitler's motives for hosting the Games were obvious, but other nations also have used them as a vehicle for national recognition. One of the organizers of the 1964 Tokyo Games admitted that "it was a national crusade for Japan to host the Olympic Games. . . . Without the magic of the Olympic name we might not have gotten the investment we needed to use as a world trade power. Our national prestige was tied to it and, yes, it was a governmental policy to make the Olympics our announcement to the world that Japan was no longer a beaten nation, that Japan had regained confidence in herself."

It was the same kind of announcement that the Soviet Union hoped to make in 1980. The Moscow Games were intended to demonstrate to the world that the Soviet system had come of age. After the invasion of Afghanistan, the United States and other boycotting nations determined that the announcement, if it were to be made at all, would not be quite so loud.

Protestors against the apartheid policy of South Africa call for action, not words. South Africa has been excluded from the Olympics since 1960. In 1976, twenty-eight nations boycotted the Montreal Games over the participation of New Zealand, which earlier had sent a rugby team to play in South Africa.

The Roll Call: Moscow 1980

On May 27, 1980, the International Olympic Committee announced the names of those nations planning to attend and those planning to boycott the 1980 Summer Olympics in Moscow. The deadline for accepting or rejecting invitations from the Moscow organization committee was May 24.

Nations Accepting Invitation—85

Afghanistan	Cyprus	India	Mongolia	Sierra Leone
Algeria	Czechoslovakia	Iraq	Nepal	Soviet Union
Andorra	Denmark	Ireland	Netherlands	Spain
Angola	Dominican Republic	Italy	New Zealand	Sri Lanka
Australia	East Germany	Jamaica	Nicaragua	Surinam
Austria	Ecuador	Jordan	Niger	Sweden
Belgium	Ethiopia	Kuwait	Nigeria	Switzerland
Benin	Finland	Laos	North Korea	Syria
Botswana	France	Lebanon	Panama	Tanzania
Brazil	Gabon	Lesotho	Peru	Trinidad and Tobago
Bulgaria	Great Britain	Libya	Poland	Uganda
Burma	Greece	Luxembourg	Portugal	Upper Volta
Cameroon	Guatemala	Madagascar	Puerto Rico	Venezuela
Colombia	Guinea	Mali	Rumania	Vietnam
Congo	Guyana	Malta	San Marino	Yugoslavia
Costa Rica	Hungary	Mauritius	Senegal	Zambia
Cuba	Iceland	Mexico	Seychelles	Zimbabwe

Nations Declining Invitation—29

Albania	China	Japan	Pakistan	Tunisia
Argentina	Gambia	Kenya	Paraguay	Turkey
Bahrain	Honduras	Liechtenstein	Philippines	United States
Bermuda	Hong Kong	Malawi	Saudi Arabia	Uruguay
Canada	Indonesia	Malaysia	Singapore	West Germany
Cayman Islands	Israel	Mauritania	Thailand	

Nations Not Replying—27

Antigua	Chad	Haiti	Neth. Antilles	Sudan
Bahamas	Chile	Ivory Coast	Norway	Swaziland
Barbados	Egypt	Liberia	Papua New Guinea	Togo
Belize	El Salvador	Monaco	Somalia	Virgin Islands
Bolivia	Fiji	Morocco	South Korea	Zaire
Central African Rep.	Ghana			

and principles, and the onslaughts on our country and on the ideas of communism and socialism."

Preparations for the Olympics were a major concern of the state. A reported $350 million were taken from government coffers for the games. Eleven new athletic centers were built and an equal number refurbished or expanded. In addition there were a spacious new Olympic Village, a television broadcast center, press headquarters, 35-story hotel, international post office, computer center, and other facilities. Roads were repaved, buildings cleaned, and historic church domes gilded. Olympic cakes appeared in bakery windows, posters were put up all over town, and taxi drivers were given crash courses in a foreign language. It was decreed that, just prior to the Games, the streets would be cleared of indigents and drunks. So that they would not be exposed to Western influence, children would be removed to camps outside the city.

All in all, it was one massive effort to make the city, its people, and the entire nation ready for a glorious occasion. Any disruption would be a major blow to the Kremlin.

For the boycotters, there would be a price to pay. A variety of U.S. concerns stood to lose millions. The National Broadcasting Company (NBC), which was to have televised the Games in the United States, would sacrifice a reported $22 million in outlays not covered by insurance, as well as untold millions in advertising revenue. Coca-Cola, designated the official soft drink of the Moscow Olympics, would not be sold there, and all American suppliers of uniforms, souvenirs, athletic

Before the start of IOC meetings in Lausanne, Switzerland, over the impending Olympic boycott, committee chairwoman Monique Berlioux (standing) joins in discussion with French representative Jean de Beaumont (left) and Vitaly Smirnov of the Soviet Union. Below, IOC members line up for their official Olympic photograph just prior to the start of the Winter Games in Lake Placid.

equipment, and technology would have to cancel important business.

The biggest losers, of course, were the athletes. Whether or not they agreed with the boycott, they were, understandably, intensely disappointed. For many it was the loss of a once-in-a-lifetime opportunity. Years of single-minded dedication and forward-looking enthusiasm—not to mention financial strains, the sacrifice of friends and education, and the sheer physical pain of training—were being brought to nothing. Swimmers and gymnasts, for example, many of whom peak in the early teens, would easily be past their prime by 1984. And others, whose sports life expectancy is not so brief, might not, after all the frustration and uncertainty, be able to muster the hope that would sustain them through four more years of preparation.

Some American athletes simply did not understand the rationale of a boycott. Politics should not interfere with the Olympics, they argued, and what difference would a boycott make, anyway? Some felt as if they were being used as pawns. "Why us?" they asked. Although most Olympic aspirants remained opposed to any boycott, a surprising number spoke out against going to Moscow. One of them, steeplechaser and USOC board member Henry Marsh, came to the heart of the dilemma. "As a patriotic citizen," he said, "I realize a boycott would be a severe blow to the Russians. But as an athlete, the very thought of a boycott breaks my heart."

From the outset there were several proposals to salvage something for the athletes. Carter first promised that every effort would be made to organize an alternate sports festival in which athletes from nonparticipating countries could compete. He offered full support, both financial and administrative, to any such

President Jimmy Carter welcomes the U.S. Winter Olympic team at the White House one day after the closing ceremonies. The athletes presented him with a petition to call off the boycott of the Summer Games.

The day President Carter set as the deadline for the withdrawal of Soviet troops from Afghanistan—February 20—brought spring-like temperatures to Lake Placid. Some spectators at the Winter Games took time out to demonstrate for the boycott.

effort. Several television networks, including NBC, announced they would be willing to provide coverage of any alternate games held outside the Soviet Union. Foreign governments, including Canada, Great Britain, and Australia, offered athletic facilities. The U.S. State Department favored an international festival, in which the events would be held in various boycotting nations. The USOC, however, opposed any alternative games as being in conflict with the formal Olympic movement, and many athletes, according to gymnastics coach Roger Counsil, would consider them "lackluster." The plans were scuttled.

A proposal which had been made in the past but which now gained more serious consideration was to move the Games to a permanent site. The enormous cost of putting on the Games, which has steadily narrowed the choice of possible host cities, and the danger of any given country using them for propagandistic purposes would be greatly reduced. The Greek government offered Olympia, the birthplace of the Olympics, as a permanent site, but the IOC stood by its commitment to Moscow for 1980. The idea of a permanent site was set aside, at least for the time being.

Some U.S. athletes proposed that they be allowed to participate in the Moscow Games but not take part in the opening or closing ceremonies or the presentation of medals. The national Olympic committees of several European countries suggested that the Games be held in Moscow but without the usual political trappings. All nations would march in under the Olympic flag; all athletes would wear the same uniforms; no national anthems would be played and no flags would be raised at the award ceremonies. The IOC decided to allow teams the option of not using their national flags or anthems at Olympic ceremonies, but further depoliticization was ruled out.

Even as all the proposals were being debated and discussed, the boycott machinery was moving into high gear. The U.S. House of Representatives and Senate overwhelmingly approved resolutions supporting Carter's stand. At a February 9 meeting of the IOC in Lake Placid, the then U.S. Secretary of State Cyrus Vance reiterated to the committee that his government would oppose sending a team to the Olympic Games ''in the capital of an invading nation.'' Days later, USOC President Robert Kane announced that his organization would ''accept any decision concerning U.S. participation in the Games the president makes. . . .''

February 20, the deadline set by President Carter for the Soviets to pull out their troops from Afghanistan, passed with no change in the status quo, and the boycott was officially on. All that remained was a vote by the USOC House of Delegates at its April 11-13 meeting in Colorado Springs. In the meantime, numerous foreign governments and several National Olympic Committees came out in support.

On April 12, the USOC delegates voted in favor of the boycott by a 2-to-1 margin. The resolution did contain a provision to send a team ''if the president of the United States advises the USOC on or before May 20 that international events have become compatible with the national interest and the national security is no longer threatened.'' It was hoping against hope, of course.

In releasing the delegate vote to the press, USOC President Kane voiced the consensus: ''I am satisfied it was a completely right decision,'' he said, ''while feeling desperately sorry for the athletes who have been hurt by it.''

At the February IOC meeting in Lake Placid, U.S. Secretary of State Cyrus Vance, right, called on the committee to move the Summer Games from Moscow. IOC President Lord Killanin, here accompanied by his wife, remained staunchly opposed.

CHRONOLOGY

Dec. 27, 1979   President Hafizullah Amin of Afghanistan is overthrown and executed in a coup engineered by the USSR. Soviet troops continue to cross into Afghanistan to put down a long-standing Muslim revolt.

Dec. 30   At a meeting in Brussels, member nations of the North Atlantic Treaty Organization (NATO) discuss the idea of a boycott of the 1980 Moscow Olympics in response to the Soviet invasion. Most representatives are cool to the idea.

IOC President Lord Killanin declares that "the athletes come first, and in no way should be prevented from competing in international competition by political, racial, or religious discrimination."

Jan. 4, 1980   In a televised address to the nation, U.S. President Jimmy Carter warns the Soviet Union that "its continued aggressive actions will endanger both the participation of athletes and the travel to Moscow by spectators who would normally wish to attend the Olympic Games."

Jan. 6   Saudi Arabia announces its withdrawal from the 1980 Olympics, becoming the first nation to boycott over the crisis in Afghanistan.

Jan. 7   The 82-member executive board of the USOC decries the idea of a U.S. boycott and votes to "resist political intrusion into the Olympic Games."

Jan 14   Lord Killanin states, "It would be physically impossible to move [the Olympics from Moscow] at this stage."

Jan. 17   Speaking before the House of Commons, British Prime Minister Margaret Thatcher announces that the Cabinet will seek a change of venue for the Games.

Jan. 20   President Carter formally calls for the 1980 Summer Olympic Games to be moved out of Moscow, postponed, or canceled if the Soviet Union does not pull its troops out of Afghanistan within one month. He also recommends that the United States not send a team if the conditions are not met and urges that the Summer and Winter Games be moved to permanent sites.

| Jan. 21 | The U.S. State Department discloses that the Carter administration has sent appeals to more than 100 heads of state for support in moving the Olympics from Moscow. |

Jan. 22   The U.S. House of Representatives Foreign Affairs Committee gives quick approval to a bill endorsing Carter's proposal to move, postpone, or cancel the 1980 Games.

The governments of Australia and New Zealand announce their support for removing the Games from Moscow.

Jan. 24   The U.S. House of Representatives votes 386–12 in favor of a nonbinding resolution backing Carter's stand.

Jan. 26   The USOC executive board votes unanimously to ask the IOC to move the Games, but also announces that it will continue to "select and prepare" an Olympic team so that athletes can compete in an alternate sports festival if they do not go to Moscow.

Canada's Prime Minister Joe Clark supports a boycott. On Jan. 11 he had announced restrictions on trade, scientific, cultural, and sports exchanges with the USSR, and launched a campaign to move the Games from Moscow, possibly to Montreal.

Jan. 28   The U.S. Senate Foreign Relations Committee votes 14–0 to urge American athletes and sports fans to stay away from the Moscow Games.

An IOC source says that barring a world war or natural disaster, the Games will stay in Moscow. The source in Lausanne, Switzerland, home of the committee, asserts that transferring the Games would be against IOC rules and that postponing them would be "absolutely impossible."

Jan. 29   The U. S. Senate votes 88–4 in favor of a resolution backing Carter on his boycott stand.

At the conclusion of an emergency meeting of The Conference of Islamic States in Islamabad, Pakistan, the foreign ministers of 36 Muslim nations issue a statement denouncing "the Soviet military aggression against the Afghan people" and supporting a boycott of the Olympics unless the USSR removes its troops.

Feb. 1   President Carter assures the nation's athletes that they will have an opportunity to compete in "athletic games of the highest caliber" if they do not compete in Moscow. While the president goes into no further details, White House sources say the administration is prepared to help organize some form of international competition or counter-Olympics.

The governments of Japan, China, and Zaire indicate their opposition to holding the Olympics in Moscow, bringing to 18 the number of countries publicly favoring a boycott.

Feb. 3   Muhammad Ali begins a five-nation African tour in an effort to drum up support for the U.S. stand against the Moscow Games. He defends his mission, saying that it would not be right to "run track with the Russians, play ball with the Russians, swim with the Russians . . . or tomorrow they may make another [military] move." Tanzanian President Julius Nyerere refuses to meet with the retired boxing champion.

Feb. 8   USOC President Kane formally asks the IOC's executive board to postpone or move the Summer Olympics from Moscow.

Feb. 9   At the opening of a three-day meeting of the IOC in Lake Placid, NY, U.S. Secretary of State Cyrus Vance pleads the case for his government's opposition to holding the Summer Olympic Games in Moscow. "To hold the Olympics in any nation that is warring on another," he says, "is to lend the Olympic mantle to that nation's actions."

Feb. 10   West Germany affirms its solidarity with the United States in the Olympic question.

Feb. 12   After three days of IOC deliberation, Lord Killanin confirms that the Moscow Games will be held as planned but that he would "keep all possible options open" until May 24, the deadline for entering teams. He calls upon "the governments of all countries, and in particular those of the major powers, to come together to resolve their differences." President Carter issues a statement urging the USOC to reach "a prompt decision against sending a team to the Games."

Feb. 13   President Carter reaffirms his February 20 deadline for the withdrawal of Soviet troops from Afghanistan. Asked whether he might change his mind about the Olympics boycott if Soviet troops are removed after the deadline, Carter snaps, "I see no possibility of that."

Feb. 14   In a prepared statement, the USOC says it will "accept any decision . . . the president makes" on not sending an American team to Moscow. Robert Kane says the decision will be legally made at the USOC House of Delegates meeting April 12 in Colorado Springs.

Feb. 20   As its deadline for the withdrawal of Soviet troops from Afghanistan passes, the Carter administration makes official the U.S. government boycott of the Moscow Olympics. In a written statement, the White House affirms that Carter's position "has been overwhelmingly supported by the United States Congress and the American people" and that USOC officials and athletes are expected to follow suit.

Feb. 21   U.S. Vice-President Walter Mondale says the United States expects to announce shortly a site for alternative Olympics, but USOC President Kane says he believes the administration's boycott decision is not irrevocable.

Feb. 25   At a White House ceremony for the U.S. Winter Olympic athletes, five-time gold-medal-winning speed skater Eric Heiden presents to President Carter a petition from them opposing a boycott of the Moscow Summer Games. "The winter athletes in general just don't feel a boycott is the right thing," says Heiden.

March 3	Representatives of the USOC's Athletes Advisory Council visit the White House to discuss a counterproposal, under which they would compete in the Games but register their protest by refusing to participate in the opening, closing, and medal ceremonies.
March 5	West German Chancellor Helmut Schmidt and U.S. President Carter issue a joint communiqué in favor of a boycott.
March 12	President Carter asks for a voluntary export ban by U.S. companies planning to send their products to Moscow for the Summer Olympics. The ban would affect 30 companies and involve $20- to $30-million worth of goods.
	The U.S. Postal Service stops the sale of stamps and postcards commemorating the Moscow Games.
March 18	The British House of Commons votes 315–147 against sending a team to the Olympics.
	At a 12-nation meeting sponsored by the United States, Great Britain, and Australia, delegates agree to proceed with plans for a world sports festival for athletes of boycotting nations. The plan was not pursued.
March 21	President Carter tells a group of American athletes that the decision to boycott is irreversible. "I can't say at this moment what other nations will not go to the Summer Olympics in Moscow," he says. "Ours will not go. I say that without any equivocation. The decision has been made."
March 22	At a meeting in Brussels, representatives of 16 European national Olympic committees vote against a boycott.
March 25	In defiance of the stand taken by Prime Minister Thatcher and the vote of the House of Commons one week earlier, the British Olympic Association votes to participate in the Moscow Games.
March 28	President Carter orders Secretary of Commerce Philip M. Klutznick to prohibit the export "of any goods or technology" to the Soviet Union for use in the Olympics.
March 30	The Olympic Committee of Norway, another country which early had supported a boycott, also votes to go.
April 12	In Colorado Springs, the House of Delegates of the USOC votes 1,604–797 in favor of a resolution to boycott the 1980 Summer Olympic Games in Moscow.
April 22	Trudeau's new government announces Canada's support of a boycott and reaffirms the January cancellation of certain exchanges with the Soviet Union.
April 26	The Canadian Olympic Association backs a boycott. Following this, organizers decide that the Canada Cup, an autumn international hockey tournament that included Russia, will be cancelled in support of boycott policy.
May 24	The nations signify their intentions to the Moscow OOC. For the list of acceptances and refusals, see page 225.

The Influence of Science

Weight training methods have greatly improved with the development of new equipment.

on Sports

Sports Medicine

GALENVS

No one who watched the skiing in the Winter Games in Lake Placid missed hearing about the snapped ankle held together with screws on which Phil Mahre was making a determined try for a medal. The televised explanation by the orthopedic surgeon who mended it, illustrated with a model foot and ankle, was a memorable example of ABC's care to supply meaningful background. It was only one of several demonstrations of one part—the most dramatic part—that medical science plays in modern recreational athletics: the treatment of injury and the rehabilitation and return to sports activity of the athlete. It is the most dramatic, but by no means the principal concern of the team of specialists working with a world class athlete. The preparation and conditioning of the athlete, and the prevention of illness or injury are of equal, or greater, concern.

In the popular mind, sports medicine is associated most strongly with recreational athletics, and particularly with the highly visible world class athletes. It is, however, a very much broader field, which includes finding—perhaps even devising—sports for the handicapped; planning programs of exercise for the unhandicapped who are physically unfit; and returning the unhealthy to physical fitness through therapy.

Sports medicine is an interest as old as sports themselves. The Yazur-Veda, a manuscript of medical learning compiled perhaps 3,000 years ago in India, described and recommended the benefits of exercise. The athletes who hoped to take part in the ancient Greek Games, at Olympia and elsewhere, put themselves in the hands of trainers who dictated the daily exercise, diet, and practice of the aspirants. The *gymnastes,* as the trainers were called, toughened their charges on the diet and living conditions characteristic of the battlefield, to give them the endurance that could separate winners from losers.

Galen of Pergamon, whose care of Roman gladiators make him the earliest team physician known, learned a good deal about the human body and the functions of many of its components, and he carefully recorded his observations. He recognized the body's need of exercise if it is to remain healthy, but he did not have a shred of the early Greeks' reverence for the professional athlete. On the contrary, he held professional athletes to be the equal of brutes, and pronounced their vigorous or violent activity more favorable to illness than health. Other voices to the contrary, it was Galen's that remained the most influential through the Middle Ages.

As it did about almost all aspects of existence, the Renaissance reopened minds about sports, and in particular, about the virtues of exercise, even the most vigorous. Gerolamo Mercuriale's 16th-century writing on the Art of Gymnastics filled six books with discussions of preventive and therapeutic exercises. His near contemporary, Cagnatus of Verone, recommended training physicians especially to supervise sports; such background, he believed, and a love of sports, were essential to the understanding of the problems of athletes.

Succeeding centuries increased the understanding of the relationship between physical exercise and health, and between nutrition and health, but it wasn't until the 20th century that any comprehensive sports medicine, as we use the term, came into being. Over and above the interests cited above—the effects of sports activities on the body, the injuries such activity may bring about, and the treatment the injuries should have; the development of exercise for rehabilitation, and the application of the correct exercise for a given end—sports medicine encompasses much more. It includes the study of muscle, nerve, heart, and breathing to develop maximum speed, endurance, and strength; the study of drugs and their effects on the body, and of ways to detect prohibited drugs that may be used by competitors in physical contests to gain a performance edge; the genotyping of athletes in athletic contests to prevent illegal entrants in events separated by sex; and even the developing of the correct sports attire.

The participation in sports by large numbers of the population is a 20th century development that reflects both increased leisure and greater general affluence. Among Americans alone, enthusiastic participants in sports sustain more than 17 million sports injuries a year. That statistic is perceived as more than adequate explanation for the emphasis today on sports medicine. But of greater importance than its treatment-oriented aspects is the sports medicine research that is directed toward assisting the athlete in proper conditioning, training, and competition.

The importance of sports medical research to athletic programs has long been acknowledged in the countries of East Europe, notably the Soviet Union and the German Democratic Republic, where the performance of athletes in international competition is viewed as a measure of national strength. But other countries as well—Canada, for example—have established strong programs of research in sports medicine, with doctor, coach, and athlete working together to improve performance.

In the Final Report of the President's Commission on Olympic Sports 1975-77, it was noted that one of the problems in countries like the United States, which do not have state-controlled sports programs, is instilling the results of research in sports medicine in the people—coaches and athletes—who can most benefit from them. To illustrate the point, take the example of nutrition.

From the time of the Greek Games, the importance of diet in the conditioning and training program was known, but what a good diet comprised was not certain. Milo of Croton, who was supposed to have developed his great strength by carrying a calf

Bicycle racing is good training for any athlete. Below, a cyclist works out at the USOC's Colorado Springs, CO, training center. The track, normally used for running, is made of a synthetic material called Chevron 400. A four-inch base of asphalt is covered with a three-quarter inch layer of polyurethane and ground, used automobile tires.

every day until it was a full-grown bull, won the wrestling competitions six times in the 6th century B.C. His diet was seen as suitable to a big winner: 20 pounds each of bread and meat a day, and 9 quarts of wine. It was a small step to the conclusion that to be a victor like Milo, one should eat like Milo.

The idea that eating a strong animal makes the eater strong took deep root, and not only among primitive people. In the late 15th century, the soldiers of the Catholic sovereigns Ferdinand and Isabella, thought to need all their strength in the battle to drive the Moors from Spain, were allowed meat on Fridays and fast days. Thereafter, Spaniards preserved that distinction from other Roman Catholics.

Right to the present time, until sports science research came to bear, the precontest meal of steak was a familiar thing. But research showed that the body does not ordinarily use protein as an energy source, which meant that the steak was unyielding of either strength or power; the athlete was better off to eat nothing before his competition.

Athletes and their coaches, keen to find any means to better performance, are often ready-made for fads. Vitamins in bulk, food supplements, various drugs, and such practices as ''blood doping'' have all had their believers and advocates. Drugs and their possible misuse led to the creation of the Medical Commission of the International Olympic Committee. The commission maintains a list of banned substances, and instituted procedures for testing athletes to be sure no such substances are in intentional use.

In 1972 in Munich Rick De Mont, a member of the U.S.

The Cybex strength-testing machine at Colorado Springs helps an athlete develop his legs. Advances in the design of training shoes have also helped improve performances.

swimming team, won a gold medal, submitted urine in a routine test, and lost the medal. Medication prescribed for asthma by his physician contained a prohibited substance.

In many instances the use of drugs is intentional. In Montreal, anabolic steroids became the main target of official concern. Anabolic steroids, which are modified male hormones, were being taken to increase weight, enhance muscle development, and augment aggressiveness and competitiveness. The women swimmers of the victorious East German team were accused of using steroids. The drug is forbidden because research shows that prolonged use can result in bone deformities, tumors, prostate problems, and impotence.

Of more recent date is the recourse to testosterone for the same purposes as anabolic steroids. The male sex hormone occurs naturally; it is not an illegal substance. But its massive use worries sports authorities. Research shows that it has the same deleterious results as the steroids when taken in massive doses.

Conditioning involves more than just the care and feeding of the athlete. The mental and emotional preparation are of immediate consequence in achieving athletic excellence. Sports psychologists help the athlete to accept and counter the pain that exertion entails, to deal with the anxieties and the tensions that precede competiton, and to handle the stress that builds up. Sports physiologists are able to help an athlete to push to his physical limits without harm, by training with such devices as a treadmill equipped with biotelemetry monitors. The physiologist can measure body performance rates in actual training and see how hard the athlete works to achieve the proper intensity of stress. Biotelemetry provides the opportunity to spot specific problems. For example, a runner who falls apart in the homestretch may see how to correlate his heart rate and his running for better results.

The recognition that sports medicine is of intensifying importance is attested to by its standing as a medical specialty in several European countries. There is no corresponding medical specialty in the United States, but several organizations support research and development in the field.

Biotelemetry, the measurement of heartbeat, muscle activity, oxygenation, and other physiological functions, is another new tool in athletic training. Miniature radio transmitters allow athletes to monitor those functions and achieve maximal levels of physical exertion and mental stress. At right, U.S. Olympic cross-country skier Beth Paxson undergoes oxygen measurement in a rigorous treadmill exercise.

Sports Technology

Made to glide on asphalt, pseudo-skates enabled Eric Heiden to practice his racing technique year-round. Makeshift as they are, they obviously worked for Heiden.

A close look at the Olympic record books demonstrates that the motto of the Games—Swifter, Higher, Stronger—has been well served over the years.· Every four winters sledders and speed skaters are a split-second faster, skiers a little stronger, and the leaps of the figure skaters a few inches higher and a touch more graceful. Since 1896 summer Olympians have been recording steadily decreasing times in running and swimming, longer distances in throwing, and greater heights in leaping. The 400-meter freestyle swimming event is just one example of how dramatically performances have improved. In 1964, Donald Schollander of the United States recorded a time of 4:12.2 to beat the previous men's Olympic record by a remarkable 6.1 seconds. At the Montreal Games only 12 years later, Petra Thuemer of East Germany won the women's version of the event in a time of 4:09.89, more than two full seconds faster than Schollander. And the growth of athletic prowess is not confined to the amateur ranks. Baseballs are hit harder, footballs thrown farther, and basketballs shot with more accuracy than ever before. The athletes themselves are bigger, stronger, and better trained.

One explanation is that conditioning methods are becoming increasingly more sophisticated, the care and development of athletes more scientific. But a frequently overlooked consideration is the effect of technological advances in equipment and facilities. Just as industry, agriculture, transportation, and daily life itself have been revolutionized by the technological developments of the last 100 years, so too has the world of sports.

Although these innovations often seem subtle and of minor consequence, their cumulative effect is to enhance athletic performances notably. The periodic breaking of records coincides with steady and ongoing advances in sports technology. The 1980 Olympic Winter Games in Lake Placid provided numerous examples of such improvements in equipment and facilities.

Speed skating, in which all nine Olympic records were broken, had the look of a science fiction movie as the racers competed in tight, nylon, one-piece, hooded suits called "skins." Introduced before the 1976 Games, the suits were refined over the next several years. Tested in wind tunnels, they cut resistance and increase a skater's speed. Another development was a specially-designed roller skate for off-season training. The wheels are lined up horizontally, and, according to U.S. coach Dianne Holum, the skate provides "a good variation in training" when an icy rink is not available. And at Lake Placid itself, skating conditions were enhanced by several miles of refrigeration pipes under the surface of the speed skating oval. Strong performances were guaranteed by a reliably fast and evenly refrigerated surface.

Technological improvements were seen also in the skiing

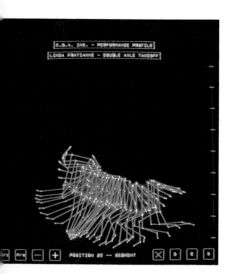

In Alpine and Nordic competition alike, the choice of wax may mean the difference between victory and defeat. The waxes are scientifically tested under different snow conditions and carefully applied the night before or on the morning of the race. Below, a computerized video-screen displays the performance profile of a double-axle takeoff by figure skater Linda Fratianne.

competitions. The effectiveness of various waxes was closely and scientifically examined by ski manufacturers and team coaches. Precise timing devices and sophisticated instruments for measuring the tensile strength of the snow were used to determine which wax to use. In the Alpine downhill race, skiers used bent poles for minimal resistance in the all-important "tuck" position. In Nordic skiing, lightweight fiberglass skis, weighing 1½ pounds each, have replaced heavier ash skis; bindings are lighter; and carbon-fiber poles have replaced the old bamboo poles. In ski jumping, several competitors used skis with a flexible rubber heel for additional lift.

Design innovations in the bobsled are being studied at the American Bobsled Research Association and elsewhere, and ways to speed up the luge have been devised. Governing bodies for these sports may have to define more precise regulations to keep up with technological advances. The situation eventually may become similar to auto racing, in which engineering improvements are sometimes outlawed by the racing associations. The practice of heating luge runners has already been declared illegal.

Indeed one can look at almost any sport and find developments that have improved or at least altered athletes' performances. Some have greater effect than others. Perhaps the greatest revolution has come in the area of ground surfaces. In baseball, Astroturf is a hitter's dream; in football, it gives halfbacks nightmares of skinned elbows and torn knee cartilage. Tartan, a synthetic resin surface, replaced the traditional cinder track and the effect was dramatic. The material was first used in the Olympics at the 1968 Mexico City Games, and the running and jumping events saw new Olympic or world records, several of which still stand. The best example was Bob Beamon's long jump of 29′ 2½″, more than 21 inches longer than the previous world mark. Specialists are now engaged in research on new synthetic materials for indoor and outdoor courts and for improved running tracks. A West German firm has developed an artificial turf called poligras, which does not accumulate static electricity and which absorbs moisture better than the original Astroturf. The French taraflex, used for indoor volleyball and handball at the Montreal Olympics, was further improved by the Soviets (their version is called taraflex-sport-VB) for use in the volleyball tournament at the 1980 Moscow Games. Soviet and West German engineers also have been working on a track surface with small steel spirals woven into a thick mat for added spring and traction.

Fiberglass vaulting poles, foam rubber landing pits, better designed running shoes, metal tennis racquets and more visible yellow balls, wave-reducing lane dividers in swimming pools, photo-electric timing devices, and domed stadiums are just some other relatively recent developments that have fundamentally affected the pursuit of athletic excellence. As for the future, new innovations no doubt will emerge from the laboratories, testing grounds, wind tunnels, and scientifically-controlled experimental environments of equipment manufacturers and amateur researchers. The final results, of course, will be seen in the arenas of athletic competition.

In track and field, pole vaulters were enabled to achieve new heights with the fiberglass poles introduced in the early 1960's. Left, the use of foam rubber in the landing pit allowed high jumpers to adopt new techniques. The sand or sawdust used previously would have been most uninviting to the Fosbury Flopper.

WINTER GAMES

Gold Medalists	Silver Medalists	Bronze Medalists

Alpine Skiing

Men's Downhill

	Gold	Silver	Bronze
1948	Henri Oreiller (FRA)	Franz Gabl (AUT)	Karl Molitor (SUI)
			Ralph Olinger (SUI)
1952	Zeno Colò (ITA)	Othmar Schneider (AUT)	Christian Pravda (AUT)
1956	Anton Sailer (AUT)	Raymond Fellay (SUI)	Anderl Molterer (AUT)
1960	Jean Vuarnet (FRA)	Hans-Peter Lanig (GER)	Guy Périllat (FRA)
1964	Egon Zimmermann II (AUT)	Léo Lacroix (FRA)	Wolfgang Bartels (GER)
1968	Jean-Claude Killy (FRA)	Guy Périllat (FRA)	Jean-Daniel Dätwyler (SUI)
1972	Bernhard Russi (SUI)	Roland Collombin (SUI)	Heini Messner (AUT)
1976	Franz Klammer (AUT)	Bernhard Russi (SUI)	Herbert Plank (ITA)
1980	Leonhard Stock (AUT)	Peter Wirnsberger (AUT)	Stephen Podborski (CAN)

Men's Giant Slalom

	Gold	Silver	Bronze
1952	Stein Eriksen (NOR)	Christian Pravda (AUT)	Toni Spiss (AUT)
1956	Anton Sailer (AUT)	Anderl Molterer (AUT)	Walter Schuster (AUT)
1960	Roger Staub (SUI)	Josef Stiegler (AUT)	Ernst Hinterseer (AUT)
1964	François Bonlieu (FRA)	Karl Schranz (AUT)	Josef Stiegler (AUT)
1968	Jean-Claude Killy (FRA)	Willy Favre (SUI)	Heini Messner (AUT)
1972	Gustavo Thoeni (ITA)	Edmund Bruggmann (SUI)	Werner Mattle (SUI)
1976	Heini Hemmi (SUI)	Ernst Good (SUI)	Ingemar Stenmark (SWE)
1980	Ingemar Stenmark (SWE)	Andreas Wenzel (LIE)	Hans Enn (AUT)

Men's Slalom

	Gold	Silver	Bronze
1948	Edi Reinalter (SUI)	James Couttet (FRA)	Henri Oreiller (FRA)
1952	Othmar Schneider (AUT)	Stein Eriksen (NOR)	Guttorm Berge (NOR)
1956	Anton Sailer (AUT)	Chiharu Igaya (JPN)	Stig Sollander (SWE)
1960	Ernst Hinterseer (AUT)	Hias Leitner (AUT)	Charles Bozon (FRA)
1964	Josef Stiegler (AUT)	Bill Kidd (USA)	James Heuga (USA)
1968	Jean-Claude Killy (FRA)	Herbert Huber (AUT)	Alfred Matt (AUT)
1972	Francisco Fernández-Ochoa (ESP)	Gustavo Thoeni (ITA)	Roland Thoeni (ITA)
1976	Piero Gros (ITA)	Gustavo Thoeni (ITA)	Willy Frommelt (LIE)
1980	Ingemar Stenmark (SWE)	Phil Mahre (USA)	Jacques Luethy (SUI)

Women's Downhill

	Gold	Silver	Bronze
1948	Hedy Schlunegger (SUI)	Trude Beiser (AUT)	Resi Hammerer (AUT)
1952	Trude Jochum-Beiser (AUT)	Annemarie Buchner (GER)	Giuliana Minuzzo (ITA)
1956	Madeleine Berthod (SUI)	Frieda Dänzer (SUI)	Lucile Wheeler (CAN)
1960	Heidi Biebl (GER)	Penny Pitou (USA)	Traudl Hecher (AUT)
1964	Christl Haas (AUT)	Edith Zimmermann (AUT)	Traudl Hecher (AUT)
1968	Olga Pall (AUT)	Isabelle Mir (FRA)	Christl Haas (AUT)
1972	Marie-Theres Nadig (SUI)	Annemarie Proell (AUT)	Susan Corrock (USA)
1976	Rosi Mittermaier (GER)	Brigitte Totschnig (AUT)	Cindy Nelson (USA)
1980	Annemarie Moser-Proell (AUT)	Hanni Wenzel (LIE)	Marie-Theres Nadig (SUI)

Women's Giant Slalom

	Gold	Silver	Bronze
1952	Andrea Mead Lawrence (USA)	Dagmar Rom (AUT)	Annemarie Buchner (GER)
1956	Ossi Reichert (GER)	Josefine Frandl (AUT)	Dorothea Hochleitner (AUT)
1960	Yvonne Rüegg (SUI)	Penny Pitou (USA)	Giuliana Chenal-Minuzzo (ITA)
1964	Marielle Goitschel (FRA)	Christine Goitschel (FRA)	Jean Saubert (USA)
1968	Nancy Greene (CAN)	Annie Famose (FRA)	Fernande Bochatay (SUI)
1972	Marie-Theres Nadig (SUI)	Annemarie Proell (AUT)	Wiltrud Drexel (AUT)
1976	Kathy Kreiner (CAN)	Rosi Mittermaier (GER)	Danièle Debernard (FRA)
1980	Hanni Wenzel (LIE)	Irene Epple (GER)	Perrine Pelen (FRA)

Women's Slalom

	Gold	Silver	Bronze
1948	Gretchen Fraser (USA)	Antoinette Meyer (SUI)	Erika Mahringer (AUT)
1952	Andrea Mead Lawrence (USA)	Ossi Reichert (GER)	Annemarie Buchner (GER)
1956	Renée Colliard (SUI)	Regina Schopf (AUT)	Yevgeniya Sidorowa (URS)
1960	Anne Heggtveit (CAN)	Betsy Snite (USA)	Barbi Henneberger (GER)
1964	Christine Goitschel (FRA)	Marielle Goitschel (FRA)	Jean Saubert (USA)
1968	Marielle Goitschel (FRA)	Nancy Greene (CAN)	Annie Famose (FRA)
1972	Barbara Cochran (USA)	Danièle Debernard (FRA)	Florence Steurer (FRA)
1976	Rosi Mittermaier (GER)	Claudia Giordani (ITA)	Hanni Wenzel (LIE)
1980	Hanni Wenzel (LIE)	Christa Kinshofer (GER)	Erika Hess (SUI)

| | Gold Medalists | Silver Medalists | Bronze Medalists |

Biathlon

10-Kilometer Individual

| 1980 | Frank Ullrich (GDR) | Vladimir Alikin (URS) | Anatoli Aljabiev (URS) |

20-Kilometer Individual

1960	Klas Lestander (SWE)	Antti Tyrväinen (FIN)	Aleksandr Privalov (URS)
1964	Vladimir Melanin (URS)	Aleksandr Privalov (URS)	Olav Jordet (NOR)
1968	Magnar Solberg (NOR)	Alexander Tikhonov (URS)	Vladimir Gundartsev (URS)
1972	Magnar Solberg (NOR)	Hans-Jörg Knauthe (GDR)	Lars-Göran Arwidson (SWE)
1976	Nikolai Kruglov (URS)	Heikki Ikola (FIN)	Aleksandr Elizarov (URS)
1980	Anatoli Aljabiev (URS)	Frank Ullrich (GDR)	Eberhard Rosch (GDR)

Relay

1968	URS (Alexander Tikhonov, Nikolai Pussanov, Viktor Mamatov, Vladimir Gundartsev)	NOR (Ola Waerhaug, Olav Jordet, Magnar Solberg, Jon Istad)	SWE (Lars-Göran Arwidson, Tore Eriksson, Olle Petrusson, Holmfrid Olsson)
1972	URS (Alexander Tikhonov, Rinnat Safin, Ivan Bjakov, Viktor Mamatov)	FIN (Esko Saira, Juhani Suutarinen, Heikki Ikola, Mauri Röppänen)	GDR (Hans-Jörg Knauthe, Joachim Meischner, Dieter Speer, Horst Koschka)
1976	URS (Aleksandr Elizarov, Ivan Bjakov, Nikolai Kruglov, Alexander Tikhonov)	FIN (Henrik Flöjt, Esko Saira, Juhani Suutarinen, Heikki Ikola)	GDR (Karl-Heinz Menz, Frank Ullrich, Manfred Beer, Manfred Geyer)
1980	URS (Vladimir Alikin, Alexander Tikhonov, Vladimir Barnaschov, Anatoli Aljabiev)	GDR (Mathias Jung, Klaus Siebert, Frank Ullrich, Eberhard Rosch)	GER (Franz Bernreiter, Hansi Estner, Peter Angerer, Gerd Winkler)

Bobsled

2-Man

1932	USA (Hubert Stevens, Curtis Stevens)	SUI (Reto Capadrutt, Oscar Geier)	USA (John R. Heaton, Robert Minton)
1936	USA (Ivan Brown, Alan Washbond)	SUI (Fritz Feierabend, Joseph Beerli)	USA (Gilbert Colgate, Richard Lawrence)
1948	SUI (Felix Endrich, Friedrich Waller)	SUI (Fritz Feierabend, Paul Eberhard)	USA (Fred Fortune, Schuyler Carron)
1952	GER (Andreas Ostler, Lorenz Nieberl)	USA (Stanley Benham, Patrick Martin)	SUI (Fritz Feierabend, Stephan Waser)
1956	ITA (Lamberto Dalla Costa, Giacomo Conti)	ITA (Eugenio Monti, Renzo Alverà)	SUI (Max Angst, Harry Warburton)
1960	Not Held		
1964	GBR (Anthony Nash, Robin Dixon)	ITA (Sergio Zardini, Romano Bonagura)	ITA (Eugenio Monti, Sergio Siorpaes)
1968	ITA (Eugenio Monti, Luciano De Paolis)	GER (Horst Floth, Pepi Bader)	RUM (Ion Panturu, Nicolae Neagoe)
1972	GER (Wolfgang Zimmerer, Peter Utzschneider)	GER (Horst Floth, Pepi Bader)	SUI (Jean Wicki, Edy Hubacher)
1976	GDR (Meinhard Nehmer, Bernhard Germeshausen)	GER (Wolfgang Zimmerer, Manfred Schumann)	SUI (Erich Schaerer, Josef Benz)
1980	SUI (Erich Schaerer, Josef Benz)	GDR (Bernhard Germeshausen, Hans Jurgen Gerhardt)	GDR (Meinhard Nehmer, Bosdan Musiol)

4-Man

1924	SUI (Eduard Scherrer, Alfred Neveu, Alfred Schläppi, Henrich Schläppi)	GBR (Ralph H. Broome, T. A. Arnold, H. A. W. Richardson, Rodney E. Soher)	BEL (Charles Mulder, René Mortiaux, Paul van den Broeck, Victor Verschueren, Henri Willems)
1928	USA (William Fiske, Nion Tocker, Charles Mason, Clifford Gray, Richard Parke)	USA (Jennison Heaton, David Granger, Lyman Hine, Thomas Doe, Jay O'Brien)	GER (Hanns Kilian, Valentin Krempl, Hans Hess, Sebastian Huber, Hans Nägle
1932	USA (William Fiske, Edward Eagan, Clifford Gray, Jay O'Brien)	USA (Henry Homburger, Percy Bryant, Paul Stevens, Edmund Horton)	GER (Hanns Kilian, Max Ludwig, Hans Mehlhorn, Sebastian Huber)
1936	SUI (Pierre Musy, Arnold Gartmann, Charles Bouvier, Joseph Beerli)	SUI (Reto Capadrutt, Hans Aichele, Fritz Feierabend, Hans Bütikofer)	GBR (Frederick McEvoy, James Cardno, Guy Dugdale, Charles Green)

Gold Medalists	Silver Medalists	Bronze Medalists

Bobsled (continued)

	Gold Medalists	Silver Medalists	Bronze Medalists
1948	USA (Francis Tyler, Patrick Martin, Edward Rimkus, William D'Amico)	BEL (Max Houben, Freddy Mansveld, Louis-Georges Niels, Jacques Mouvet)	USA (James Bickford, Thomas Hicks, Donald Dupree, William Dupree)
1952	GER (Andreas Ostler, Friedrich Kuhn, Lorenz Nieberl, Franz Kemser)	USA (Stanley Benham, Patrick Martin, Howard Crossett, James Atkinson)	SUI (Fritz Feierabend, Albert Madörin, André Filippini, Stephan Waser)
1956	SUI (Franz Kapus, Gottfried Diener, Robert Alt, Heinrich Angst)	ITA (Eugenio Monti, Ulrico Girardi, Renzo Alverà, Renato Mocellini)	USA (Arthur Tyler, William Dodge, Charles Butler, James Lamy)
1960	Not Held		
1964	CAN (Victor Emery, Peter Kirby, Douglas Anakin, John Emery)	AUT (Erwin Thaler, Adolf Koxeder, Josef Nairz, Reinhold Durnthaler)	ITA (Eugenio Monti, Sergio Siorpaes, Benito Rigoni, Gildo Siorpaes)
1968	ITA (Eugenio Monti, Luciano De Paolis, Roberto Zandonella, Mario Armano)	AUT (Erwin Thaler, Reinhold Durnthaler, Herbert Gruber, Josef Eder)	SUI (Jean Wicki, Hans Candrian, Willi Hofmann, Walter Graf)
1972	SUI (Jean Wicki, Hans Leutenegger, Werner Camichel, Edy Hubacher)	ITA (Nevio De Zordo, Adriano Frassinelli, Corrado Dal Fabbro, Gianni Bonichon)	GER (Wolfgang Zimmerer, Stefan Gaisreiter, Walter Steinbauer, Peter Utzschneider)
1976	GDR (Meinhard Nehmer, Jochen Babok, Bernhard Germeshausen, Bernhard Lehmann)	SUI (Erich Schaerer, Ulrich Baechli, Rudolf Marti, Josef Benz)	GER (Wolfgang Zimmerer, Peter Utzschneider, Bodo Bittner, Manfred Schumann)
1980	GDR (Meinhard Nehmer, Bosdan Musiol, Bernhard Germeshausen, H. J. Gerhardt)	SUI (Erich Schaerer, Ulrich Baechli, Rudolf Marti, Josef Benz)	GDR (Horst Schoenau, Roland Wetzig, Detlef Richter, Andreas Kirchner)

Figure Skating

Pairs

	Gold Medalists	Silver Medalists	Bronze Medalists
1908	GER (Anna Hübler, Heinrich Burger)	GBR (Phyllis Johnson, James Johnson)	GBR (Madge Syers, Edgar Syers)
1920	FIN (Ludowika Jakobsson-Eilers, Walter Jakobsson-Eilers)	NOR (Alexia Bryn, Yngvar Bryn)	GBR (Phyllis Johnson, Basil Williams)
1924	AUT (Helene Engelmann, Alfred Berger)	FIN (Ludowika Jakobsson-Eilers, Walter Jakobsson-Eilers)	FRA (Andrée Joly, Pierre Brunet)
1928	FRA (Andrée Joly, Pierre Brunet)	AUT (Lilly Scholz, Otto Kaiser)	AUT (Melitta Brunner, Ludwig Wrede)
1932	FRA (Andrée Brunet, Pierre Brunet)	USA (Beatrix Loughran, Sherwin Badger)	HUN (Emilia Rotter, László Szollás)
1936	GER (Maxie Herber, Ernst Baier)	AUT (Ilse Pausin, Erik Pausin)	HUN (Emilia Rotter, László Szollás)
1948	BEL (Micheline Lannoy, Pierre Baugniet)	HUN (Andrea Kékessy, Ede Király)	CAN (Suzanne Morrow, Wallace Diestelmeyer)
1952	GER (Ria Falk, Paul Falk)	USA (Karol Kennedy, Michael Kennedy)	HUN (Marianna Nagy, László Nagy)
1956	AUT (Elisabeth Schwarz, Kurt Oppelt)	CAN (Frances Dafoe, Norris Bowden)	HUN (Marianna Nagy, László Nagy)
1960	CAN (Barbara Wagner, Robert Paul)	GER (Marika Kilius, Hans-Jürgen Bäumler)	USA (Nancy Ludington, Ronald Ludington)
1964	URS (Ludmilla Beloussova, Oleg Protopopov)	GER (Marika Kilius, Hans-Jürgen Bäumler)	CAN (Debbi Wilkes, Guy Revell)
1968	URS (Ludmilla Beloussova, Oleg Protopopov)	URS (Tatjana Schuk, Aleksandr Gorelik)	GER (Margot Glockshuber, Wolfgang Danne)
1972	URS (Irina Rodnina, Aleksei Ulanov)	URS (Ludmilla Smirnova, Andrei Suraikin)	GDR (Manuela Gross, Uwe Kagelmann)
1976	URS (Irina Rodnina, Aleksandr Zaitsev)	GDR (Romy Kermer, Rolf Österreich)	GDR (Manuela Gross, Uwe Kagelmann)
1980	URS (Irina Rodnina, Aleksandr Zaitsev)	URS (Marina Cherkosova, Sergei Shakrai)	GDR (Manuela Mager, Uwe Bewersdorff)

Men's Singles

	Gold Medalists	Silver Medalists	Bronze Medalists
1908	Ulrich Salchow (SWE)	Richard Johansson (SWE)	Per Thorén (SWE)
1920	Gillis Grafström (SWE)	Andreas Krogh (NOR)	Martin Stixrud (NOR)
1924	Gillis Grafström (SWE)	Willy Böckl (AUT)	Georges Gautschi (SUI)
1928	Gillis Grafström (SWE)	Willy Böckl (AUT)	Robert van Zeebroeck (BEL)
1932	Karl Schaefer (AUT)	Gillis Grafström (SWE)	Montgomery Wilson (CAN)
1936	Karl Schaefer (AUT)	Ernst Baier (GER)	Felix Kaspar (AUT)
1948	Richard Button (USA)	Hans Gerschwiler (SUI)	Edi Rada (AUT)
1952	Richard Button (USA)	Helmut Seibt (AUT)	James Grogan (USA)
1956	Hayes Alan Jenkins (USA)	Ronald Robertson (USA)	David Jenkins (USA)
1960	David Jenkins (USA)	Karol Divin (TCH)	Donald Jackson (CAN)

Gold Medalists	Silver Medalists	Bronze Medalists
1964	Manfred Schnelldorfer (GER)	Alain Calmat (FRA)	Scott Allen (USA)
1968	Wolfgang Schwarz (AUT)	Timothy Wood (USA)	Patrick Péra (FRA)
1972	Ondrej Nepela (TCH)	Sergei Chetveroukhin (URS)	Patrick Péra (FRA)
1976	John Curry (GBR)	Vladimir Kovalev (URS)	Toller Cranston (CAN)
1980	Robin Cousins (GBR)	Jan Hoffmann (GDR)	Charles Tickner (USA)

Women's Singles

1908	Madge Syers (GBR)	Elsa Rendschmidt (GER)	Dorothy Greenhough-Smith (GBR)
1920	Magda Julin-Mauroy (SWE)	Svea Norén (SWE)	Theresa Weld (USA)
1924	Herma Planck-Szabó (AUT)	Beatrix Loughran (USA)	Ethel Muckelt (GBR)
1928	Sonja Henie (NOR)	Fritzi Burger (AUT)	Beatrix Loughran (USA)
1932	Sonja Henie (NOR)	Fritzi Burger (AUT)	Maribel Vinson (USA)
1936	Sonja Henie (NOR)	Cecilia Colledge (GBR)	Vivi-Anne Hultén (SWE)
1948	Barbara Ann Scott (CAN)	Eva Pawlik (AUT)	Jeanette Altwegg (GBR)
1952	Jeanette Altwegg (GBR)	Tenley Albright (USA)	Jacqueline du Bief (FRA)
1956	Tenley Albright (USA)	Carol Heiss (USA)	Ingrid Wendl (AUT)
1960	Carol Heiss (USA)	Sjoukje Dijkstra (HOL)	Barbara Roles (USA)
1964	Sjoukje Dijkstra (HOL)	Regine Heitzer (AUT)	Petra Burka (CAN)
1968	Peggy Fleming (USA)	Gabriele Seyfert (GDR)	Hana Mašková (TCH)
1972	Beatrix Schuba (AUT)	Karen Magnussen (CAN)	Janet Lynn (USA)
1976	Dorothy Hamill (USA)	Dianne de Leeuw (HOL)	Christine Errath (GDR)
1980	Anett Poetzsch (GDR)	Linda Fratianne (USA)	Dagmar Lurz (GER)

Ice Dancing

1976	URS (Ludmila Pakhomova, Aleksandr Gorshkov)	URS (Irina Moiseeva, Andrey Minenkov)	USA (Colleen O'Connor, James G. Millns)
1980	URS (Natalia Linichuk, Gennadi Karponosov)	HUN (Krisztina Regoczy, Andras Sallay)	URS (Irina Moiseeva, Andrey Minenkov)

Ice Hockey

1920	CAN	USA	TCH
1924	CAN	USA	GBR
1928	CAN	SWE	SUI
1932	CAN	USA	GER
1936	GBR	CAN	USA
1948	CAN	TCH	SUI
1952	CAN	USA	SWE
1956	URS	USA	CAN
1960	USA	CAN	URS
1964	URS	SWE	TCH
1968	URS	TCH	CAN
1972	URS	USA	TCH
1976	URS	TCH	GER
1980	USA	URS	SWE

Luge

Men's Singles

1964	Thomas Koehler (GER)	Klaus Bonsack (GER)	Hans Plenk (GER)
1968	Manfred Schmid (AUT)	Thomas Koehler (GDR)	Klaus Bonsack (GDR)
1972	Wolfgang Scheidl (GDR)	Harald Ehrig (GDR)	Wolfram Fiedler (GDR)
1976	Detlef Guenther (GDR)	Josef Fendt (GER)	Hans Rinn (GDR)
1980	Bernhard Glass (GDR)	Paul Hildgartner (ITA)	Anton Winkler (GER)

Men's Doubles

1964	AUT (Josef Feistmantl, Manfred Stengl)	AUT (Reinhold Senn, Helmut Thaler)	ITA (Walter Aussendorfer, Sigisfredo Mair)
1968	GDR (Klaus Bonsack, Thomas Koehler)	AUT (Manfred Schmid, Ewald Walch)	GER (Wolfgang Winkler, Fritz Nachmann)
1972	ITA (Paul Hildgartner, Walter Plaikner) GDR (Horst Hörnlein, Reinhard Bredow) (tie)	no medal	GDR (Klaus Bonsack, Wolfram Fiedler)
1976	GDR (Hans Rinn, Norbert Hahn)	GER (Hans Brandner, Balthasar Schwarm)	AUT (Rudolf Schmid, Franz Schachner)
1980	GDR (Hans Rinn, Norbert Hahn)	ITA (Peter Gschnitzer, Karl Brunner)	AUT (Georg Fluckinger, Karl Schrott)

Gold Medalists	Silver Medalists	Bronze Medalists

Women's Singles

Luge (continued)

	Gold	Silver	Bronze
1964	Ortrun Enderlein (GER)	Ilse Geisler (GER)	Helene Thurner (AUT)
1968	Erica Lechner (ITA)	Christa Schmuck (GER)	Angelika Dünhaupt (GER)
1972	Anna-Maria Müller (GDR)	Ute Rührold (GDR)	Margit Schumann (GDR)
1976	Margit Schumann (GDR)	Ute Rührold (GDR)	Elisabeth Demleitner (GER)
1980	Vera Zozulia (URS)	Melitta Sollmann (GDR)	Ingrida Amantova (URS)

Nordic Skiing

Men's 15-Kilometer Cross-Country

	Gold	Silver	Bronze
1924	Thorleif Haug (NOR)	Johan Gröttumsbraaten (NOR)	Tapani Niku (FIN)
1928	Johan Gröttumsbraaten (NOR)	Ole Hegge (NOR)	Reidar Odegaard (NOR)
1932	Sven Utterström (SWE)	Axel T. Wikström (SWE)	Veli Saarinen (FIN)
1936	Erik-August Larsson (SWE)	Oddbjörn Hagen (NOR)	Pekka Niemi (FIN)
1948	Martin Lundström (SWE)	Nils Östensson (SWE)	Gunnar Eriksson (SWE)
1952	Hallgeir Brenden (NOR)	Tapio Mäkelä (FIN)	Paavo Lonkila (FIN)
1956	Hallgeir Brenden (NOR)	Sixten Jernberg (SWE)	Pavel Koltschin (URS)
1960	Haakon Brusveen (NOR)	Sixten Jernberg (SWE)	Veikko Hakulinen (FIN)
1964	Eero Mäntyranta (FIN)	Harald Grönningen (NOR)	Sixten Jernberg (SWE)
1968	Harald Grönningen (NOR)	Eero Mäntyrana (FIN)	Gunnar Larsson (SWE)
1972	Sven-Åke Lundbäck (SWE)	Fjodor Simaschew (URS)	Ivar Formo (NOR)
1976	Nikolai Bajukov (URS)	Evgeni Beliaev (URS)	Arto Koivisto (FIN)
1980	Thomas Wassberg (SWE)	Juha Mieto (FIN)	Ove Aunli (NOR)

Men's 30-Kilometer Cross-Country

	Gold	Silver	Bronze
1956	Veikko Hakulinen (FIN)	Sixten Jernberg (SWE)	Pavel Koltschin (URS)
1960	Sixten Jernberg (SWE)	Rolf Rämgård (SWE)	Nikolai Anikin (URS)
1964	Eero Mäntyranta (FIN)	Harald Grönningen (NOR)	Igor Worontschichin (URS)
1968	Franco Nones (ITA)	Odd Martinsen (NOR)	Eero Mäntyranta (FIN)
1972	Vyacheslav Vedenin (URS)	Paal Tyldum (NOR)	Johs Harviken (NOR)
1976	Sergei Saveliev (URS)	William Koch (USA)	Ivan Garanin (URS)
1980	Nikolai Zimyatov (URS)	Vasili Rochev (URS)	Ivan Lebanov (BUL)

Men's 50-Kilometer Cross-Country

	Gold	Silver	Bronze
1924	Thorleif Haug (NOR)	Thoralf Strömstad (NOR)	Johan Gröttumsbraaten (NOR)
1928	Per Erik Hedlund (SWE)	Gustaf Jonsson (SWE)	Volger Andersson (SWE)
1932	Veli Saarinen (FIN)	Väinö Liikkanen (FIN)	Arne Rustadstuen (NOR)
1936	Elis Viklund (SWE)	Axel Wikström (SWE)	Nils-Joel Englund (SWE)
1948	Nils Karlsson (SWE)	Harald Eriksson (SWE)	Benjamin Vanninen (FIN)
1952	Veikko Hakulinen (FIN)	Eero Kolehmainen (FIN)	Magnar Estenstad (NOR)
1956	Sixten Jernberg (SWE)	Veikko Hakulinen (FIN)	Fjodor Terentjev (URS)
1960	Kalevi Hämäläinen (FIN)	Veikko Hakulinen (FIN)	Rolf Rämgård (SWE)
1964	Sixten Jernberg (SWE)	Assar Rönnlund (SWE)	Arto Tiainen (FIN)
1968	Ole Ellefsaeter (NOR)	Vyacheslav Vedenin (URS)	Josef Haas (SUI)
1972	Paal Tyldum (NOR)	Magne Myrmo (NOR)	Vyacheslav Vedenin (URS)
1976	Ivar Formo (NOR)	Gert-Dietmar Klause (GDR)	Benny Soedergren (SWE)
1980	Nikolai Zimyatov (URS)	Juha Mieto (FIN)	Aleksandr Zavjalov (URS)

Men's Combined

	Gold	Silver	Bronze
1924	Thorleif Haug (NOR)	Thoralf Strömstad (NOR)	Johan Gröttumsbraaten (NOR)
1928	Johan Gröttumsbraaten (NOR)	Hans Vinjarengen (NOR)	John Snersrud (NOR)
1932	Johan Gröttumsbraaten (NOR)	Ole Stenen (NOR)	Hans Vinjarengen (NOR)
1936	Oddbjörn Hagen (NOR)	Olaf Hoffsbakken (NOR)	Sverre Brodahl (NOR)
1948	Heikki Hasu (FIN)	Martti Huhtala (FIN)	Sven Israelsson (SWE)
1952	Simon Slättvik (NOR)	Heikki Hasu (FIN)	Sverre Stenersen (NOR)
1956	Sverre Stenersen (NOR)	Bengt Eriksson (SWE)	Franciszek Gron-Gasienica (POL)
1960	Georg Thoma (GER)	Tormod Knutsen (NOR)	Nikolai Gusakov (URS)
1964	Tormod Knutsen (NOR)	Nikolai Kiselev (URS)	Georg Thoma (GER)
1968	Franz Keller (GER)	Alois Kälin (SUI)	Andreas Kunz (GDR)
1972	Ulrich Wehling (GDR)	Rauno Miettinen (FIN)	Karl-Heinz Luck (GDR)
1976	Ulrich Wehling (GDR)	Urban Hettich (GER)	Konrad Winkler (GDR)
1980	Ulrich Wehling (GDR)	Jouko Karjalainen (FIN)	Konrad Winkler (GDR)

Men's 40-Kilometer Cross-Country Relay

	Gold	Silver	Bronze
1936	FIN (Sulo Nurmela, Klaes Karppinen, Matti Lähde, Kalle Jalkanen)	NOR (Oddbjörn Hagen, Olaf Hoffsbakken, Sverre Brodahl, Bjarne Iversen)	SWE (John Berger, Erik A. Larsson, Artur Häggblad, Martin Matsbo)
1948	SWE (Nils Östensson, Nils Täpp, Gunnar Eriksson, Martin Lundström)	FIN (Lauri Silvennoinen, Teuvo Laukkanen, Sauli Rytky, August Kiruru)	NOR (Erling Evensen, Olav Ökern, Reidar Nyborg, Olav Hagen)

Gold Medalists	Silver Medalists	Bronze Medalists
1952 FIN (Heikki Hasu, Paavo Lonkila, Urpo Korhonen, Tapio Mäkelä)	NOR (Magnar Estenstad, Mikal Kirkholt, Martin Stokken, Hallgeir Brenden)	SWE (Nils Täpp, Sigurd Andersson, Enar Josefsson, Martin Lundström)
1956 URS (Fyedor Terentjev, Pavel Koltschin, Nikolai Anikin, Vladimir Kusin)	FIN (August Kiuru, Jorma Kortalainen, Arvo Viitanen, Veikko Hakulinen)	SWE (Lennart Larsson, Gunnar Samuelsson, Per-Erik Larsson, Sixten Jernberg)
1960 FIN (Toimi Alatalo, Eero Mäntyranta, Väinö Huhtala, Veikko Hakulinen)	NOR (Harald Grönningen, Hallgeir Brenden, Einar Östby, Haakon Brusveen)	URS (Anatoli Scheljuchin, Gennadi Waganow, Aleksei Kusnjetsow, Nikolai Anikin)
1964 SWE (Karl-Åke Asph, Sixten Jernberg, Janne Stefansson, Assar Rönnlund)	FIN (Väinö Huhtala, Arto Tiainen, Kalevi Laurila, Eero Mäntyranta)	URS (Ivan Utrobin, Gennadi Waganow, Igor Worontschichin, Pavel Koltschin)
1968 NOR (Odd Martinsen, Paal Tyldum, Harald Grönningen, Ole Ellefsaeter)	SWE (Jan Halvarsson, Bjarne Andersson, Gunnar Larsson, Assar Rönnlund)	FIN (Kalevi Oikarainen, Hannu Taipale, Kalevi Laurila, Eero Mäntyranta)
1972 URS (Vladimir Woronkov, Juri Skobov, Fedor Simaschov, Vyacheslav Vedenin)	NOR (Oddvar Braa, Paal Tyldum, Ivar Formo, Johs Harviken)	SUI (Alfred Kälin, Albert Giger, Alois Kälin, Eduard Hauser)
1976 FIN (Matti Pitkänen, Juha Mieto, Pertti Teurajärvi, Arto Koivisto)	NOR (Paal Tyldum, Einar Sagstuen, Ivar Formo, Odd Martinsen)	URS (Evgeni Beliaev, Nikolai Baschukov, Sergei Saveliev, Ivan Garanin)
1980 URS (Vasili Rochev, Nikolai Bazhukov, Evgeni Beliaev, Nikolai Zimyatov)	NOR (L.E. Eriksen, P.K. Aaland, O. Aunli, O. Braa)	FIN (H. Kirvesniemi, Pertti Teurajarvi, Matti Pitkanen, Juha Mieto)

Men's Ski Jumping (70-Meter)

Gold Medalists	Silver Medalists	Bronze Medalists
1924 Jacob Tullin Thams (NOR)	Narve Bonna (NOR)	Thorleif Haug (NOR)
1928 Alfred Andersen (NOR)	Sigmund Ruud (NOR)	Rudolf Burkert (TCH)
1932 Birger Ruud (NOR)	Hans Beck (NOR)	Kaare Wahlberg (NOR)
1936 Birger Ruud (NOR)	Sven Eriksson (SWE)	Reidar Andersen (NOR)
1948 Petter Hugsted (NOR)	Birger Ruud (NOR)	Thorleif Schjelderup (NOR)
1952 Arnfinn Bergmann (NOR)	Torbjörn Falkanger (NOR)	Karl Holmström (SWE)
1956 Antti Hyvärinen (FIN)	Aulis Kallakorpi (FIN)	Harry Glass (GER)
1960 Helmut Recknagel (GER)	Niilo Halonen (FIN)	Otto Leodolter (AUT)
1964 Veikko Kankkonen (FIN)	Toralf Engan (NOR)	Torgeir Brandtzaeg (NOR)
1968 Jiři Raška (TCH)	Reinhold Bachler (AUT)	Baldur Preiml (AUT)
1972 Yukio Kasaya (JPN)	Akitsugu Konno (JPN)	Seiji Aochi (JPN)
1976 Hans-Georg Aschenbach (GDR)	Jochen Danneberg (GDR)	Karl Schnabl (AUT)
1980 Anton Innauer (AUT)	Hirokazu Yagi (JPN) Manfred Deckert (GDR) (tie)	no medal

Men's Ski Jumping (90-Meter)

Gold Medalists	Silver Medalists	Bronze Medalists
1964 Toralf Engan (NOR)	Veikko Kankkonen (FIN)	Torgeir Brandtzaeg (NOR)
1968 Vladimir Beloussov (URS)	Jiři Raška (TCH)	Lars Grini (NOR)
1972 Wojciech Fortuna (POL)	Walter Steiner (SUI)	Rainer Schmidt (GDR)
1976 Karl Schnabl (AUT)	Anton Innauer (AUT)	Henry Glass (GDR)
1980 Jouko Tormanen (FIN)	Hubert Neuper (AUT)	Jari Puikkonen (FIN)

Women's 5-Kilometer Cross-Country

Gold Medalists	Silver Medalists	Bronze Medalists
1964 Claudia Boyarskikh (URS)	Mirja Lehtonen (FIN)	Alevtina Koltschina (URS)
1968 Toini Gustafsson (SWE)	Galina Kulakova (URS)	Alevtina Koltschina (URS)
1972 Galina Kulakova (URS)	Marjatta Kajosmaa (FIN)	Helena Šikolová (TCH)
1976 Helena Takalo (FIN)	Raisa Smetanina (URS)	Nina Baldicheva (URS
1980 Raisa Smetanina (URS)	Hilkka Riihivuori (FIN)	Kveta Jeriova (TCH)

Women's 10-Kilometer Cross-Country

Gold Medalists	Silver Medalists	Bronze Medalists
1952 Lydia Wideman (FIN)	Mirja Hietamies (FIN)	Siiri Rantanen (FIN)
1956 Ljubovj Kozyreva (URS)	Radya Jeroschina (URS)	Sonja Edström (SWE)
1960 Maria Gusakova (URS)	Ljubovj Kozyreva (URS)	Radya Jeroschina (URS)
1964 Claudia Boyarskikh (URS)	Eudokia Mekschilo (URS)	Maria Gusakova (URS)
1968 Toini Gustafsson (SWE)	Berit Mördre (NOR)	Inger Aufles (NOR)
1972 Galina Kulakova (URS)	Alevtina Olunina (URS)	Marjatta Kajosmaa (FIN)
1976 Raisa Smetanina (URS)	Helena Takalo (FIN)	Galina Kulakova (URS)
1980 Barbara Petzold (GDR)	Hilkka Riihivuori (FIN)	Helena Takalo (FIN)

Women's 20-Kilometer Cross-Country Relay
(1956–1972 15 Kilometers)

Gold Medalists	Silver Medalists	Bronze Medalists
1956 FIN (Sirkka Polkunen, Mirja Hietamies, Siiri Rantanen)	URS (Ljubovj Kozyreva, Alevtina Koltschina, Radya Jeroschina)	SWE (Irma Johansson, Anna-Lisa Eriksson, Sonja Edström)
1960 SWE (Irma Johansson, Britt Strandberg, Sonja Ruthström-Edström)	URS (Radya Jeroschina, Maria Gusakova, Ljubovj Baranova-Kozyreva)	FIN (Siiri Rantanen, Eeva Ruoppa, Toini Pöysti)
1964 URS (Alevtina Koltschina, Eudokia Mekschilo, Claudia Boyarskikh)	SWE (Barbro Martinsson, Britt Strandberg, Toini Gustafsson)	FIN (Senja Pusula, Toini Pöysti, Mirja Lehtonen)

Gold Medalists	Silver Medalists	Bronze Medalists

Nordic Women's Relay (continued)

	Gold Medalists	Silver Medalists	Bronze Medalists
1968	NOR (Inger Aufles, Babben Enger Damon, Berit Mördre)	SWE (Britt Strandberg, Toini Gustafsson, Barbro Martinsson)	URS (Alevtina Koltschina, Rita Atschkina, Galina Kulakova)
1972	URS (Ljubov Muchatscheva, Alevtina Olunina, G. Kulakova)	FIN (Helena Takalo, Hilkka Kuntola, Marjatta Kajosmaa)	NOR (Inger Aufles, Aslaug Dahl, Berit Lammedal-Mördre)
1976	URS (Nina Baldycheva, Sinaida Amossowa, Raisa Smetanina, Galina Kulakova)	FIN (Liisa Suihkonen, Marjatta Kajosmaa, Hilkka Kuntola, Helena Takalo)	GDR (Monika Debertshäuser, Sigrun Krause, Barbara Petzold, Veronika Schmidt)
1980	GDR (Marlies Rostock, Carola Anding, Veronika Hesse, Barbara Petzold)	URS (Nina Baldycheva, Nina Rocheva, Galina Kulakova, Raisa Smetanina)	NOR (Brit Pettersen, Anette Boe, Marit Myrmael, Berit Aunli)

Speed Skating

Men's 500 Meters

	Gold	Silver	Bronze
1924	Charles Jewtraw (USA)	Oskar Olsen (NOR)	Roald Larsen (NOR) Clas Thunberg (FIN) (tie)
1928	Clas Thunberg (FIN) Bernt Evensen (NOR) (tie)	no medal	Johnny Farrell (USA) Roald Larsen (NOR) Jaakko Friman (FIN) (tie)
1932	John A. Shea (USA)	Bernt Evensen (NOR)	Alexander Hurd (CAN)
1936	Ivar Ballangrud (NOR)	Georg Krog (NOR)	Leo Freisinger (USA)
1948	Finn Helgesen (NOR)	Ken Bartholomew (USA) Thomas Byberg (NOR) Robert Fitzgerald (USA) (tie)	no medal
1952	Kenneth Henry (USA)	Donald McDermott (USA)	Arne Johansen (NOR) Gordon Audley (CAN) (tie)
1956	Yevgeni Grishin (URS)	Rafael Gratsch (URS)	Alv Gjestvang (NOR)
1960	Yevgeni Grishin (URS)	William Disney (USA)	Rafael Gratsch (URS)
1964	Richard McDermott (USA)	Yevgeni Grishin (URS) Vladimir Orlov (URS) Alv Gjestvang (NOR) (tie)	no medal
1968	Erhard Keller (GER)	Magne Thomassen (NOR) Richard McDermott (USA) (tie)	no medal
1972	Erhard Keller (GER)	Hasse Börjes (SWE)	Valery Muratov (URS)
1976	Yevgeni Kulikov (URS)	Valery Muratov (URS)	Daniel Immerfall (USA)
1980	Eric Heiden (USA)	Yevgeni Kulikov (URS)	Lieuwe De Boer (HOL)

Men's 1,000 Meters

	Gold	Silver	Bronze
1976	Peter Mueller (USA)	Jörn Didriksen (NOR)	Valery Muratov (URS)
1980	Eric Heiden (USA)	Gaetan Boucher (CAN)	Froede Roenning (NOR) Vladimir Lobanov (URS) (tie)

Men's 1,500 Meters

	Gold	Silver	Bronze
1924	Clas Thunberg (FIN)	Roald Larsen (NOR)	Sigurd Moen (NOR)
1928	Clas Thunberg (FIN)	Bernt Evensen (NOR)	Ivar Ballangrud (NOR)
1932	John A. Shea (USA)	Alexander Hurd (CAN)	William F. Logan (CAN)
1936	Charles Mathiesen (NOR)	Ivar Ballangrud (NOR)	Birger Wasenius (FIN)
1948	Sverre Farstad (NOR)	Åke Seyffarth (SWE)	Odd Lundberg (NOR)
1952	Hjalmar Andersen (NOR)	Willem van der Voort (HOL)	Roald Aas (NOR)
1956	Yevgeni Grischin (URS) Yuri Mikhailov (URS) (tie)	no medal	Toivo Salonen (FIN)
1960	Yevgeni Grischin (URS) Roald Aas (NOR) (tie)	no medal	Boris Stenin (URS)
1964	Ants Antson (URS)	Cornelis Verkerk (HOL)	Villy Haugen (NOR)
1968	Cornelis Verkerk (HOL)	Ard Schenk (HOL)	Ivar Eriksen (NOR)
1972	Ard Schenk (HOL)	Roar Grönvold (NOR)	Göran Claeson (SWE)
1976	Jan Egil Storholt (NOR)	Yuri Kondakov (URS)	Hans van Helden (HOL)
1980	Eric Heiden (USA)	Kai Arne Stenshjemmet (NOR)	Terje Andersen (NOR)

Men's 5,000 Meters

	Gold	Silver	Bronze
1924	Clas Thunberg (FIN)	Julius Skutnabb (FIN)	Roald Larsen (NOR)
1928	Ivar Ballangrud (NOR)	Julius Skutnabb (FIN)	Bernt Evensen (NOR)
1932	Irving Jaffee (USA)	Edward S. Murphy (USA)	William F. Logan (CAN)
1936	Ivar Ballangrud (NOR)	Birger Wasenius (FIN)	Antero Ojala (FIN)
1948	Reidar Liaklev (NOR)	Odd Lundberg (NOR)	Göthe Hedlund (SWE)
1952	Hjalmar Andersen (NOR)	Kees Broekman (HOL)	Sverre Haugli (NOR)
1956	Boris Shilkov (URS)	Sigvard Ericsson (SWE)	Oleg Gontscharenko (URS)
1960	Viktor Kosichkin (URS)	Knut Johannesen (NOR)	Jan Pesman (HOL)
1964	Knut Johannesen (NOR)	Per Ivar Moe (NOR)	Fred Anton Maier (NOR)

Gold Medalists	Silver Medalists	Bronze Medalists
1968 Fred Anton Maier (NOR)	Cornelis Verkerk (HOL)	Petrus Nottet (HOL)
1972 Ard Schenk (HOL)	Roar Grönvold (NOR)	Sten Stensen (NOR)
1976 Sten Stensen (NOR)	Piet Kleine (HOL)	Hans van Helden (HOL)
1980 Eric Heiden (USA)	Kai Arne Stenshjemmet (NOR)	Tom Erik Oxholm (NOR)

Men's 10,000 Meters

1924 Julius Skutnabb (FIN)	Clas Thunberg (FIN)	Roald Larsen (NOR)
1932 Irving Jaffee (USA)	Ivar Ballangrud (NOR)	Frank Stack (CAN)
1936 Ivar Ballangrud (NOR)	Birger Vasenius (FIN)	Max Stiepl (AUT)
1948 Åke Seyffarth (SWE)	Lauri Parkkinen (FIN)	Pentti Lammio (FIN)
1952 Hjalmar Andersen (NOR)	Kees Broekman (HOL)	Carl-Erik Asplund (SWE)
1956 Sigvard Ericsson (SWE)	Knut Johannesen (NOR)	Oleg Gontscharenko (URS)
1960 Knut Johannesen (NOR)	Viktor Kosichkin (URS)	Kjell Bäckman (SWE)
1964 Jonny Nilsson (SWE)	Fred Anton Maier (NOR)	Knut Johannesen (NOR)
1968 Jonny Hoeglin (SWE)	Fred Anton Maier (NOR)	Örjan Sandler (SWE)
1972 Ard Schenk (HOL)	Cornelis Verkerk (HOL)	Sten Stensen (NOR)
1976 Piet Kleine (HOL)	Sten Stensen (NOR)	Hans van Helden (HOL)
1980 Eric Heiden (USA)	Piet Kleine (HOL)	Tom Erik Oxholm (NOR)

Women's 500 Meters

1960 Helga Haase (GER)	Natalia Dontschenko (URS)	Jeanne Ashworth (USA)
1964 Lidia Skoblikova (URS)	Irina Jegorowa (URS)	Tatyana Sidorova (URS)
1968 Ludmila Titova (URS)	Mary Meyers (USA)	no medal
	Dianne Holum (USA)	
	Jennifer Fish (USA) (tie)	
1972 Anne Henning (USA)	Vera Krasnova (URS)	Ludmila Titova (URS)
1976 Sheila Young (USA)	Cathy Priestner (CAN)	Tatiana Averina (URS)
1980 Karin Enke (GDR)	Leah Poulos Mueller (USA)	Natalia Petruseva (URS)

Women's 1,000 Meters

1960 Klara Guseva (URS)	Helga Haase (GER)	Tamara Rylova (URS)
1964 Lidia Skoblikova (URS)	Irina Jegorowa (URS)	Kaija Mustonen (FIN)
1968 Carolina Geijssen (HOL)	Ludmila Titova (URS)	Dianne Holum (USA)
1972 Monika Pflug (GER)	Atje Keulen-Deelstra (HOL)	Anne Henning (USA)
1976 Tatiana Averina (URS)	Leah Poulos (USA)	Sheila Young (USA)
1980 Natalia Petruseva (URS)	Leah Poulos Mueller (USA)	Silvia Albrecht (GDR)

Women's 1,500 Meters

1960 Lidia Skoblikova (URS)	Elwira Seroczynska (POL)	Helena Pilejczyk (POL)
1964 Lidia Skoblikova (URS)	Kaija Mustonen (FIN)	Berta Kolokolzewa (URS)
1968 Kaija Mustonen (FIN)	Carolina Geijssen (HOL)	Christina Kaiser (HOL)
1972 Dianne Holum (USA)	Christina Baas-Kaiser (HOL)	Atje Keulen-Deelstra (HOL)
1976 Galina Stepanskaya (URS)	Sheila Young (USA)	Tatiana Averina (URS)
1980 Annie Borckink (HOL)	Ria Visser (HOL)	Sabine Becker (GDR)

Women's 3,000 Meters

1960 Lidia Skoblikova (URS)	Valentina Stenina (URS)	Eevi Huttunen (FIN)
1964 Lidia Skoblikova (URS)	Valentina Stenina (URS)	Pil Hwa Han (PRK)
1968 Johanna Schut (HOL)	Kaija Mustonen (FIN)	Christina Kaiser (HOL)
1972 Christina Baas-Kaiser (HOL)	Dianne Holum (USA)	Atje Keulen-Deelstra (HOL)
1976 Tatiana Averina (URS)	Andrea Mitscherlich (GDR)	Lisbeth Korsmo (NOR)
1980 Bjoerg Eva Jensen (NOR)	Sabine Becker (GDR)	Beth Heiden (USA)

THE OLYMPIC WINTER GAMES

YEAR	SITE	NUMBER OF NATIONS REPRESENTED	NUMBER OF ATHLETES PARTICIPATING
1924	Chamonix, France	16	293
1928	St. Moritz, Switzerland	25	491
1932	Lake Placid, N.Y., USA	17	307
1936	Garmisch-Partenkirchen, Germany	28	756
1948	St. Moritz, Switzerland	28	713
1952	Oslo, Norway	30	732
1956	Cortina d'Ampezzo, Italy	32	924
1960	Squaw Valley, Calif., USA	30	693
1964	Innsbruck, Austria	36	1,332
1968	Grenoble, France	37	1,272
1972	Sapporo, Japan	35	1,125
1976	Innsbruck, Austria	37	1,054
1980	Lake Placid, N.Y., USA	37	1,283

INDEX

A

Aas, Roald (Norwegian speed skater) 248

ABC *see* American Broadcasting Company

Albrecht, Silvia (East German speed skater) 169, 178, 195, 249

Albright, Tenley (U.S. figure skater) 8, 245
Illus. 8

Ali, Muhammad (U.S. boxer) 231

Alikin, Vladimir (Soviet biathlete) 78, 81, 243
Illus. 78

Aljabiev, Anatoli (Soviet biathlete) 77, 76, 78, 80, 81, 243
Illus. 75, 77, 78, 80, 81

Allen, Lisa-Marie (U.S. figure skater) 106

Allen, Scott (U.S. figure skater) 245

ALPINE SKIING 45–72
gold, silver, and bronze medalists 242
skis and boots 161
technology 240

Altwegg, Jeanette (British figure skater) 245

Amantova, Ingrida (Soviet luger) 142, 143, 246
Illus. 143

American Broadcasting Company (ABC) 14
McKay, Jim 211

Anabolic steroids (hormones) 238

Andersen, Alfred (Norwegian skier) 247

Andersen, Hjalmar (Norwegian speed skater) 183, 248, 249

Andersen, Reidar (Norwegian skier) 247

Andersen, Terje (Norwegian speed skater) 186, 195, 248

Anderson, Karl (U.S. skier)
Illus. 46

Anderson, Sture (Swedish ice hockey player) 118

Andersson, Volger (Swedish skier) 246

Anding, Carola (East German skier) 154, 165

Anikin, Nikolai (Soviet skier) 246

Antson, Ants (Soviet speed skater) 248

Aochi, Seiji (Japanese skier) 247

Argentina
biathlon 76

Arledge, Roone (U.S. television executive) 14

ARTS FESTIVAL 196–99

Arwidson, Lars-Göran (Swedish biathlete) 243

Aschenbach, Hans-Georg (East German skier) 247

Ashworth, Jeanne (U.S. speed skater) 249

Asplund, Carl-Erik (Swedish speed skater) 249

Associated Press 25

Astroturf (synthetic ground surface) 240

Aufles, Inger (Norwegian skier) 247

Aunli, Ove (Norwegian skier) 148, 165, 246

Austria 27
bobsledding 88
downhill, men's 47 following, 72
downhill, women's 50 following, 72
giant slalom, men's 56, 57, 72

giant slalom, women's 61, 63
luge 139, 143
ski jumping, 159, 160, 165
slalom, men's 65, 66
slalom, women's 68

Averina, Tatiana (Soviet speed skater) 183, 249

B

Baas-Kaiser, Christina (Dutch speed skater) 249

Babilonia, Tai (U.S. figure skater) 93 following
Illus. 93, 94

Bachler, Reinhold (Austrian skier) 247

Bäckman, Kjell (Swedish speed skater) 249

Baier, Ernst (German figure skater) 244

Bajukov, Nikolai (Soviet skier) 150, 246

Baker, Bill (U.S. ice hockey player) 125, 113, 117, 118
Illus. 125

Ballangrud, Ivar (Norwegian speed skater) 183, 248, 249

Balderis, Helmut (Soviet ice hockey player) 115

Baldycheva, Nina (Soviet skier) 148, 154, 247

Ballangrud, Ivar (Norwegian speed skater) 248, 249

Bancroft, Leslie (U.S. skier) 148, 154

Bartels, Wolfgang (German skier) 242

Bartholomew, Ken (U.S. speed skater) 248

Bazhukov, Nikolai (Soviet skier) 153, 165
Illus. 153

Beamon, Bob (U.S. jumper) 241

Beck, Hans (Norwegian skier) 247

Becker, Sabine (East German speed skater) 169, 184, 195, 249
Illus. 169

Behle, Jochem (West German skier) 153

Beiser, Trude (Austrian skier) 242

Beliaev, Evgeni (Soviet skier) 150, 153, 155, 165, 246
Illus. 153

Beloussov, Vladimir (Soviet skier) 247

Benz, Josef (Swiss bobsledder) 84, 91

Berge, Guttorm (Norwegian skier) 242

Berglund, Bo (Swedish ice hockey player)
Illus. 120

Bergmann, Arnfinn (Norwegian skier) 247

Berlin Games, 1916 (cancelled) 221

Berlin Summer Games, 1936 220

Berlioux, Monique (French Olympic official) 204
Illus. 204

Berthod, Madeleine (Swiss skier) 242

Bewersdorff, Uwe (East German figure skater) 99, 111
Illus. 97

BIATHLON 73–81
gold, silver, and bronze medalists 243

Biebl, Heidi (German skier) 242

Biellmann, Denise (Swiss skater), 106

Biotelemetry 238

Blegen, Julius (U.S. coach)
Illus. 32

Blondeau, Yves (French biathlete) 78

BOBSLEDDING 82–91
gold, silver, and bronze medalists 243

Bobsleds 85, 240

Bochatay, Fernande (Swiss skater) 242

Böckl, Willy (Austrian figure skater) 244

Bonlieu, François (French skier) 242

Bonna, Narve (Norwegian skier) 247

Bonsack, Klaus (East German luger) 245

Borckink, Annie (Dutch speed skater) 168, 173, 179, 184, 195
Illus. 169

Börjes, Hasse (Swedish speed skater) 248

Boucher, Gaetan (Canadian speed skater) 175, 182, 183, 195, 204, 248
Illus. 181, 182, 205

Bower, John (U.S. Nordic ski team leader) 148, 152, 159

Boyarskikh, Claudia (Soviet skier) 247

Boycott, of the 1980 Moscow Olympics 216

Bozon, Charles (French skier) 242

Braa, Oddvar (Norwegian skier) 147

Brandner, Hans (West German luger) 245

Brandtzaeg, Torgeir (Norwegian skier) 247

Brenden, Hallgeir (Norwegian skier) 246

Brodahl, Sverre (Norwegian skier) 246

Broekman, Kees (Dutch speed skater) 248, 249

Bronze medalists 242 following

Brooks, Herb (U.S. ice hockey coach) 125, 113 following, 130, 132, 134, 136
Illus. 125

Broten, Neal (U.S. ice hockey player) 125, 124, 134
Illus. 125

Bruggmann, Edmund (Swiss skier) 242

Brundage, Avery (U.S. Olympic official) 220, 223

Brunner, Karl (Italian luger) 139, 143, 245

Brusveen, Haakon (Norwegian skier) 246

Buchner, Annemarie (German skier) 242

Bulau, Horst (Canadian skier) 160

Bulgaria 27
cross-country skiing 147, 165

Bumberger, Alois (Austrian coach) 50

Burger, Fritzi (Austrian figure skater) 245

Burka, Petra (Canadian figure skater) 245

Burka, Sylvia (Canadian speed skater) 168, 184

Burke, Lynn (U.S. swimmer) 8
Illus. 8

Burkert, Rudolf (Czech skier) 247

Button, Dick (U.S. figure skater, television commentator) 14, 96, 97, 244

Byberg, Thomas (Norwegian speed skater) 248

C

Caldwell, Tim (U.S. skier) 154

Calmat, Alain (French figure skater) 245

Canada 27
bobsledding 88
Boucher, Gaetan 204
cross-country skiing 148, 151, 152, 154
downhill, men's 48, 72
ice hockey 115, 118, 120 following, 124, 128, 133, 135
luge 141, 143
Moscow Olympics boycott 217, 230, 233
opening ceremonies 40
Podborski, Steve 214
ski jumping 160, 162
speed skating 168, 169, 175, 182, 184, 195

Carey, Hugh (New York governor) 19, 40

Carlos, John (U.S. runner) 223

Carruthers, Peter and Caitlin (U.S. figure skaters) 99
Illus. 96

Carter, Jimmy (U.S. president) 12, 18, 132, 136
Moscow Olympics boycott 216 following, 227, 230 following

Cazacu, Traian (Rumanian ice hockey player) *Illus.* 120

Chenal-Minuzzo, Giuliana (Italian skier) 242

Cherkosova, Marina (Soviet figure skater) 99, 111
Illus. 98

Chetveroukhin, Sergei (Soviet figure skater) 245

Children's art 199

China
Moscow Olympics boycott 231
slalom, women's 26, 72
speed skating 169

Christian, Bill (U.S. ice hockey player) 114

Christian, Dave (U.S. ice hockey player) 125, 114, 117, 124, 136
Illus. 125, 133

Christian, Roger (U.S. ice hockey player) 114

Christoff, Steve (U.S. ice hockey player) 125, 134
Illus. 125, 130

Claeson, Göran (Swedish speed skater) 248

Clark, Joe (Canadian prime minister) 217, 230

Cleary, Bill (U.S. ice hockey player) 114

CLOSING CEREMONY 200–03

Cochran, Barbara (U.S. skier) 242

Colledge, Cecilia (British figure skater) 245

Colliard, Renée (Swiss skater) 242

Collins, Stephen (Canadian skier) 160

Collombin, Roland (Swiss skier) 242

Colò, Zeno (Italian skier) 242

Cooper, Christin (U.S. skier) 61, 63, 68, 72
Illus. 60

Corrock, Susan (U.S. skier) 242

Costa Rica 26

Coubertin, Baron Pierre de (French sportsman) 197, 221, 224

Photo Credits

Unless otherwise acknowledged below, all photographs included in this volume were supplied by The Associated Press. Special photo research by Central Picture Services, Grolier Incorporated.

Page(s): 30—The Bettmann Archive; 32—Brown Brothers; Photoworld, Brown Brothers; 33—Brown Brothers (top left), Photoworld (top right); 122—Paul Sutton, Duomo; 148—Focus on Sports; 161—Kneissl (left), Christopher G. Knight (right); 166 and 169—Paul Sutton, Duomo; 169 (bottom)—Steven Sutton, Duomo; 170—Oberhamer Shoe Company; 172 and 174—Paul Sutton, Duomo; 181—Gail Constable, Duomo; 183—Steven Sutton, Duomo; 196—The National Art Museum of Sport. Courtesy, The New York Telephone Company; 197—Long Wharf Theatre; 198—Louis A. Claudio; 199—XIII Olympic Winter Games National Fine Arts Commission (right). Adrian Byran-Brown; 205—Canadian Press Wide; 210—Duomo; 220—Photoworld, F.P.G. (top), The Bettmann Archive; 221—Eastfoto; 222—Joseph McKeown, Black Star; 223—Zimmerman, Freelance Photographers Guild; 224—L. Eby, Alpha Photo Associates; 234—Joe DiMaggio/JoAnne Kalish, Focus on Sports; 235—The Bettmann Archive; 236—J. DiMaggio/J. Kalish, Courtesy, United States Olympic Committee (USOC); 238—Laura Viscome, Lake Placid News; 239—USOC; 240—Paul J. Sutton, Duomo (top), Dan McCoy, Rainbow; 241—Steven Sutton, Duomo (pole vault), Rick Clarkson, "Sports Illustrated."